*Unsettled Minds*

# Unsettled Minds

*Psychology and the American Search for
Spiritual Assurance, 1830–1940*

CHRISTOPHER G. WHITE

*University of California Press*

BERKELEY    LOS ANGELES    LONDON

University of California Press, one of the most distinguished university presses in the United States, enriches lives around the world by advancing scholarship in the humanities, social sciences, and natural sciences. Its activities are supported by the UC Press Foundation and by philanthropic contributions from individuals and institutions. For more information, visit www.ucpress.edu.

Parts of this book also appear in Christopher G. White, "Minds Intensely Unsettled: Phrenology, Experience, and the American Pursuit of Spiritual Assurance, 1830–1880," *Religion and American Culture* 16:2 (Summer 2006): 227–61, and "A Measured Faith: Edwin Starbuck, William James, and the Scientific Reform of Religious Experience," *Harvard Theological Review* (forthcoming).

University of California Press
Berkeley and Los Angeles, California

University of California Press, Ltd.
London, England

Library of Congress Cataloging-in-Publication Data

White, Christopher G., 1969–
    Unsettled minds : psychology and the American search for spiritual assurance, 1830–1940 / Christopher G. White.
        p.      cm.
    Includes bibliographical references and index.
    ISBN 978-0-520-25679-8 (cloth : alk. paper)
    1. Psychology, Religious—United States.    2. Psychology and religion—United States.    3. Christianity—Psychology.
4. Liberalism (Religion)—United States.    5. United States—Religion—History.    I. Title.
    BL53.W5185    2009
    201'.6150973—dc22                                        2008009380

Manufactured in the United States of America

17    16    15    14    13    12    11    10    09    08
10    9    8    7    6    5    4    3    2    1

The paper used in this publication meets the minimum requirements of ANSI/NISO Z39.48-1992 (R 1997) (*Permanence of Paper*).

*For Clay and Carole White*
*and in memory of Arthur and Nura Ioas*

# Contents

# Illustrations

# Acknowledgments

I am deeply indebted to the many people and agencies who helped make this book possible. I am grateful, first of all, to Harvard University, the National Endowment for the Humanities, and Georgia State University for generous grants that made possible research travel and time to think and write about the history of psychology and faith in America. I also am grateful to the Center for the Study of Religion and American Culture and their Young Scholars program, which provided rich conversations and supportive colleagues at a crucial time at the end of my writing.

Many people read and commented on drafts and chapters. John Corrigan, Richard Fox, Philip Goff, David Hall, William Hutchison, James Kloppenberg, John Lardas Modern, Robert Orsi, Jon Roberts, Leigh Schmidt, Ann Taves, and Tracy Bagley White—all of them read sections or chapters and helped me think about them. A smaller group read the entire manuscript— Courtney Bender, John Corrigan, Joseph Creech, Curtis Evans, David Hall, and Louis Ruprecht. Two anonymous reviewers also scoured the manuscript and presented me with a set of remarkably helpful ideas. I am tremendously grateful to all these readers. Others in Harvard Divinity School's American Colloquium, wonderful mentors and friends, offered rousing encouragement and shrewd advice as I tested out ideas. I also thank John Corrigan and Judith Weisenfeld and colleagues in the 2005–6 cohort of Young Scholars in American Religion at the Center for the Study of Religion and American Culture. Their perceptive comments shaped individual chapters. Finally, though I really began this book after graduate school, I owe my deepest debt to advisors and mentors at Harvard—David Hall, William Hutchison, and Jim Kloppenberg. So much of this project, and my way of thinking about it, was influenced by their ideas and work. There is no way to repay them for their high expectations, their faith in my abilities, and their ways of teaching and exemplifying integrity and hard work. David Hall in particular helped shape the book at almost every stage along the way.

I also thank the community of students and scholars at Quincy House, with whom Tracy and I lived for seven years while in graduate school, a reliable source of conviviality, intellectual stimulation, and (not least) babysitting help.

Then there were research librarians and student assistants who tracked down obscure sources, gave advice, and in other ways helped prepare the book. I thank librarians from the following archives and libraries: the Andover-Harvard Theological Library, the Clark University Archives, the Congregational Library and Archives (Boston, Mass.), the Episcopal Diocese Archive (Boston, Mass.), Harvard University Archives, Houghton Library, the Oberlin College Archives, the Ohio Historical Society, the Springfield College Archives, Widener Library, the University of Southern California Archives, the Yale University Archives, the Yale Divinity School Archives and Special Collections, and the University of Iowa Special Collections. A number of research assistants did difficult detective work and even less glamorous tasks without complaint—Jeannie Alexander, Scott Hodgman, Dennis LoRusso, Kat Milby, Holly Phillips, Ari Stern, and Trig Throntveit.

Without fail, my editors at the University of California Press were insightful, professional, and patient. I am grateful especially for Reed Malcolm's ongoing enthusiasm for the project, Kalicia Pivirotto's help in steering this book toward production, and Jacqueline Volin's incredible attention to detail as publication deadlines neared. It is a privilege to publish this book with the University of California Press.

My greatest personal debts are to family and friends, who over the years reinforced my flagging energies and always supported my work. All of the Whites and Bagleys and our many friends—the Ahdiehs, Avanessians, Grants, Kianis, Sharifis, and Yamartinos in particular—have supported me all the way through. Colleagues at Georgia State University's Department of Religious Studies and especially our chair, Tim Renick, did everything in their power to support me and make time available for research and writing. My family, and especially my wife, Tracy, will never know the extent of my gratitude; she has been unfailingly supportive of this book and of my academic career more generally, even when both took me away from other priorities that we share. Our two boys came along at the beginning and middle of the process, and they have been reliable diversions and cherished reminders of the best things in life. Finally, for his vision of cooperation between scientists and believers, I thank Bahá'u'lláh; and, for making everything possible, including what I know of science and faith, I owe the greatest debt to my parents and grandparents.

# Introduction

What is the fate of young people who try earnestly to believe but find themselves exhausted or bewildered by their parents' religions? Can these unsettled young believers eventually recover something comforting or useful from their childhood faiths? Can those who have given up altogether on older theologies, seeking not to reform but obliterate them, find new ways of achieving religious certainty or assurance? How? Out of what raw materials can wholly new views on issues of crucial importance, issues such as the meaning of the moral life, the nature and possibilities of human nature, and the problem, so unsolvable, of death, be developed? This book examines these questions by turning to the religious lives of nineteenth- and twentieth-century Americans who rejected older religious traditions and turned to scientific psychologies to help them formulate new ideas about the self and new practices concerning spiritual growth. It begins with the unsettled reflections of a group of early-nineteenth-century Christians who found themselves unable to conform to their parents' evangelical Calvinism. Christians in this situation, full of self-doubt and anxious religious reflections, eventually redirected their suspicions outward, pronouncing their natal evangelicalism unhealthy, irrational, or in other ways defective. Quickly, their intense dislike for older traditions propelled them in novel directions, fueling a range of theological reformulations and emendations, and especially new views of the self and spiritual growth. I follow their changing attitudes, aspirations, and new formulations carefully.

These liberal believers were aided in their spiritual innovations in three principal ways by psychological sciences and their new methods for mapping and controlling the emotional self. First, scientific psychologies sometimes suggested the existence of powerful spiritual energies and mental faculties that captured or husbanded them. Christians laboring with Calvinist convictions of impotence and inability embraced this possibility as a liberation. Second, scientific psychologies demystified the confounding inner spaces of the self by offering new ways to detect, measure, and map them. In particular, scientific psychologies linked mental (and spiritual) states to the body, bringing mysterious emotions and religious states to the surfaces of the self, where they could be more easily understood and reflected upon. Inner conditions could be discerned in the contours of the head or body. They could be seen in one's characteristic attitudes, facial expressions, and postures. Thus, new sciences made confounding inner spaces visible again. Third, by developing new ways of thinking about mental and nervous functioning, different psychologies helped liberals fashion new guidelines concerning spiritual health, overcoming sin, and resisting modern temptations. In short, religious liberals used scientific psychologies to develop clearer ways of thinking about the self and better methods for developing its spiritual capacities. The powerful new discourses they produced changed how twentieth-century Americans thought about healthy and unhealthy forms of religion, faith and healing, gender, irrationality, and race.

The stories I tell in this book present alternatives to conventional narratives about science, religion, and therapeutic culture in the United States. Older narratives on science and religion tended to treat these entities as hypostatized essences always in conflict with one another. Historians writing these "conflict" narratives recalled clashes between new scientific theories and old religious doctrines, examined acrimonious debates between believers and skeptics, and chronicled how religion was displaced, privatized, or marginalized by increasingly powerful publicly funded scientific activities. Though conflicts, sharply drawn debates, and extreme voices (on both sides) continue to capture scholarly and popular attention, several commentators recently have wondered if the rhetoric of conflict coming from scientific and religious leaders has distracted us from the strategies most people use to negotiate their various commitments. Most people combine, harmonize, and live with ambiguity. In this book I am interested less in the polemics of intolerant extremists than I am in the mediating strategies that most believers employ. I am interested in efforts to borrow psychology's prestige, use its methods, incorporate its promises of certainty, and perhaps most urgently, control its meanings. In the end I want to draw attention to the more or less successful ways believers used science (and enlightenment categories generally) to produce new forms of religious meaning or assurance. In many cases, believers used psychology to produce new ways of seeing clearly religious emotions, new ways of mapping more precisely religious growth, new ways of acquiring religious competencies and guarantees. I am interested, then, less in the religion-science conflict or religious decline than I am in trying to make clear how religious Americans, and especially religious liberals, used science to buttress faith.[1]

It is true, of course, that sometimes efforts to reshape psychological insights for religious purposes faltered or failed completely, and the sciences that believers used to reinforce belief became sources of doubt and consternation. This is a crucial part of my story as well. Believers battled constantly to control science and its meanings, and sometimes the end result was unexpected, strangely ironic, or deeply distressing.

The group of religious Americans in which I am interested turned to science for new metaphors for spirit and spiritual growth. Essentially romantics, religious liberals believed that nature was alive with spiritual forces. Science was the way to probe carefully these forces and the eternal truths they reflected. For example, in the case of phrenology, the first scientific psychology, science helped liberals establish an alternative mental philosophy, one anchored not in dogmatic truths about depravity but in the struggle to uncover eternal divine-human correspondences that could be discerned in the physiological self. When phrenologists looked at human nature, they saw not a sinfulness to be disciplined but a set of capacities—for "veneration" and morality, for example—to be developed and expressed. Religious liberals in general were certain that scientific reflection on nature would yield powerful religious insights. "Theology cannot remain content with repeating the old phrases for faith," one liberal proclaimed, "when science offers a richer natural language for the expression of spiritual truth." These new perspectives often were expanded into more comprehensive "natural styles" that reoriented how liberals thought about mind, body, and spirituality. Many embraced natural personal styles that incorporated a range of things—freer modes of emotional expression, unaffected spontaneity and creativity, and interest in outdoor or casual forms of worship. That this natural style contrasted with older norms of decorum and restraint is illustrated well in two photographs, taken between 1845 and 1860, of Lyman Beecher and his progressive son, Henry Ward (figure 1). The natural style that Henry cultivated liberated him from both the artificial constraints of Calvinism and the unnatural, urban environment he inhabited.

Other religious liberals borrowed *the natural* for similar purposes, using nature and its study to identify the unhygienic or vitiating aspects of modern life and find edifying alternative mental and spiritual practices. Religious

Figure 1. From older forms of restraint to newer, natural styles. Henry Ward Beecher (left) and Lyman Beecher, circa 1845–60. The image of Henry Ward Beecher is from the Yale Collection of American Literature, Beinecke Rare Book and Manuscript Library, call no. Za St78 869A; the image of Lyman Beecher is from the Library of Congress, Prints and Photographs Division, call no. LC-USZ62-109964.

liberals such as Luther Gulick and Josiah Strong called for recuperative play in natural environments and a new strenuosity that might enhance neuromuscular mass and, by extension, nervous and spiritual health. Other psychologically informed believers developed normative discourses of religious experience by identifying how all human beings naturally develop through the life cycle. Religious systems that artificially stimulated or retarded these natural processes were seen as unhealthy and irrational. These were some of the ways that religious liberals used conceptions of the natural to develop normative discourses of spirit and spiritual development.[2]

While liberal believers reflected on nature (or its study) to understand better how the divine operated in the world and the self, later observers have linked their project to different forms of religious decline or cultural malaise. Commentators have pointed to different liberal deficiencies. By being too eager to reconcile revelation and nature, or too willing to interpret Christian symbols in scientific idioms, or too adept at translating theological categories into psychological ones, these believers sacrificed their distinctively religious message and, the argument goes, the institutional power of Christianity as well. For all these reasons, commentators have argued that liberal religious missteps led to the secularization of religion, the marginalization of theology in public discourse, and the decline of the assumption (in American culture) that God exists. Others have implicated liberals in another decline narrative more directly relevant to this study, the transformation of Christian salvation into "self-realization."[3] Recently, evangelical historians in particular have successfully promoted the link between religious liberals (especially liberal Protestants) and one or another form of decline. While it is impossible here to evaluate the merits of these decline narratives, there is no question that they have turned attention away from liberal religious subjects and their spiritual lives.[4] I am not the first to complain that the scholarship on these believers has become "dark with metaphors of spiritual decay" and that liberal aspirations, beliefs, and enduring religious conceptions have been obscured.[5]

A final word needs to be said about the literature on psychology, religion, and therapeutic culture in America, a literature that also has produced its share of decline narratives and nostalgic lamentations. Several historians, including T. J. Jackson Lears, have argued that the rise of consumer culture in the early twentieth century cannot be accounted for unless we first understand changes in American religious cultures, and especially the "shift from a Protestant ethos of salvation through self denial to a therapeutic ethos stressing self realization in this world, which was focused on psychic and physical health." The most ambitious effort to document the turn to the therapeutic in American Christian cultures was E. Brooks Holifield's book on pastoral care, a definitive book that examined Protestant clerics who borrowed psychological insights as they reconceptualized ways of curing and edifying fellow believers. Holifield's is a complicated and nuanced book; but it, too, tries to persuade readers that liberal believers were overly eager to reduce theological categories to psychological ones. Holifield also remonstrates against liberals who were too willing to exchange older styles of salvation for a newer culture of solipsism and self-realization. Holifield and historians with similar preoccupations may have been taking cues from the wider critical environment, an environment tinged with consternation about psychological discourses that seemed to cannibalize all other symbol systems. Philip Rieff was not the first to point to this problem, but his trenchant *Triumph of the Therapeutic* (1966) set the tone for Americans increasingly anxious that psychology, and specifically Freudianism, usurped our sense of the transcendent and forced us to exchange meaningful religious commitments that inculcated responsibility for therapeutic ones that encouraged individualism and the selfish pursuit of gain. Several scholars and critics, often conservative, continue to lament the fact that psychological discourses have obliterated more traditional religious or civic traditions of duty and responsibility.[6]

A couple of more recent historical works, however, including especially Ann Taves's brilliant and wide-ranging *Fits, Trances, and Visions*, have opened up other possibilities. Because Taves treated psychology as an interpretive system that changed over time, she was better able to probe how psychological and religious glosses of apparently involuntary acts (such as trances and fits) were situated in specific historical contexts. Psychology in Taves's analysis is not a hegemonic system but a changing discourse that, like other human discourses, orders and accounts for human life. Taves's innovation was not in interpreting psychology as a fully historical phenomenon; this is a commonplace in the history and philosophy of science. Her real contribution was in using this idea to understand how competing discourses, psychological and religious, accounted for people's ecstatic experiences during different periods in American history. My book builds on Taves's work in particular, for I too am interested in religious and psychological glosses on experience. But the issues I deal with, and my arguments, are different. My focus is less on the history of interpretations of ecstatic experiences than it is on the ways religious believers tried to use science, and psychology in particular, to improve their religious positions and especially see more clearly the self and its religious possibilities.[7]

This fact makes my analysis different from Taves's in several additional ways, the most important of which is that it is less focused on the unconscious and how people have reflected on that part of the self. This is the case partly because I am less interested in people's explanations of ecstatic experiences and partly because I am curious about other mediating categories, including free will (chapters 2 and 4), nervous energies (chapter 3), and the concept of the "mind" itself. Believers used each of these categories, and others, to resist fully physiological accounts of the self. A final reason I am less attentive to the unconscious is that I think many liberal believers, while accepting the unconscious when it emerged in the twentieth century, were wary of it. In this book I try to understand why that was the case, and I argue that because religious liberals, and especially liberal Protestants, were confounded by religious feelings and experiences, they were less interested in exploiting the deep parts of the self (e.g., the unconscious) than they were anxious about controlling and measuring them. For this reason, I point to the ways that religious liberals borrowed again and again from consciousness psychologies—psychologies that emphasized rationality, willpower, and self-control. In the last chapter of the book, I do turn to the unconscious, but even here I am interested mainly in techniques that believers developed to control and measure it.

In summing up this book's relationship to other work on psychology, religion, and American culture, I would say that the book represents a countersecularization narrative, a narrative that examines not how enlightenment discourses minimized or obliterated religious belief but how they abetted religiousness in unexpected ways. Its starting point is not apprehension about psychological hegemony but a dawning awareness that religion and psychology, especially in the twentieth century, flourished together. To me, the conspicuous feature of modern America, and thus the feature that must be explained, is not religious decline but an astonishing American religious efflorescence, an efflorescence often buttressed by psychological and popular psychological notions. Would anyone claim that America, especially when compared to other Western nations, is particularly or even notably irreligious? Isn't it more urgent to probe not Christian decline but how religiousness has grown, burst out of older forms, changed over time and incorporated new elements? To answer these questions we must understand better the spirituality first cobbled together by religious liberals over a century ago—an amalgam of Christian themes, world religious teachings, and popular psychological glosses on self and self-culture. This is a powerful spiritual tradition pulsing through Christian and non-Christian communities, a tradition we need to analyze and relate to other currents in American history. This is what I attempt to do in this book.

· · ·

The most enthusiastic borrowers of psychological notions were liberal Protestants, post-Protestant metaphysical believers, and a collection of spiritualists, mental healers, theosophists, deists, and others on the religious left. In this book I cast all of them into a single category—*religious liberals*—even though scholars in the past have tried to sort them out. Some have attempted to categorize them by their levels of Christian commitment. Henry Van Dusen and then Kenneth Cauthen did this several generations ago. Cauthen argued that evangelical liberals stood squarely within the Christian tradition, while their "modernistic liberal" brethren were best thought of as intelligent moderns who incorporated what they could of Christianity. Later, William Hutchison rightly protested that this distinction distorted modernist Protestant intentions; but even his ecumenical vision encompassed only the Protestant spectrum. There were few, if any, spiritualists or Quakers in his classic analysis of liberal religion. The same is true for Gary Dorrien's more recent history of liberal theology. Others have had a hard time under-standing intra-Protestant liberalisms without trying to incorporate radicals into their analyses. Marie Caskey found real theological and psychologi-cal differences among her liberal Protestants, but she also noted important commonalities, or "family resemblances," as well.[8] The radical liberals—the freethinkers, deists, and spiritualists—have had their historians too, and though there are synoptic analyses of radical liberals, no one has recognized the important similarities between these radicals and more conventional liberal Protestants. The exception is Leigh Schmidt, who has recently writ-ten a book that draws on a wide range of religious liberals to limn out a set of shared liberal interests in nondogmatic religion, individualistic spiritual practices, mysticism, and the edifying study of world religions.[9]

I too am interested in this shared liberal culture. In fact, seeing religious liberalism as a whole is crucial to this project, because religious liberals across the board were interested in using psychological sciences when developing new ideas and spiritual practices. (As they are today.) Of course, diverging experiences and theological interests meant that liberals used psychology in quite different ways. That I combine them in this book does not mean I am inattentive to differences or to the fact that liberals often disagreed or intensely disliked one another.

Nevertheless, while being careful about these differences, I use the term *religious liberal* to describe believers who usually have the following char-acteristics: confidence in human nature and its spiritual capacities; a belief in God's immanence in nature and human nature; a universalistic or at least ecumenical conviction that ultimate truth can be found in different forms or religions; and an interest in harmonizing religion, nature, and science. The first characteristic marks liberals off dramatically from evangelical Calvinists and other traditional Christians; in fact, many have pointed to optimism about human nature as the defining liberal characteristic. If this is true, then probing the psychological dimensions of liberalism will help us better understand the origins of their distinctive style. It is also worth saying that liberal views on human nature were employed as anti-Calvinist weapons; complaints about Calvinism often centered on notions of human sin and inability. The logic of the second characteristic, liberal interest in God's immanence, sometimes led directly to a universalism that is noted in the third characteristic; and often it generated interest in the religious experiences of savants, mystics, and other religious specialists. Sometimes this interest stimulated eclectic spiritual pursuits and hybrid forms of devotionalism or meditative practices; sometimes it undergirded the comparative study of religious experiences; and sometimes, as Leigh

Schmidt has shown, it is hard to tell the difference between the two.[10] This fact becomes clear in later chapters of my book.

. . .

My narrative begins with a group of unsettled nineteenth-century Americans who developed new discourses of spiritual progress built on insights gleaned from the first scientific psychology, phrenology. I point out that, beginning in this early period (ca. 1830–1880), a broad coalition of religious liberals used phrenology to find in external, especially bodily, conditions signs of inner spiritual states. The result was a series of physiological charts that mapped how spiritual forces pulsed through the body, especially the head and brain. Religious liberals in this period produced a range of new religious positions. Liberal Protestants tended to harmonize phrenology with traditional Christian categories. They believed that, though the Holy Spirit drove the process of regeneration, it worked through secondary, material causes, and its actions therefore could be seen best in the physiological self. Other liberals had tired of rehabilitating Christian categories and found that, when reading spiritual signs in the physiological self, it was better to develop a new nomenclature for these things. Radicals such as Andrew Jackson Davis, a recovering Methodist, did just that, as did other itinerant preachers and peddlers of new psychological notions. In chapter 1, as in others, I show how psychological ideas were used by a range of believers to understand their inner lives, map them out more precisely, and promote new ways of thinking about spiritual growth.

Later in the century, ideas about the mind changed. Starting in the 1870s and 1880s, psychologists began locating the mind not in the brain but in the entire neuromuscular system. For these so-called "new psychologists," the arc of nervous transmission, from stimulus to muscle contraction, represented the basic unit of the self. This meant that experience, and religious experience as well, was produced less by faculties in the brain and more by nervous impulses organized in the nervous system and muscles. The benefit of reducing the self to stimulus-response units was apparent from the beginning: all mental events could be monitored, tested, and measured experimentally. New psychologists were known for measuring reflexes, calculating reaction times, and testing sensation and perception. But there were difficulties, too, in reducing the self to mechanical stimulus-response patterns. Many of the founders of scientific psychology wondered how a soul or spirit might operate in a fully stimulus-response world. Was mind or spirit merely matter? Were higher mental functions simply the result of biological, electrical, and chemical reactions? In chapter 2, I examine the ambivalence of psychologists who, while wanting to believe in God and the human spirit, also built a science of the self on merely physiological principles. I focus in particular on the lives and ideas of two key American psychologists, G. Stanley Hall and William James, and I point to the ways they tried to control the meanings of psychology and harmonize it with religious commitments. That they were successful is clear from the many American religious figures who embraced their psychological notions as ways of more precisely understanding self-culture, the proper emotions of faith, and the stages of personal, spiritual transformation. Still, though theologians and lay believers embraced the new science as a way to understand spiritual development with scientific exactitude, the new psychology was a sharp edge tool. It could aid faith or take it away. Religious Americans battled constantly to control the meanings of a science that reduced the self to physiological processes.

In the third and fourth chapters, I slow the book's chronology in order to consider in detail the impact of the new psychology on American culture. I pause in particular to consider how religious liberals in the period from 1880 to 1915 used the new psychology to reimagine faith, religious duties, self-culture, and modern temptations. In chapter 3, I begin by considering a mediating category that reduced tensions between mechanistic and spiritual models of the self, the category *nervous energies*. Was nervous energy an electrical charge, a subtle fluid, or a pervasive, ethereal substance? Was it material or spiritual? Because it was never precisely defined, the category served believers and unbelievers, professional scientists and cultural critics, equally well, anchoring a pervasive discourse about the self and how to expend and conserve its vital forces. This discourse, in many ways a carryover from earlier vitalist discourses, was skillfully put to use by purveyors of moral and spiritual advice willing to satisfy the public's need for information about the body and its relation to spiritual health. In chapter 3, I examine liberal religious advice literatures that incorporated ideas about nervous energies and how to manage them. I am interested in how believers used discourses of nervousness and nervous depletion to flag the moral and spiritual dangers of alcohol, tobacco, sexuality, intemperate evangelical "enthusiasms," and other modern temptations. I point here to the ways that liberal Christians and other religious liberals used scientific psychologies to find new ways to cultivate belief and faithfully navigate modern temptations and the particularly unholy diversions of the city.

Depleted nervous energies could be restored by various disciplines for strengthening that mental capacity most closely linked to the muscles, a capacity called *the will*. In chapter 4, I begin by investigating how liberals in this same period (1880–1915) embraced the will as a crucial category. I point out that they used the will to free themselves from deterministic systems, religious and scientific. The will was the source of our freedom, the proof that we transcended mere materiality. I also examine both why physicians and psychologists linked the will to neuromuscular fitness and the different ways muscular Christians borrowed from this literature to promote programs of physical and spiritual fitness. In particular I discuss a group of thinkers and organizers involved in that quintessential muscular Christian organization, the YMCA. Many have studied muscular Christianity, but few have examined the physiological literatures that undergirded this movement. When experience becomes embodied, or imprinted on the neuromuscular self as it does here, other kinds of discourses suddenly become central to spiritual development. One of those discourses was that of habit, so crucial to religious liberals, a discourse about sedimenting in the body certain religious attitudes and dispositions. When believers repeated moral acts, practiced forms of self-control, or rehearsed the right religious sentiments, these acts were engraved physically in the neuromuscular system. Neurons and muscles took shape around them. But linking spiritual states so closely to bodily ones raised other issues, especially about whose bodies were the most spiritually attuned. Is one kind of body better suited to spiritual perfection? Without a doubt, religious liberals, muscular or not, built notions of spiritual development on metaphors of race and gender, using the white male body as the symbol of both outer strength and inner perfection. This meant that women and other "primitive" persons were cast in spiritually inferior roles. According to liberal schemes, they had to work harder to achieve will and muscle strength and corresponding spiritual states.

In chapter 5, I edge forward into the early decades of the twentieth century, examining how one group of religious liberals, psychologists of religion, developed new discourses about religious experience by analyzing these experiences with new, scientific methods. Yearning for intense religious feelings, yet disgusted by the excessive forms they often took, these religious liberals used scientific methods to lift ecstatic experiences out of their many unpalatable contexts. The psychologist of religion Edwin Starbuck did this most impressively in his early studies of evangelical conversion, studies that reduced the ecstatic experiences of American Methodists to natural moments that brought adjustment and maturity to adolescents. In publishing such studies, Starbuck, like James and other psychologists, made these intense experiences available to wider audiences, who read about them (as James did) and lived out their intense moments vicariously. But Starbuck and others also domesticated these experiences as stages in much longer processes of spiritual development. The fits and ecstatic trances of American believers were expressions of primitive impulses in all of us, impulses that ought to be cultivated—but only at an immature stage of life. Eventually, these feelings had to be superseded by more refined sensibilities cultivated in the intellect and the will. This, too, was a normative discourse, one that associated emotional, superstitious, and childlike sensibilities with immature stages that had to be rationally managed and overcome.

The sixth and final chapter takes a last look at the ambiguities of psychological perspectives on faith by turning to a single case, to how, in the early decades of the twentieth century, human suggestibility was measured by scientists and developed into faith therapies by liberal believers. There are two parts to this chapter. The first analyzes how believers and scientists used personality inventories and experimental tests to measure levels of suggestibility. Individuals involved in this process were fashioning a debunking discourse, a way of redescribing religious experiences (and human susceptibility to them) as the consequences of biological or psychological forces. The second part of the chapter, however, shows how psychological categories like suggestion were difficult to control and how religious figures in this situation, as in others, borrowed these categories and used them to their advantage. Many religious liberals developed techniques for building suggestibility in the self. Others developed elaborate systems of suggestions and affirmations that, when administered over time, built up spiritual sensitivities. In the end, this was another situation in which religious liberals used scientific notions to reorganize and rebuild spiritual sensibilities and practices.

I conclude the book with an epilogue that examines how scientific psychology fragmented and diversified in the twentieth century. I also look at how this psychological fragmentation encouraged an efflorescence of new religious ways of using psychological notions to think about the self and spiritual assurance.

# 1   Minds Intensely Unsettled

In 1841, at a Congregational church near Granville, Massachusetts, a regrettable incident occurred. A lecturer then touring New England, a man named Nelson Sizer, said he could see into people's hearts. He offered to be blindfolded, which he was, and two men stepped forward as volunteers. Sizer touched their bodies and heads, running his hands through their hair and around their ears, alighting on particular locations, the significance of which was known only to him. The congregation waited silently. When done, he announced that the first man was "a harmonious, careful, upright man," an assessment that appeared to please the congregation. But the case of the second man was more complicated. At first Sizer used terms such as *talent* and *self-reliance* to describe the man, but quickly his tone changed. This second man showed signs of pride and selfishness, and Sizer thought he seemed "too low in Conscientiousness to be just and honest in his dealings, and too large in Secretiveness to be open, frank and truthful." That revelation stunned the congregation—for everyone knew that that both men were "well related by blood and marriage, and had unblemished reputations." Sizer noticed people shifting in their seats and looking "at each other and at me with round eyes." He tried to explain. "By what is known of these men I suppose you all think I have made a mistake in the last one. If any one else had made the examination, and said the same things I should have said it must be a mistake, but I told you when you put on the blind I would give my true opinions hit or miss. Those are the indications, and I should say the same thing if I were to meet the same form of head anywhere." He had said his peace, but he left the place full of sadness. "I regretted the occurrence, as it placed me and my subject in an unpleasant light."

Though Sizer left Granville accompanied by unbelieving glances, it was not long before he was vindicated. Eighteen months later, he returned to Granville and inquired about his two volunteers. As it happened, the second man had "borrowed money of many people, some of it before I examined his head," and there were "some other seriously crooked matters which were spoken of respecting him with bated breath." The man had left town in a hurry, probably also with bated breath, never to return. Nothing negative was said again in Granville about Nelson Sizer and his remarkable new science.[1]

This incident illustrates one way that Americans in the early nineteenth century experimented with new ways of understanding the self. As a science of seeing clearly the mind and spirit, phrenology had an obvious appeal for Americans in general, and religious Americans in particular. Who wouldn't want to see clearly the inner dynamics of reason, willpower, or faith? This was true especially for Americans confounded by the morphologies of conversion prescribed by evangelical Calvinism—morphologies that included stages such as abasement, vocation, and sanctification. By the middle of the century, many were unable to see the signs of these stages in their hearts. This chapter examines how a group of religious Americans developed new discourses of spiritual progress built on insights gleaned from new psychologies such as phrenology. Beginning in this period, a broad coalition of religious liberals used these new psychologies to find in external, especially bodily, conditions signs of inner spiritual states.

## UNSETTLED BELIEVERS

The early nineteenth century was a time of religious experimentation, an era dominated by the spiritual yearnings of believers alienated by their parents' Calvinism. Nelson Sizer and other itinerant phrenologists were responding to this restlessness and helping create it, and like other peddlers and evangelists, they promoted new ways of thinking about the self and salvation. They spoke at colleges, churches, open-air meetings, poorhouses, and prisons.[2] Probably the most pervasive solution to the perceived coldness of Calvinism was religious revival, which in this period gathered explosive force as both a movement for religious renewal and a forceful critique of the inherited tradition. Surveying a vast landscape of visions, dreams, and prophesies, Nathan Hatch and Ann Taves have demonstrated that Americans in this period, eager to put behind them "respectable" churches and frowning clergymen, found in Arminian religions and revival experiences new certainties about God and experience. One of them, Henry Alline, discovered that the Calvinism of his youth had deprived his soul of God's sweet love. Now free of old constraints, his soul was "ravished with a divine ecstasy beyond any doubts or fears, or thoughts of being then deceived." He and others blamed Calvinist clergymen for cramping people's minds with ordered schemes of religious experience and rigid theological systems. For such freewheeling believers, visions, dreams, and other revival-inspired illuminations were normal channels of divine guidance. "I know the word of God is our infallible guide, and by it we are to try all our dreams and feelings," the Methodist believer Freeborn Garrettson conceded. "I also know," he added defiantly, that "things of a divine nature have been revealed to me."[3] Without a doubt, Methodists and other Arminians found in revival religion release from sin and Calvinism at the same time.

But revivals also were destabilizing events, and revived believers could do unpredictable things. They might suddenly realize that old friends and ministers were corrupt and admonish (or avoid) them; they might argue that older theologies were deadening and harshly criticize them; they might pronounce old churches impure and form new ones. Foreign observers and American participants alike commented on this strange state of affairs, this chaos of come-outers, critics, and new religious movements. "Every theological vagabond and peddler may drive here his bungling trade, without passport or license, and sell his false wares at pleasure," one observer noted. "What is to come of such confusion is not now to be seen."[4] Even indigenous evangelicals such as Robert Baird, writing to counter foreign criticism, admitted that, "in some of the divisions of Churches that have taken place in the United States, men have at times permitted themselves to speak and write with an acrimony unbecoming the Gospel." Though contending sects appeared to him as diverse "divisions of one vast army," he admitted that Christian soldiers sometimes turned on one another. The multiplication of sects was a serious evil, he said; it rendered the churches small and ineffective, and it led to disagreeable collisions and "unbrotherly jealousy."[5] While Baird thought that on "essential points there is little disputation," he had to concede that one matter in particular divided the evangelical army—namely, "the constitution of the human mind, the analysis of responsibility and moral agency, and the old question of 'fate and free-will.'"[6] Without a doubt, the period's volatile religious discussions grew out of this main concern of all revivalists—personal religious experiences and how they worked. Even an apologist for the revivals could see opinions on these matters had dangerously multiplied.

In the end, then, there was a doubleness to revivals, for though they gave spiritual comfort they also could take it away. Even the Calvinism of foreign-born Scots such as Alexander Campbell could be unsettled by

America's rough-and-tumble atmosphere. Reflecting on his seven years on the frontier, Campbell wrote that during "this period of years my mind and circumstances have undergone many revolutions. . . . I have . . . renounced much of the traditions and errors of my early education." Elsewhere he remembered that his "mind was, for a time, set loose from all its former moorings. It was not a simple change: but a new commencement[;] . . . the whole landscape of Christianity presented itself to my mind in a new attitude and position."[7] Others endured similar anxieties. Confused by the contradictory theologies promoted by different sects, a son of the great evangelist Lyman Beecher also felt his mind gradually becoming "intensely unsettled." In the 1850s he slipped deeper into uncertainty. Still others, such as the Methodist La Roy Sunderland, were bewildered by dissonant voices, human and divine, projecting themselves outward from revivals.[8] He was vexed in particular about ecstatic experiences—how and why people had them. Like others he would journey toward liberalism and its ways of interpreting experience.[9]

## OUT OF ORTHODOXY

Those journeying toward liberalism followed diverse paths in and out of Calvinist and Arminian groups but shared a sense of loss and a consciousness of their own spiritual failure. Almost all of them had failed to experience conversion in its prescribed forms. This meant of course that these Christians were interested in critiquing the old-time religion (usually evangelical Calvinism) and experimenting with alternatives. The discourses of critique and reform they produced were characterized by a common set of preoccupations: acute fears of a distant or wrathful God; inability to produce (or discover within) a sense of sin; and unusually high levels of confidence in the natural rhythms of nature and the powers of human nature. If we include a few other notions, such as a belief in God's immanence and a more individualistic and experimental religious attitude, we have a serviceable definition of the religious liberalism of this period. It is worth probing this liberal style for a moment to see how it contributed to the formation of new discourses of experience and spiritual assurance.

Liberal complaints about youthful anxiety were so frequent that they might seem meaningless tropes, but as Michael McGiffert has said of Puritan religious narratives, repetitive discourses can powerfully reshape the self and inner experience.[10] And so we might begin by considering liberal complaints and their ominous pronouncements concerning orthodoxy.[11] Undoubtedly, religious liberals missed few opportunities to deride offensive doctrines being delivered by coldhearted Calvinist doctors of divinity. The Unitarian educator and phrenologist Horace Mann remembered his childhood minister as a "man of pure intellect, whose logic was never softened in its severity by the infusion of any kindliness of sentiment. He expounded all the doctrines of total depravity, election, and reprobation, and not only the eternity, but the extremity of hell-torments, unflinchingly and in their most terrible significance."[12] Of course, the precise sources of Mann's fear lay not just in the prevailing Calvinism but also in the ways young liberals misunderstood, reacted to, and worried about that system. Imagining only the darker implications of Calvinism, glossing its doctrines as cruel and spiritually deadening, Mann was representative of the larger group. His childhood minister presented the doctrines matter-of-factly, he recalled, but "in the way in which they came to my youthful mind, a certain number of souls were to be forever lost, and nothing—not powers, nor principalities, nor man, nor angel, nor Christ, nor the Holy Spirit, nay, not God himself—could save them." Surely he, or his parents or siblings, would go to hell. "To my vivid imagination, a physical hell was a living reality, as much so as though I could have heard the shrieks of the tormented, or stretched out my hand to grasp their burning souls."[13] Liberals across the spectrum—from frontier Universalists and Congregationalists to urbane Unitarians—thought Calvinism promoted an unhealthy piety that made believers hopeless and mentally unstable. Different symptoms resulted—an infirm body, poor mental development, depression, insomnia, insanity. Perspicacious believers escaped before severe sicknesses set in, but even milder afflictions could be recalled later with resentment. "The dinners I have lost because I could not go through 'sanctification,' and 'justification,' and 'adoption,' and all such questions, lie heavily on my memory," one recovering Calvinist remembered. "I do not know that they have brought forth any blossoms. I have a kind of grudge against many of those truths that I was taught in my childhood, and I am not conscious that they have worked up a particle of faith in me."[14]

In point of fact, Calvinist doctrines were intended to produce an anxious alertness, an unsettling conviction of total sinfulness. Only after achieving this state could one learn to rely entirely on God; one had to wait, plead, and supplicate, and hope for God's intervention. Though feelings of worthlessness could put believers through harrowing psychological exercises, these emotions also laid the groundwork for compensating moments of comfort. This was so because abasement was an important inner sign that God had (already) saved you. Thus, the deeper the anxiety about abasement, the more certain believers might be that they were saved. These were the paradoxical comforts of perceiving the depths of your own worthlessness.

The trouble for liberals was that they could not master these alternating rhythms of abasement and contentment. They could not feel the depths of their sinfulness, and they thus could not start the process of conversion. This led to a different kind of anxiety—an anxiety that resulted not from a conviction of sin *but from an inability to achieve this conviction*. We can see this clearly in the life of someone like Andrew Jackson Davis (1826–1910), who, before becoming the famous spiritualist and seer, was a Presbyterian-turned-Methodist with a mind "painfully agitated" about a number of spiritual questions. As a youth he prayed to become aware of his sinfulness, hoping that a deep conviction of sin would generate new religious feelings. His pastor did his best to help.

> After being in this state of suspense for a long time, the residing and much esteemed Pastor came one day where I was engaged at my work, and inquired:
> "Well, brother Davis, how do you feel?"
> "Very well, Sir," said I.
> "No, no, I have reference to your spiritual welfare—have you made peace with your God?"
> It seemed impossible to answer. I never have had any disturbance with him in all my life, thought I.

Didn't he fear God? Didn't he worry about sin? Quickly his pastor gave up—"'O, unconverted youth, I fear the day of grace is past. I fear you will be damned forever!' On thus saying, he turned and left me. O, reader, can you imagine my thoughts, as he closed this sentence? The love of my nature was chilled into the coldest hate."[15] In moments like these, Christians like Davis gave up not on salvation but on the possibility that Calvinist notions might get them there.

Davis's cold hate propelled him in novel directions, as we will see; but the impulse to rethink experience proceeded along more ordinary paths as well, unsettling some even in the religious mainstream. Most of Lyman Beecher's remarkable children participated in this process. Catharine's revolt, played out in a fascinating correspondence with her father, has been analyzed elsewhere,[16] but the anxieties of her brother Henry Ward speak more clearly to the issue at hand—namely, why unsettled believers turned to new psychologies. Henry Ward shared emotional problems with Davis and his sister Catharine, and though Catharine comforted him by insisting that "you are not required to feel or to do anything that your willing or choosing will not secure," Henry Ward brooded.[17] He had been chary of open rebellion and had joined his father's church, but in college a spiritual darkness descended, and he reviewed "the almost childish experiences under which he had joined the church, as possibly deceptive," trying and disciplining "himself by those profound tests with which the Edwardean theology had filled the minds of New England." Had he found inner dispositions of total sinfulness? Without them, could he proceed legitimately? "A black despair was the result," Harriet remembered of this time in Henry's life, a despair that, like Andrew Jackson Davis's, resulted not because he had found a deeply sinful nature but because he had not. When Henry Ward consulted the president of the college, one of his father's friends, Henan Humphrey, the man misunderstood the sources of Henry's sadness. He congratulated him, saying that "his present feelings were a work of the spirit," and that Henry "should not interfere." So Henry continued to wait for abasement, and the spiral of "blank despair" quickened.[18] His spiritual failure, he remembered, "came near [to] wrecking me; for I became skeptical, not malignantly but honestly, and it was to me a matter of great distress and anguish. It continued for years and no logic ever relieved me." "During all that time," he confided to his sister, "my mind was *intensely* unsettled in theology."[19]

People in this situation had a choice—either they could admit that they had not produced the characteristic emotions of faith, or they could rethink how the whole process worked. Many were inclined to do the latter, gradually developing, as Henry Ward did, "a very different mental philosophy from that of the framers of theology." This new mental philosophy was based on natural philosophy and new physiological studies, both of which raised the possibility that the world, and the self, were not fallen at all, or fallen only in a restricted sense. These new mental philosophies stressed the beauty and order of the universe, and they drew on the natural sciences and romantic and natural theological glosses on them. Beecher, and many others, drew on Coleridge—and Paley. "I am delighted in studying the doctrines lately . . . and, in reading in science, in nature. I am searching for comparisons and analogies and similar principles to unfold, explain, and confirm the various truths of Scripture," he wrote.[20] This too was part of his liberation from Calvinism. Other liberals as well—Emerson and other Transcendentalists, Andrew Jackson Davis and other Spiritualists, Horace Bushnell and other Christian romantics—sought correspondences between the natural and the spiritual worlds. And others came, haltingly at first, to trust intuitions that nature, and human nature, if seen correctly, might be "a symbol of invisible spiritual truths."[21] The natural world was attuned to divine things.

It was not difficult to move from these convictions to new ideas on that most perfect of all created things, human nature, and how human nature might symbolize divine realities. Excited by this possibility, many turned to physiological studies to explore theological questions about mind and spirit and how they worked in regeneration.[22] God could remain transcendent, but tokens of his nature could be discerned in the forms of the human body, and especially in the human mind. "Human nature," one liberal wrote, "illustrates divine nature." "Divine attribute [sic] corresponds to our idea of human faculty. The terms are analogous."[23] Beecher for one believed that the physiology of the brain corresponded to the faculties of the mind, which in turn corresponded to the attributes of God. The correspondences were laid out for him in the science that attracted him above all others, a new physiological science called phrenology. As a system of correspondences that localized spiritual and mental capacities in regions of the head, phrenology hypothesized that the brain was the organ of the mind; that the brain was made up of distinct parts, each of them serving task-specific faculties; that the size of the different parts of the brain indicated the relative strength of the faculties they served; and that mental faculties could grow or atrophy depending on whether they were used.[24] (Localizing mental capacities in this way was a possibility developed much earlier in physiological studies, alluded to by Paley, and, in the nineteenth century, explored by different schools of anatomists and physiologists, including the Austrian anatomist Franz Joseph Gall [1758–1826]).[25] Beecher allowed this psychology to displace older mental philosophies; it became a new starting point. "My pride is a little humbled," he admitted, writing to his sister, "when I think that my great things are too small to be as first principles with father." Nevertheless, he concluded, "I mean to continue, for by such labor the subject is to my own mind expanded and made plain."[26]

Of course minds thus made plain were not the same minds mapped out by earlier, more orthodox believers. These psychological traditions were new discoveries. Those journeying out of orthodoxy embraced them as such, using them to find new capacities within themselves and better ways of thinking about how these capacities worked. Many finally found confirmation that they had natural abilities to perceive spiritual things. One young man, learning about phrenology from a friend, was surprised to realize that "he possessed at least an average amount of natural talent." This discovery caused "a new light" to break upon his mind and he "began to see that, as ignorant as he was, he had formerly underrated his abilities. He resolved to commence the cultivation of his mind at once." An expert phrenological examination, conducted by none other than Nelson Sizer, added to his confidence. His religious views changed entirely, for while he "formerly regarded his Maker as a mere tyrant, whom it was almost impossible to please," a God that sought "every opportunity to discover a defect in our conduct," he now saw clearly that these were symptoms of a "dark and benighted mind." He saw good possibilities in himself and corresponding qualities in God.[27] Other believers unable to work themselves into convictions of their sin (or out of them) embraced phrenology for similar reasons. The young Elizabeth Cady Stanton was terrified about salvation and caught in a paralyzing conviction of her inability. Though she somehow mustered a moment of joyful conversion, her relief, according to her, was cut short by Charles G. Finney's incessant harpings on "the depravity and deceitfulness of the human heart." Had her heart fooled her into thinking she was saved? How could she know? Only an encounter with phrenological studies by Gall, Johann Spurzheim, and George Combe released her from not knowing what to do or whether she could do it. Another young man, a student at Harvard Divinity School named James Freeman Clarke, saw clearly the ways that phrenology aided stalled believers. "One of the real benefits of [my study of phrenology] was that it inspired courage and hope in those who were depressed by the consciousness of some inability."[28]

But phrenology helped struggling believers in other ways. If it convinced some that powerful spiritual faculties existed in the self, it attracted others for another reason: It brought the mysterious inner dynamics of the self to the surfaces of the body, where these dynamics could be more easily observed and understood. In short, it made inner, invisible things visible again. "If . . . we can know the condition of the physical organism at any time, we can determine therefrom the condition of the mind," one enthusiastic Universalist wrote. In this new procedure lay "the mysterious pathway to the court of the soul." Others agreed that without the new psychological sciences everything else was "conjecture, speculation, theoretical abstraction." Another religious liberal said it plainly: as a guide to regeneration and practical spirituality, the older metaphysics were impenetrable.[29] The ambitious maps of mind and spirit that these believers produced—the busts, charts, and inventories of spiritual powers—are eloquent testimony that those confounded by the messy inwardness of Calvinism no longer wished to grope in spiritual darkness.

## PHRENOLOGICAL IMPROVEMENTS

On the face of it, liberals formulating new discourses of the self were doing what believers had done for centuries—borrowing ideas from mental philosophy to think about theological problems. But scientific psychologies like phrenology represented a new kind of mental philosophy, and borrowing from these psychologies resulted in formulations that also were new. To be sure, in the early nineteenth century, older philosophical traditions rooted in Christian theological concerns were giving way to mental philosophies that related human mental, emotional, and even spiritual life to physiological—especially neurological—processes. Phrenology was a part of this broader impulse in transatlantic culture. The principal stimulus behind this impulse was the professionalization of the medical sciences and the rising prestige of biological explanations of human life in general. By the middle of the century, this prestige was appropriated by influential social scientists like Herbert Spencer and Alexander Bain, thinkers investigating the human neuromuscular system and how it influenced cognition, feelings, and to some extent, beliefs. Bain in particular wanted to collapse physiology and psychology, seeking what he once called in a letter to his friend John Stuart Mill the "physiological basis of mental phenomena."[30] These phenomena included religion, though Bain recognized the complexity of belief, explaining that it was caused by feelings, mental processes of association, *and* the physiology of muscular and nervous activity. Even with these caveats, however, it was clear that these more physiological psychologies linked mental and spiritual realities to material phenomena; Bain's widely read textbook, *The Emotions and the Will,* for example, pointed out that belief had its "basis and ultimate criterion" in physiological activities.[31] The presupposition behind the work of Bain and Spencer was one shared with phrenologists—namely, that different emotional and mental capacities could be localized in different physiological structures. In fact, Bain and Spencer both took phrenology seriously, entering into sustained arguments about particular mental faculties and how they might be localized.

Scientific debate over phrenology continued until just after the middle of the century, when other physiological psychologies emerged and replaced what suddenly seemed an outdated and speculative science.[32] But phrenology lingered longer in popular culture, its categories and assumptions continuing to inform lay discourses on mind and personality. One historian has remarked that by midcentury "phrenology held a place in the American mind not unlike that occupied by psychiatry in the 1930s":

"its terminology and tenets entered the language of daily conversation"; "it proved a convenient means of summarizing behavior and character" in literature; and it offered a vocabulary of divine-human correspondence that undergirded art and painting in particular.[33] Its reach into American literature was extensive. Sometimes literary references were superficial and humorous—as in Melville's discussion of the phrenology of the white whale in *Moby Dick*—and sometimes more substantial, as in Caroline Lee Hentz's 1869 popular novel *Eoline.* Hentz filled out her principal characters with appropriate cranial topographies: one character's vocational choice— she was a schoolteacher—was vindicated by a phrenological consultation which demonstrated that "her organs of Self-Esteem and Firmness were, indeed, most wonderfully developed." Walt Whitman was perhaps the most famous borrower, using phrenological categories to understand himself, his generation, and his art. He kept his phrenological chart until the end of his life and published it five times with *Leaves of Grass.* It was a good thing he did; the phrenological language the book contains is hard to handle without it.[34]

Works by Bain and Spencer, and other major phrenological texts, were discussed in religious and secular magazines, and these works were cited and reviewed in the major Christian periodicals. It is clear that phrenology attracted audiences with a broad range of religious convictions, from Mormons and Adventists to Methodists, Presbyterians, and Congregationalists. Though there were exceptions, most positive reviews appeared in periodicals sponsored either by liberal denominations, mainline denominations rapidly becoming liberal (e.g., Congregationalists), or groups espousing a popular rationalism. In general, discussion about phrenology was more active in places dominated by evangelicalism (and evangelical offshoots), probably because the issue of religious experience mattered more in these contexts. If there was one group that embraced phrenology without hesitation, it was the Universalists. Confirming basic ideas about the goodness of human nature and the universality of salvation, phrenologists bolstered Universalist criticisms of orthodoxy and abetted rationalist approaches to experience. While Universalists enthusiastically embraced this new spiritual science, reaction in other denominations was mixed. Positive reviews were more likely in popular periodicals; professional theologians writing in approved journals could be cagey, and they usually took notice of the unseemly "excesses" and sensational demonstrations of crusading lecturers like Nelson Sizer and Edward Zeus Franklin Wickes, of whom more will be said later. In any event, religious interest in the new science was considerable.[35]

American believers embraced phrenology as a scientific alternative to the unsettled spiritual categories of American sectarianism. Ways of thinking about mind and spirit proliferated in contradictory patterns; newer, scientific psychologies overcame contradiction and doubt. Henry Ward Beecher urged "the study of man from the scientific side," preaching early and late in life that one of the most promising developments for religious people was the "founding of mental philosophy upon physiology." Linking the mind to the physical world—to a world of reliable facts and predictable laws—brought a new kind of certainty. Older systems had succeeded one another in vertiginous arrays. He was dizzy.[36] Others complained of similar forms of spiritual vertigo. Horace Mann said early in the century that he was "a hundred times more indebted to phrenological [sic] than to all the metaphysical works I ever read," pointing out that the "principles of Phrenology lie at the bottom of all sound mental philosophy, and all the sciences depending upon the science of the Mind; and all of sound theology too."[37] The Unitarian reformer Samuel Gridley Howe, the liberal physician Charles Caldwell, and in the last quarter of the century, the erudite Boston Unitarian James Freeman Clarke all agreed that phrenology was a significant improvement on older systems. For his part, Clarke was willing to repeat old liberal encomiums to phrenology even as new physiological psychologies displaced it. Phrenology had revolutionized mental philosophy, he wrote, for "metaphysics, a doubtful, uncertain study heretofore, with small practical results, at once became interesting and adapted to daily use."[38] To be sure, Americans like Clarke were merely repeating discourses initiated by phrenology's European founders.[39] No longer was the mind lost in darkness and indeterminacy. One could look at it; one could feel it.

In these ways, and for these reasons, believers embraced phrenology as an objective foundation for piety. Taking "the Bible for his chart in theology; Christ as his pattern in divinity; and Phrenology as his guide in Philosophy," the well-known Universalist writer George Weaver, for example, promoted phrenology because it linked subjective realities to objective ones. "The great error with past metaphysicians, has been, in neglecting to acquaint themselves with the material connections of mind, and through these to seek an acquaintance with the principles of mentality." "There can be no doubt," Weaver insisted, "that every exertion of the intellect, every flight of the imagination, . . . every feeling of sympathy, every emotion of joy or pleasure, calls into action some portion of the physical organism." The mind and spirit manifested their powers in the brain and nervous system in particular. Weaver saw as inescapable the conclusion that the "mind does manifest its states and changes through the material organism with which it is united," and reasoned that, if we "can know the condition of the physical organism at any time, we can determine therefrom the condition of the mind." The state of the body, and especially of the brain, "opens the passage that leads to the sanctuary of thought and feeling." "The mysterious pathway to the court of the soul," he said, had "been made plain."[40]

## SCIENTIFICALLY SORTING SINNERS AND SAINTS

The end result of this kind of reasoning was a dramatic reworking of the practical matters of religious experience—how to have one, and how to tell if yours was genuine. While for Weaver it was enough to argue and prove that "mind or spirit . . . molds matter," and that therefore the brain was an index of the mind, others were interested in practical matters.[41] How might phrenology help Christians understand how to gain and sustain faith? How might it help them better understand the dark, confounding spaces of their inner lives?

Using diagrammed busts of George Washington as illustrations, the Unitarian educator John Hecker brought those confounding inner spaces to the surface by mapping conversion onto the physiological self (see figure 2). Like other phrenologists, Hecker localized "spiritual faculties" in the upper regions of the brain, intellectual faculties in the midbrain, and instinctual and sensuous faculties near the bottom. Depravity, sin, disorder, and animality were associated with the dominance of the lower faculties; this was our "fallen nature." Regeneration and spiritual insight were associated with higher faculties. Against deists like the European phrenologists Combe and Spurzheim, Hecker argued that believers had to proceed through spiritual stages that resembled old-time morphologies of conversion. He pointed out that the "spiritual group [of faculties] is not predominant in activity" until energized by the Holy Spirit; that some kind of abasement was required to begin regeneration; that abasement led to an experience of passivity; and that therefore the Holy Spirit, when it entered the mind or brain, was the active force. When the Holy Spirit acted on the brain in this way, it united and harmonized discordant relations among the faculties and strengthened our higher, spiritual faculties. With self-culture, those faculties came to be the dominant forces in the brain.[42]

Hecker's was a middle position not uncommon in America, a call for a new spiritual science located between the anticlerical deism of European phrenologists and the antimodern sentiments of American evangelicals

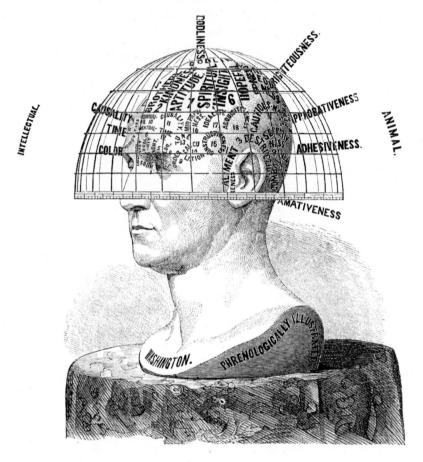

Figure 2.   Mapping spiritual and religious capacities on the head. From John Hecker, *The Scientific Basis of Education*, 1868.

who rejected phrenology vociferously. His way of producing this middle position involved borrowing orthodox nomenclatures and altering their significations. For instance, the abasement he talked about was a natural capacity lodged within us. It could be stimulated, trained, and cultivated in a way that allowed human beings to participate actively in generating the proper baseline emotions. So what at first appears to be an emphasis on passivity turns out to be a spirituality of activity and control. Phrenologists like Hecker were caught in this tension—a tension between accepting the

Holy Spirit as an active force and wanting to regulate spiritual dynamics more precisely. Still, the imperatives of personal development and social progress moved individuals like Hecker toward more liberal formulations of older spiritual dilemmas. He stressed human abilities, the beauty of human nature, moral activity, and self-culture. The moment of regeneration itself was less a moment in which grace was given, and more a moment in which God reshuffled and harmonized existing faculties. As this happened, believers could use natural abilities—they could cultivate religious emotions throughout the process, feelings like meekness, abasement, "religious impressibility," and moral sensitivity. These inner abilities also could be stimulated by various mental and physical exercises. And finally, the dynamics of conversion could be measured with certainty by attending to the shape of one's head. "The external manifestations of the gifts of the Spirit, in conduct, physiognomy, mien, bearing, language and expression, enable the observer to examine religion objectively."[43] This was the sine qua non of the believing phrenologist's position: You could map the physical contours of spiritual processes that eluded you. Hecker's formulations were similar to those promoted by key figures in the movement, including Orson Fowler, Lorenzo Fowler, and Samuel Wells.

Though liberals could compromise with orthodoxy, they were uninterested in temporizing on certain issues. The doctrine of total depravity was one of these. On this issue they delighted in subverting cherished older formulations. (Their frustration on this matter, and their impatient denunciations of the dynamics of sinfulness, probably had their origins in youthful evangelical failures, as we have seen.) Though the mood in Orson Fowler's key phrenological journal and in his popular religious publications is moderate, there was no way to be a phrenologist and a believer in total depravity. Anticipating that his opinions on "the constitutional elements of the sinfulness of sin" and the "causes and cure of human depravity" would be "directly in the teeth of all prevailing notions of this subject," Fowler pointed out that his notions were "founded in *Truth*" and "built upon FACTS," and that these facts revealed (as they did to Spurzheim and Combe) that "no [mental] faculty is *constitutionally* bad," that every faculty "as originally constituted, is *good* and *right*, and that the *legitimate* exercise of any and every faculty, upon its own appropriate object, and in a proper degree, is virtuous." The highest level of spiritual development was represented by a natural equilibrium in which all the mind's faculties, each in its proper place, worked harmoniously together, and in which the mind's organs of "marvellousness" and "veneration" were cultivated.[44]

Like Hecker, Fowler retained older words like *sin* and *depravity* and wholly redefined them. On this issue he insisted that human beings were sinful *"not* because they have *depraved faculties,* but because they make a *depraved use* of *good faculties."* All human beings partook in this disorder or depravity. "Phrenology certainly recognizes [sin] in the fact that the natural exercise and function of [each person's] faculties are more or less perverted and distorted in nearly or quite all mankind." This formulation made some form of redemption necessary, but the redemption that Fowler had in mind was not a sudden change in the nature of the faculties—all of them already were good—but a change in how they were organized and how their energies were directed. Conversion was God's way of reorganizing the relative strengths of mental faculties, stimulating moral and religious faculties in particular until they became dominant, and energizing those faculties so that they might organize all mental activity. Conversion "consists simply in the *spiritualization* of our natures already pointed out, the main medium of which is [the faculty of] marvellousness. By operating upon this faculty and organ, it extends the range of its action so as to quicken benevolence, veneration, hope, conscientiousness, and the whole moral group; and that gives them ascendancy over the propensities which we have already shown to constitute virtue, the product of which is 'joy in the Holy Ghost,' moral purity, and consequently happiness." Fowler's emphasis on spiritual faculties, intuition, and natural balance was reproduced by many others—the Beechers, the Protestant reformer (and grandfather of J. P. Morgan) John Pierpont, James Freeman Clarke, and itinerant lecturers of the sort who visited Granville, Massachusetts, in 1841.[45]

Of course the most powerful phrenological innovation had nothing to do with theories of sin or the self, but with practical ways of clearly seeing inner experience. Was it possible now to discern certain signs of inner changes? Did the Spirit's activity in the brain change the head physically? A writer for the African American *Christian Recorder* thought it logical that a change as dramatic as conversion might result in physical changes. "I cannot pretend to describe all that change, but I am of the opinion that this emotion rises higher and seems so sweet and new, not only because it is from God and inspired by such grand themes, but also because in its bursting forth it effects some physical change." Conversion was a new growth, a new exercise of the brain's faculties, a truly new birth. This writer offered some evidence, not as proof, but as a legitimate subject to consider. He said that "it is the testimony of all, that in conversion a perceptible change occurs, a change that can be felt." It was common for converts to say that "something seemed to come down and strike me right on the top of my head and run all over." Some said that "a ball of fire seemed to strike me on the top of my head," or that "the Spirit seemed to touch me on the top of the head." Might these sensations be caused by "the breaking away or releasing of these organs of the brain into joyful exercise?" The top of the head was, after all, the location of the spiritual faculties. Finally, this writer suggested that the permanence of the change might be explained by a physical change undergirding it.[46]

While popular phrenologists could debate whether and how Christians who had been regenerated by the Holy Spirit were reshaped physically,[47] most of them agreed that the outer body, and especially the head, somehow showed signs of saving inner emotions. They also learned to perceive signs of counterfeit experiences, deception, and hypocrisy. Exposing crooks, criminals, and religious fakes is a common theme in phrenological literature. When lecturing in churches, for instance, phrenologists took opportunities to assess the religious merits of ministers and church officials. One phrenologist discovered an enormous organ of Acquisitiveness (greed) in a Methodist minister; he was a thief, and he later admitted as much.[48] Others were surprised to find similar proclivities in outwardly pious preachers. In one shocking public examination of a deacon who handled the church's business affairs, a phrenologist found the man to be "grasping and selfish, but smooth and inclined to be tricky in his dealings." Onlookers gasped—but they were persuaded when this deacon disappeared with all their money. On other occasions, itinerant phrenologists advised churchgoers and church officials about their personality deficits and helped sort sinners from saints.[49]

Triumphalist stories circulated about seeing clearly the inner self. Many of them dramatized the victory of new, scientific certainties over older superstitions. Few of them match those of an outspoken former Baptist minister from Vermont, Josiah M. Graves. After lecturing in a Middletown, Connecticut, church, Graves had himself blindfolded and then offered to perform readings. He happened to have an uncle in the congregation, a temperance man and deacon of the church who was "regarded as a model in most things by every person in all that region." Someone thought it would be amusing to have Graves's uncle step forward, and the uncle obliged. Josiah Graves had a peculiar way of examining people that included vigorously rubbing different parts of the head and sampling resulting odors. Being a temperance man, Graves was interested in particular in detecting the liquor habit, which he did "by rubbing the organ of Alimentiveness" (appetite) and smelling his fingers. He reproduced the procedure on his uncle, to titters of laughter, and announced, "This man drinks!" Shouts of laughter. "He drinks rum, brandy, something hot and alcoholic!" The audience laughed mostly at Graves's eccentricities, but his uncle, feeling the heat of the spotlight, became angry. How could his nephew accuse him of such things? "Now, uncle, I smell the odor of dead liquor when I rub your organ of Alimentiveness, and I believe you have taken liquor within forty-eight hours. On your honor now, in the presence of this painfully silent audience, tell me, have you not taken liquor within forty-eight hours?" After a moment, Graves's uncle admitted he "had a bad turn of colic night before last, and I got up at 12 o'clock and took some brandy and cayenne pepper to relieve it." The audience erupted. Temperance advocates gasped. Everyone else laughed at the embarrassing and anomalous spectacle.[50]

If these stories dramatize the power of phrenology to read properly one's inner states, they also demonstrate the bravery and skill of a new class of teachers and preachers. Phrenologists willing to tell the truth had a lot to lose—and some of them became prophets without honor in their own countries. One newspaper told of a traveling phrenologist who first lectured to a large audience and then examined the head of a "stout, two-fisted fellow." "Sir, your phrenological developments are those which belong to an infamous villain—destructiveness and combativeness enormous, conscientiousness very small, and all the moral and reflective region perfectly contemptible," the phrenologist reported. All the man lacked, he continued, was an "opportunity to become a rascal." With that, the man rose and "by a well directed blow with his fist, knocked the Doctor flat upon the floor." Collecting himself, the phrenological doctor announced to a stunned audience that *here* was "the strongest proof of the truth of phrenology I have ever seen in the entire course of my career. The villain has proved every word I told him to be the truth."[51] Such stories incorporated spectacular and humorous elements and drew attention to intriguing possibilities. Could new spiritual sciences see within?

Liberal pastors also were intrigued by these new possibilities, using phrenology to understand personality types, spiritual difficulties, and religious experience. A range of liberal-leaning ministers was involved, including an especially strong showing among Universalists and other rural, anti-Calvinists. In 1852 the *Universalist Quarterly* recalled that, "when Phrenology became prevalent in our country, one could hardly enter a Universalist minister's study, but there hung the chart, or stood the bust, like the guardian angel of the place, with the 'organs' all marked out and numbered on the cranium."[52] Some would physically or intellectually stimulate their parishioners' skulls to help develop certain faculties—of veneration, for instance.[53] Others stopped short of this, borrowing phrenology only as a system of seeing more clearly people's inner states and organizing them into different classifications. Henry Ward Beecher used phrenology in this way. He assigned basic phrenological texts to his ministerial students, one of whom remembered that Beecher promoted the new science as a more factual way to understand "the mysteries of mind" and experience, and as a better way of diagnosing and preaching to parishioners. Beecher assigned Combe to his homiletics students. He used phrenological insights to understand human nature and tailor his sermons to his parishioners' needs and desires.[54] An outspoken and popular promoter of phrenology, Beecher was challenged by Catholics, Baptists and others, especially on this issue and others related to understanding experience. In one exchange, a writer for the *Catholic Herald*, while not dismissive of Beecher's claims, argued that there was another, more certain way of probing the inner self: confession. Pointing to well-known problems with phrenology, this writer argued simply that "no bumps are studied, and no characteristic is guessed at. The penitent says plainly and distinctly, 'Thus and thus I thought, and thus and thus I did.' 'So I acted, and so I failed to act.'" A perfectly clear window into the self! It was not necessary "that the confessor should know that there is a bump of accretiveness"; and if someone was violent, it was not necessary to guess at the dimensions of a bump of "combativeness." Besides, this writer continued, sins of thought (as opposed to action) were hard to see on the head but easy to probe in pastoral encounters. Beecher thought this solution was simplistic: how would it solve the problems of hypocrisy and dissimulation? But Beecher had to admit that phrenology, too, was imperfect; it was "crude," he said, and "needed revising."[55] Little did he know how completely it would be cast away.

## CERTAIN BRAIN-SPIRIT CORRESPONDENCES

While most American phrenologists compromised with Christianity, there were some who, believing they had solved the riddle of religious experience, felt no need to harmonize new and old. In their self-assured pronouncements and ambitious maps of metaphysical forces, these believers left Christian symbols behind altogether.

It is easy to find the language of complete certainty in handbills, broadsides, and pamphlets produced by itinerants in this period. Popular itinerants like Edward Zeus Franklin Wickes offered this certainty in public lectures and in a number of new technologies for measuring the self—including personality charts, tables of mental faculties, and simple theological principles correlating nature, human nature, and divine realities. If Wickes's printed pronouncements are any indication, he found appreciative audiences by promising complete religious certainty. His promotional materials, and presumably his "entertaining and instructive" lectures, were productions of an inspired and iconoclastic prophet. Everything "in nature is compelled to bear its character at mast-head," Wickes exclaimed; and new spiritual sciences would help us finally "see secret thoughts and intents of the hearts."[56] At first glance, Wickes's ways of seeing inner thoughts resembled those of other popular phrenologists—charts, busts, and tables. A sample of Wickes's "Improved Phreno-Chart" is in figure 3. As with other charts, his is organized with the spiritual capacities at the crown of the head and the lower, animal propensities at the base and near the ears. But Wickes's system is more ambitious than most. His system of correspondences links the human head not just to an inner, spiritual geography but also to the regions of the earth and to Swedenborg's spiritual essences, love and wisdom. (Wickes's liberation from Christianity, like that of other freethinkers, was abetted by the ideas of the Swedish seer Emmanuel Swedenborg, who, in a series of angelic revelations, outlined the material-spiritual correspondences that constituted the universe. His system was taken up and modified by many phrenologists, mesmerists, and freethinkers in this period.) Like Swedenborg, Wickes exuded confidence; he found answers to all human problems, personal, business, and marital, in the correspondences between the cosmos and the body.

Wickes's theological perspective, which he never explicitly stated, is important to ponder. Unlike Hecker and other mediators, Wickes does not use Christian terminology. Essentially a deist, he assumes that nature, not revelation, is the source of religious knowledge: "Nature's symbolical bible of truth with her life-like pictures is ever open to all; printed by the great Architect of the universe without errors, interpolations or pious frauds." As a source of truth, nature was an improvement on the ministry and the church; nature was incapable of dissimulation or hypocrisy. With his spiritual guidebooks and pamphlets split about evenly between salvation and healing, Wickes promoted a system in which all mental, spiritual, and physical events were a part of the same creation. Health and salvation were achieved by understanding natural forces and harmonizing one's own energies with them. "No rational mind can doubt that God controls all things by fixed, unchangeable laws, which are His will and word, instituted by the Creator for the preservation of the beauties and harmonies of nature, by

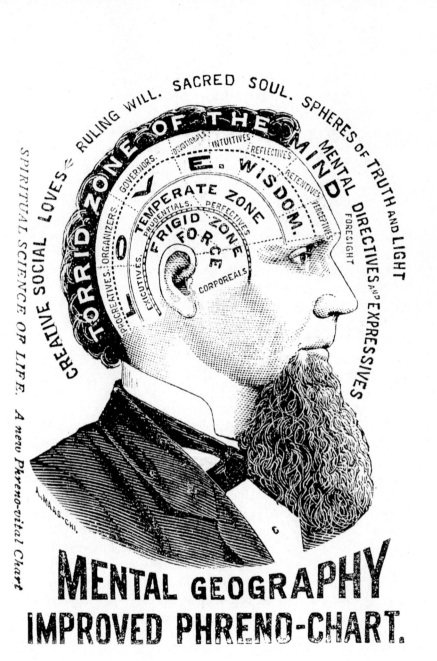

Figure 3.    Seeing secret inner things on the outer self. From Edward Zeus
Franklin Wickes, *Improved Phreno-Chart and Compass of Life,* circa 1883.
(Taken from Charles Colbert, *A Measure of Perfection: Phrenology and the Fine
Arts in America* [Chapel Hill: University of North Carolina Press, 1997], 32).

which the winds blow and the tides of ocean measure." Wickes, like most radicals, combined phrenological charts with techniques for manipulating immaterial forces, forces that he sometimes glossed as magnetic or electrical. These forces could be redirected and shaped to bring balance to the map of faculties. In this context, self-culture involved an array of techniques for observing, measuring, and redistributing cosmic forces.[57]

This was precisely the case for Andrew Jackson Davis, whose spiritual peregrinations I already have touched on. Certain that orthodoxy hampered "the spontaneous development of Nature's own religion," Davis learned to listen to inner impressions. Among other things, these impressions told him that the "four pillars upon which the theological superstructure is sustained"—"original sin, atonement, faith and regeneration"—were a "mass of disgusting rubbish," and that "nature, reason and intuition are the only infallible mediums of revelation, the only church, creed and religion natural to the mind of man." Davis was more combative than most, more willing to trash older theologies, and more willing to engage in invidious comparisons between revelation and nature. When challenged by moderates, Davis assured them that "the best of Harmonial Philosophers are among those who have tried the old system thoroughly." They had tried it, they had tested "experimental" orthodoxy, but this system had failed them.[58] Intolerant of compromise, he criticized his neighbor in Hartford, Horace Bushnell, for his temporizing tome, *Nature and the Supernatural* (1858).[59] Davis would not have been sympathetic to Christian phrenologists either. In any case, the mature Davis, inner voice firmly in command, was overcome with a certainty that impelled him to write things down and tell others about his spiritual discoveries. His resulting formulations made human beings the critical link between all other material and spiritual realities—far from sinful or inhibited, human beings were mediators between heaven and earth. His views on these matters are illustrated in the image adorning the first pages of his *Present Age and Inner Life* (figure 4), as is his strong conviction, won during the long spiritual struggle with orthodoxy, that inspiration was unmediated—that the unaided self could communicate directly with the spirit world. The self connects the material world with the regions of love and wisdom—again, Swedenborg's nomenclature—and the concourse of angels. Angels communicate directly with the spiritual mental faculties.

The other aspect of Davis's image worth noting is the dynamic nature of the forces impinging on the self. This image makes it clear that there is an ongoing commerce between spiritual and mental forces, and that these forces converge on the human body in particular. Combining phrenology,

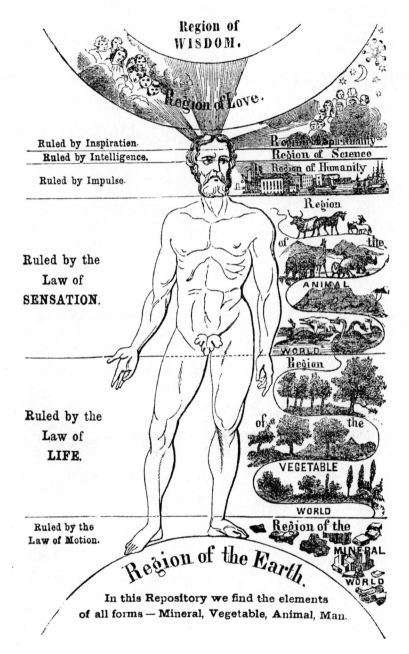

Figure 4.    Andrew Jackson Davis's map of the spiritual self. From Andrew Jackson Davis, *The Present Age and Inner Life*, 1869.

physiological studies, mesmerism, and other spiritual sciences, Davis, like Wickes and others, extended brain-spirit correspondences outward from the head, mapping mental and spiritual states on the entire body.[60] Regeneration became a discipline of manipulating these forces and using them to move believers through four different hypnotic (or "mesmeric" or "magnetic") states. In the first, individuals "lose none of their senses, but are susceptible to all external impressions. They have also the full power of muscular action; and if situated nearly midway between the first and second states, they are inclined to happy feelings." In stage 2, individuals lose sensation and muscular power but keep their intellectual powers. Stage 3 brings unconsciousness. Finally, in stage 4, the mind is freed "from all inclinations which the body would subject it to, and only sustains a connexion [to the body] by a very minute and rare medium, the same that connects one thought with another." In this stage, the mind is "capable of receiving impressions of foreign or proximate objects."[61] This is the state in which Davis himself received his spiritual impressions. Needless to say, the model of spiritual development Davis recommended here was quite different from older ways of thinking about regeneration.

. . .

I have deliberately transgressed boundaries between popular and official, high culture and low, in order to limn out a shared culture of religious psychological experimentation in this period. My argument is that scientific psychologies like phrenology helped liberals put an end to their religious difficulties by opening up new ways of thinking about the self and salvation. Radical liberals and churched liberals both testified to this—that this science and others helped them recover a sense of spiritual vitality. Near the end of his life, Henry Ward Beecher summed up these claims in an article, "Progress of Thought in the Church," for the *North American Review*. He celebrated the passing of "hideous doctrines" like the doctrine of total depravity in particular. "No ingenuity or eloquence can persuade [believers] that a God, who for ten thousand years has labored to produce an infinite population of damnable souls, can with decency be called our Father. The common sense, the humanity, the moral sense which have grown out of the Gospel are judging theology." But the heavy lifting had been done by something other than common sense. Part of the transformation, Beecher himself confirmed, was fueled by "recent scientific researches and disclosures respecting the mind of man," by which Beecher meant not just phrenology—even he knew that that theory was, like depravity, losing its luster—but by *all* new psychologies "developed within the scope of our experience and observation" by which we might better "deduce conceptions of the great mind." Psychological sciences were becoming the alembic transforming older theological formulas, the methodology that uncovered the original essence of religious truth. The natural world and human nature were revealing new things, tearing down and building up. If properly understood and used, our mental faculties in particular could produce certainty about God and spiritual matters. This is what Beecher meant when he claimed that the moral sense was "judging theology." Transitions were difficult—"positive faith may stagger while old things are passing away"—but there was a "larger reason, higher morality, deeper spirituality" possible through "this advanced and purified nature of man," one that might give old truths "clearer and more rational interpretation."[62] This modernist agenda was embraced by liberal laypeople and clergy across the board.

Nevertheless, it is worth reinforcing an obvious point—that not all liberals pursued this course as single-mindedly as Henry Ward Beecher. Putting aside for a moment orthodox complaints and recriminations, which occurred continuously until the 1870s, liberals too had questions about how to handle properly the sharp-edged tools of modern psychology. There is no question that liberals used phrenology to redescribe mysterious inner processes in physiological terms. When they did this, they found themselves able to perceive their experiences more clearly and understand and manage them. They developed techniques for training and manipulating the body and its vital forces and considered these techniques ways of shaping the inner self. This procedure solved their spiritual problems, but it raised other difficulties. Liberals not blinded by enthusiasm for newfound psychological systems of salvation worried about this. Had all spiritual things been reduced to natural forces? Were the movements of spirit merely physical in origin? John Hecker wrestled with this question, hoping to preserve autonomy for spiritual forces by translating standard phrenological terms for mental faculties (inherited from Spurzheim) into more religious ones (e.g., by translating the faculty of "marvellousness" into "spiritual insight" and "veneration" into "Godliness"). Others, like the onetime Methodist minister La Roy Sunderland, were not able to keep the natural and supernatural apart and slid into fully naturalistic accounts of the self.[63] Some wondered if the demise of Sunderland and others like him was the natural result of experimenting with such notions.[64]

Radicals like Davis brought these disagreements into sharp focus. Davis raised one crucial question in particular: Were personal religious experiences sufficient testimony? Or should they be checked by other sources of religious authority—by the Bible, the ministry, a circle of learned practitioners? When Davis cultivated his faculties in ways that led to sensational visions and revolutionary denunciations of the status quo, many liberals took umbrage. Horace Mann, Henry Ward Beecher, and other open-minded liberals thought Davis a ridiculous imposter.[65] Others called for Davis to submit to a phrenological reading—to see if his putative abilities could be verified by a scientific reading of his cranium. Arguments about experience among phrenologists also incorporated class dimensions, with professional theologians (and psychologists) increasingly ashamed of the intemperate enthusiasms of rationalistic rabble-rousers in their own ranks. Popular lecturers were accused of being merely entertainers. Itinerants like Wickes and delusional radicals like Davis were giving science a bad name. Sophisticated defenders of the new science made more measured claims, admitting that precise correspondences were "hit and miss," even if the basic procedures were sound. Body and spirit were linked in *some* way. Besides, though imperfect, phrenology was the only useful system for classifying and understanding mental capacities.[66] For this reason and others, many held on to it as a way to better understand inner dynamics of mind and spirit.

There was one final irony here, though, not noticed by most liberals embracing this new knowledge—namely, that moving the site of experience outside its dark, interior spaces and onto the outer surfaces of the brain did not solve the problem of seeing spiritual things clearly. For the brain and how to understand it was changing too, and even if the truths found by employing some form of phrenology provided spiritual comfort, the sand was shifting. In very short order, phrenological terminology and practices would take their turn at being old, imprecise, and "speculative," and these formulations, like the ones they displaced, would be casually cast aside. In the 1860s and 1870s, a new physiological psychology emerged, one that provided better ways of understanding the self, its vital forces, and how to develop them. This newer psychology, essentially modern scientific psychology, was, as Lucy Hartley has shown, phrenology's logical outcome and the source of its dissolution.[67]

## 2    Fragments of Truth

Not many of those comforted spiritually by psychological sciences such as phrenology could have guessed that these sciences, when fully developed, contained possibilities more dreadful than those that had been foisted upon them by older, ironclad orthodoxies. And so, for a while, in part because scientific psychology offered such powerful liberations, believers ignored their concerns about its hazards and risks. But such ignorance was not possible forever. A second generation of religious liberals, growing up in an age of science, both understood psychology's possibilities better and felt more intensely its spiritual dangers. As they extended the range and power of psychological explanations, this second generation began to see that psychological glosses on the self and experience would have to be qualified with a number of sobering caveats and warnings.

The change from first- to second-generation thinking on these matters took place in a thousand different locations—in the minds of children mystified by older theologies; in ways that pastors and parents tried to translate their religions into newer idioms; in the intellectual lives of seminarians avidly absorbing new knowledge of all kinds. In this last category was a young student at New York's Union Theological Seminary, a son of Massachusetts Puritans suddenly living far away enough from home to explore, with minimal discomfort, notions that his parents found dangerous or offensive. "My life before had been so restricted," he remembered of this time, that "all the accumulated curiosity of years to see the world and what it really was and meant was irresistible." His emancipated curiosities propelled him in astonishing directions: He consulted phrenologists, interviewed mediums, attended séances, and worshipped with Jews, Catholics, Seventh-Day

Adventists, Theosophists, and Holy Rollers. Soon he became part of a group of seminarians that attended Henry Ward Beecher's church and met with the great, progressive pastor for discussions in his study. He gratefully recalled both the kind reception he received at this church and Beecher's "disagreement with many of the things we were taught at the seminary." Here was a religious group he could join. When Beecher examined him for membership, Beecher asked if theological studies had made him more or less devout. "Less," the seminarian admitted, without elaborating. Unruffled, Beecher commended him for honesty and welcomed him to the congregation. Beecher also knew this young man had interests akin to his own—philosophical interests in mental science and physiology and a desire, but not the means, to study these subjects in Germany. About the young man's plans for study abroad, Beecher wondered—would such study make him less religious? "I said I thought it would make me religious in a larger sense," the young man recalled. This answer apparently satisfied Beecher, who gave him a note to take to Henry W. Sage, a wealthy parishioner also interested in mental science. When confronted with Beecher's note, Sage grumbled something to the effect that his "pastor took amazing liberties with his purse," scribbled a check for one thousand dollars, and presented it to the astonished young man. G. Stanley Hall departed for Europe the very next day, apparently without bidding anyone good-bye.[1]

In time, G. Stanley Hall (1844–1924) would become one of the most powerful American theorists and organizers of phrenology's replacement, the "new psychology." By locating the mind not in the brain, as phrenologists had, but in the entire neuromuscular system, Hall and the German scientists he learned from changed how people thought about the mind. In their formulations, the arc of nervous transmission, from stimulus to muscle contraction, represented the basic unit of the self. This concept was called the "reflex arc," and it was a crucial innovation, for it made it possible to explain complex human behaviors by resolving them into simple, physiological elements. The problem was that reducing the self to basic physiological elements led to distressing intellectual and religious difficulties. Was it possible to reconcile theistic commitments with a fully physiological self? Could spirit operate in a mechanistic world made up of stimulus-response patterns? Hall, William James, and other key psychologists worked through these tensions and, in different ways, developed compromises and solutions that were later borrowed by American religious believers.

## THE NEW PSYCHOLOGY

When Stanley Hall arrived in Germany in 1869, finding physiological correlates for mental states was still on the agenda, even if very few intellectuals believed in the simplistic correspondences suggested by phrenologists. In Germany and elsewhere, phrenology had declined. Observations had shown that mental faculties and cranial "bumps" did not correlate. And more important, physiologists had experimentally tested several phrenological hypotheses and found them erroneous. A French anatomist and professor of natural history at the College de France, Pierre Flourens (1794–1867), took the lead in dismissing the localizations of Gall and other phrenologists. Flourens performed experiments on animals, removing cerebral hemispheres, and noting changes in brains of recently deceased human beings with psychopathologies. From his studies Flourens was convinced that the cerebrum functioned as an integrated whole. And though efforts to localize mental capacities continued, the emphasis shifted from searching for discrete psychological "organs" to finding and understanding the simplest motor and sensory elements.[2] Europeans who did this, and Americans like Stanley Hall who copied them, believed that this procedure led to better and more scientific explanations. To be good scientists they would have to do what other scientists did: they would have to explain complex phenomena by reducing them to their most basic elements. In the hindsight of the midcentury, phrenology did not seem to do this; the new psychology did.

In the 1860s and 1870s the new psychology was worked out by several German physiologists and psychologists, most notably Gustav Fechner (1801–1887) and Wilhelm Wundt (1832–1920). In 1860 Fechner published his landmark *Elemente der Psychophysik,* a book that tried to express mathematically the connection between intensity of stimulus and intensity of (perceived) sensation. Here was one way to express uniform relations between natural and human worlds, and in particular between material and mental phenomena—in Fechner's words, it was one way to arrive at "an exact science of the functional relations of dependency between mind and body." Assuming that mental life was always accompanied by nervous and physiological changes, Fechner and several other Germans—Ernst Heinrich Weber (1795–1878), Hermann Lotze (1817–1881), and Hermann von Helmholtz (1821–1894)—measured the velocity of nervous impulses and examined how subjects associated ideas, produced memories, and perceived space and time. In this and other ways, Fechner and others showed that human beings, when properly instructed, could be reliable laboratory subjects—in other words, that they could produce data reducible to lawful description. This was the crucial matter: that activities of the mind could be observed (in the body) and then studied in terms of lawful interactions. Fechner hoped to qualify psychophysics "for membership in the select circle of the . . . experimental sciences," and he therefore rigidly adhered to quantitative experimental methods. Wundt, whose training was in physiology and neurophysiology, praised Fechner for showing "how a 'mathematical psychology' may, within certain limits, be realized in practice." But while agreeing that the mind should be studied experimentally, Wundt also called for a broader focus on consciousness rather than discrete mental events. With consciousness as its subject, Wundt's *Physiologischen Psychologie* included not just analyses of simple laws of sensation but also experimental investigations of thinking, feeling, remembering, and so on. (Wundt used the terms *psychology, experimental psychology,* and *physiological psychology* interchangeably.) As the holder of the chair of philosophy at the University of Leipzig for forty years, Wundt occupied a major position in German academic culture; his version of psychology dramatically influenced psychologists up until World War I. He is generally considered the founder of modern scientific psychology.[3]

The sine qua non of the new psychology was the "reflex arc" or "reflex action." The reflex arc played "a role in modern psychological and physiological theorizing," one historian has observed, that was comparable "with the part played by the fundamental explanatory principles of physics and chemistry."[4] It was the basic unit of the self, the simplest sensorimotor process, and it was composed of a nervous impulse traveling through sensory nerves to the central nervous system, which then guided these impulses into motor nerves that, finally, led to muscular reactions. This was the physiological replacement for concepts such as "association" that had been posited by philosophers such as Mill and Bain. To new psychologists, simple mental events were imagined as simple reflex arcs; complex mental processes were imagined as layers or combinations of these reflex arcs. Of course, this was not solely a creation of German anatomists and scientists, even though Germans led the world in making it operational within the context of laboratory experiments. Though the new psychology represented an advance over phrenology in many ways, it was nevertheless the case that linking thoughts or feelings to sensorimotor processes, as these new psychologists did, was not so different from linking mental functions to brain structures, as phrenologists did. Both moved the pattern of the mind's experience into the body, where it might be better observed, studied, and understood.

Fechner, Wundt, and their students produced a great deal of early psychological research on the brain, mind, and behavior, and their approaches profoundly influenced a generation of scientific psychologists in Europe and America. But they left behind a double legacy. Fechner, Wundt, and other psychologists of their generation felt disappointed in certain ways by the systems they had devised. Wundt is known both for carrying forward and systematizing the scientific procedures of Fechner and Helmholtz *and* pursuing a second, quite distinct, agenda, arguing in different contexts that significant events in human history—and in fact significant events within the mind itself—were beyond the reach of experimental methods. He was acutely aware of the limitations of Fechner's procedures and of British associationism; and he was disdainful of the premise that psychology could definitively settle philosophical matters like the mind/body problem. Sure that human history did not proceed exclusively according to causal laws, he thought that fully understanding life required different methods and explanatory principles.[5] This was why he had insisted on a broader subject matter—consciousness—and a science that considered more than just stimulus-response chains and the laws that might determine them. In many ways, these were paradoxical positions for a scientific psychologist to hold.

Fechner had his own ways of avoiding the implications of the science he was helping create. There were, as Ralph Barton Perry correctly remembered, two Gustav Fechners: one, the author of psychophysical laws and inventor of techniques to measure them; and the other, a metaphysical Fechner, one who "conceived of the universe as a series of overlapping souls from God down through the earth-soul to man, and from man to the unobservable psychic states." Fechner was troubled by materialism and felt a calling to refute it in its various forms, partly because he nursed long-standing interests in the *Naturphilosophie* of his home country and partly because he experienced a miraculous cure of debilitating ailments, an astounding event that raised his interest in the soul and religious consciousness. German psychology always had been metaphysical; Fechner followed in this tradition, as did Hermann Lotze, who was seminal for American religious thinkers and believing psychologists, and who worked out a "physiology of the soul." Fechner's solution to the problems raised by scientific materialism was a "panpsychism" that affirmed the identity of mind and matter and argued that the entire universe was alive with spirit. Consciousness was in everything.[6]

Fechner's was not an uncommon middle position, and on his different journeys to Germany, Hall listened to it sensitively. (And repeatedly: for a time in 1879 and 1880, Hall and his young wife lived next door to Fechner, and they conversed often.) A more mature Hall learned to do what other scientists were doing—to look askance at Fechner's notions. Eventually Hall would deride, in particular, Fechner's eccentric "dreameries about souls of molecules, plants and planets." Fechner thought everything was alive with spirit. But there is no question that the younger Hall saw Fechner's ideas as a way around scientific materialism. In addition, Hall's mature philosophical position, an idealism that interpreted mind and matter as different ways of seeing the same substance, was in many respects a restatement of Fechner's basic position. But Hall moved slowly to this formulation. During his first trip to Germany (1869–1870) he studied theology and philosophy and occasionally preached to an American congregation near Berlin. From Berlin he reassured his parents that he was not falling prey to lax German theologies: "I meet rationalism everywhere in the lectures of the professors, even here in the family, but thanks in part to my early training and still more to a higher faith as I trust, it leaves no mark on me." The higher faith he had glimpsed briefly in Beecher's study was coming into focus.[7]

There was, however, a final piece missing in this higher faith. This element was supplied by a philosopher who had helped many transcend older dogmas, the German Christian romantic Georg Wilhelm Friedrich Hegel (1770–1831). Hall thought Hegel's philosophy encompassed all things in a universal "explanatory solvency" that harmonized reason and the divine spirit. Hegel's Christianity showed how spirit and matter, Christ and culture, were coextensive. "All conventionalities, and ideal institutions of society, church, state, family, schools, duty, etc.," Hall wrote, "cease to exist merely and alone as brute material facts, and become clothes which the mind has made for itself rather than integuments which cannot be put off without vital lesion." (A typical Hall passage—obscurely written and impassioned. "Hall is a wonderful creature," William James once wrote. "Never an articulate conception comes out of him.") To be fair to Hall, these were difficult problems to conceptualize. The divine manifested itself in all things in the world, and especially in the human mind and its diverse intellectual and creative activities. "Hall loved to conceive the Divine as the system of 'reason which underlay and shaped all things,'" one of Hall's biographers has written, and to "interpret Hegel's concept of history as 'God coming to consciousness in man.'"[8] Though Hall was chary of theologians and thought the "theological stage" had been superceded, he continued to overlay his Hegelian idealism with Christian theological terms. His idealism incorporated Christian motifs.

The higher faith that Hall developed transported him beyond the confines of Puritan doctrine and practice, and in letters home he could not always hide his transformations. Once he made the mistake of offhandedly telling his parents that he was socializing with women and dancing, facts that his father found "astounding." He warned Stanley to resist temptation, gently requested a fuller accounting of his daily activities, and implied that he should come home. When Stanley insisted that such matters were trivialities because his motives were innocent, it probably provided little reassurance. Stanley found himself enjoying these activities, drinking beer, and continuing to read Hegel. His parents were not the only ones witnessing his internal revolutions. Even before Germany, Hall had preached a "trial sermon" at Union, after which the seminary's president had "knelt and prayed that I might be shown the true light and saved from mortal errors of doctrine." Then, Hall remembered, the discomfited president "excused me without a word."[9]

Hall's doctrinal departures were more striking than his moral ones, for he remained to the end, despite the beer, a person of exacting self-restraint. He was especially chary of sexual impulses, which he mistakenly allowed to overtake him in adolescence, acquiring for a time a habit of masturbation that so filled him with shame that he continued to talk about it in old age. Perhaps it was this shame that led him to monitor so studiously his sexual impulses and other emotions. Perhaps it was this shame that also caused him to make the remarkable comment that, of all the worthwhile activities in life, sexual sublimations represented "the best things in the human world." Given these facts, it is hard not to speculate that a heroic set of sublimations and repressions powered his stupendous experimental productivity. Hall was a tremendously industrious scientist. Of course, experimental psychology, unlike almost every other vocation, offered one additional benefit to someone confounded by powerful inner emotions. What other field made it possible to tame these mysterious inner things by turning them into disembodied statistics neatly organized in scientific charts?[10]

There was one final reason that Hall, as he returned from Germany in 1870, was turning with enthusiasm to scientific psychology. His theological and philosophical study still left him with questions, especially on the matter of mind and body. In Germany he saw that psychological experimentation might resolve these questions, but when he returned to America he was uncertain about how to proceed. In 1872, he took a job teaching at a Unitarian college in Ohio, Antioch College, where he also preached in the college chapel. (It was really "essay reading," he assured a biographer in 1914; "I still have a big bunch of those *quasi* sermons all on philosophical subjects.") Hall overstated his youthful religious emancipations, for in fact these quasi sermons were the typical liberal Christian repertoire—"Comparative Religions," "The Philosophy of the Christian Fathers," "Christianity without Myth or Miracle."[11] He corresponded with and visited several prominent American Hegelians and pondered different ways to reconcile the mind/matter problem. Was it possible to link these persuasively through the study of objective and subjective processes, as experimentalists like Wundt were doing in Europe? Hall came to believe that Hegel had failed to resolve these and other crucial questions, and he wondered if the new psychology might be able to answer them once and for all. Could new physiological studies lift philosophy out of its interminable vagueness? Could scientific study of human sensation and perception reveal how outer and inner, objective and subjective, matter and mind, were related? Hall's German education strengthened his belief that this might be possible—that the mind carried within it the pattern of its experience, and that this pattern could be studied by analyzing the body. Hall took these questions to the only place in America where they could be studied from physiological angles. In 1876, he traveled to Cambridge, Massachusetts, and enrolled at Harvard University.

## HOPES FOR A SCIENCE

So much of the early history of scientific psychology was, for believers at least, both good news and bad news. The good news for Hall as he moved to Harvard was that it was possible there (and only there) to pursue psychological study from experimental and physiological angles. The bad news was that, while this kind of study was possible, it was exceedingly difficult.

It is no exaggeration to say that the circumstances surrounding the beginnings of the new psychology in its American form were inauspicious in the extreme. To begin with, the first courses offered in the subject could not find a departmental home. Given in the 1875–1876 school year as "natural history" classes, they were in the next year (April 1877) transferred to the philosophy department, a department then pursuing psychological knowledge and instruction in entirely different modes. At this point, arguments about how to teach psychology became a feature of the university. Complicating matters further, both new courses were offered by an assistant professor trained not in philosophy or epistemology but in anatomy and physiology, a young man named William James (1842–1910). James had an effervescent personality but could be given to fits of anxiety and indecision. His privileged, cosmopolitan family offered him every kind of experience and new knowledge, American and European, but the lessons he learned during his transatlantic upbringing both enriched and disoriented him. There were too many choices. As a result, he cycled through several vocational false starts: art school, chemistry, physiology, and medical school. Each one, in turn, was unappealing. In the middle of medical school, he pronounced the curriculum "humbug." He picked up enough of it, however, to graduate and begin teaching anatomy, and he gradually moved his courses, which always focused on physiology and psychology, into the philosophy department. He was, again, in a betwixt and between situation, an anatomist working in a philosophy department, and he felt his in-between status at Harvard acutely.

This was hardly the end of James's problems. Between medical school and physiological and psychological studies in Germany, he found himself caught in a set of ambivalences familiar to scientific psychologists. Though in 1867 and 1868 he could write to friends that he hoped to help physiologize psychology by adding scientific facts about the nervous system to older studies of mind—the "time has come for psychology to begin to be a science," he said—the more he learned, the more unsettled he became. The spiritual crisis that resulted did not merely vex or annoy him, as such crises had done for Fechner and others; it entirely took away his will to live. In the years around 1870, just as Hall was soaking up science and liberal religion in Germany, James descended into a crippling despair, waking every day, he said, with a "horrible dread." To a close friend he confided that he felt "swamped in an empirical philosophy" to such an extent that he wondered if "not a wiggle of our will happens save as the result of physical laws."[12] Was free will an illusion? Was everything in life the result of ironclad, mechanical forces? Suddenly the implications of the new scientific worldview seemed to crush him: if scientific views were correct, perhaps there was nothing he could control, nothing he could decide, nothing he might choose. Terrified and irresolute, James skidded in and out of a crippling depression. It lasted one year, then another.

Then something extraordinary happened. Somehow he transformed his deep despair into a towering inner assurance, performing a remarkable inner change not unlike an evangelical conversion. "Today I about touched bottom," James wrote in his diary on February 1, 1870, "and perceive plainly that I must face the choice with open eyes: shall I frankly throw the moral business overboard[,] ... or shall I follow it, and it alone, making everything else merely stuff for it?" James did not have the answer—were our lives wholly determined or were we free and thus moral agents? Though he could not find indubitable warrants for freedom, he discovered a way out of his dilemma in the ideas of the important French neo-Kantian philosopher Charles Renouvier (1815–1903). Perhaps he should try *acting* free. "I finished the first part of Renouvier's second Essais," James logged in his diary on April 30, 1870, "and see no reason why his definition of free will—'the sustaining of a thought because I choose to when I might have other thoughts'—might not be illusion. At any rate, I will assume for the present—until next year—that it is no illusion. My first act of free will shall be to believe in free will." For this powerful act of turning, James was indebted not just to Renouvier but also to his good friend Charles Peirce, who was known to define belief in terms of actions and habits. "The feeling of believing," Peirce was sure, "is a more or less sure indication of there being established in our nature some habit which will determine our actions."[13] Peirce, as James himself recognized, drew these insights from new psychologists such as Alexander Bain, intellectuals who thought that the terminus of belief in action was more important than the source of belief in reason. In any case, James's moment of insight is fascinating because it illustrates what I identify as a key liberal method of overcoming spiritual problems: making a choice, performing a willful act. I discuss this in chapter 4 in particular, a chapter on the muscular cultivation of willpower. In any case, in the end, James's experiment worked: as he acted with freedom, his energy increased.

Something of the power of James's transformation is illustrated by the fact that, instead of fearfully abandoning science, he assiduously built a place for it at Harvard and in the United States more generally. By the middle of the 1870s, about the time Hall arrived in Cambridge, James was promoting the new psychology as a middle way between materialistic science, on the one hand, and outmoded religious and philosophical pursuits, on the other. This involved a delicate set of negotiations worth explaining briefly here, for they illustrate a crucial point I return to again and again: the new psychology contained meanings that, when not properly understood, could destroy cherished comforts and certainties. James knew this firsthand.

James's careful negotiations began in the philosophy department, where faculty using older approaches had to be gingerly sidestepped or placated. Professor Francis Bowen, a sophisticated historian of modern philosophy and the first ever to teach a course on psychology at Harvard, represented the old way of doing things. He was, as Bruce Kuklick has written, "wearisome in propagandizing for Christian theism and laborious in his defense of religious fundamentals." "All of Bowen's courses were constructive in that they expounded his religious thought and disproved the skeptics." When the scientific milieu changed in the rush of events after Darwin's *Origin*, Bowen's contributions seemed reactionary. He feared the practical consequences of Darwin's "dirt-philosophy" and warned that a society "not based upon Christianity is big with the elements of its own destruction." Though James had his own reasons to dislike materialism, they weren't specifically Christian ones; and James was wary of academics with theological commitments. He worried that his psychology might be subject to the onerous constraints of Christian philosophers like Bowen, while Bowen, for his part, detested James's empirical orientation. The resulting tensions were noticed by students and faculty. Stanley Hall arrived at precisely this moment, and, siding quickly with James, reported in Alexander Bain's journal *Mind* that James's psychology course "was admitted not without some opposition into the department of philosophy, and is up to the present time the only course in the country where students can be made familiar with the methods and results of recent German researches in physiological psychology." James's new psychology was genuinely new, and it attracted attention. "The first lecture in psychology that I ever heard," James once said, not untruthfully, "was the first lecture I ever gave."[14]

In the end, James convinced Harvard's new president, the chemist Charles W. Eliot, that mental philosophy was being handled inadequately by "professors whose education has been exclusively literary or philosophical" and who therefore "are too apt to show a real inaptitude for estimating the force and bearing of physiological arguments when used to help define the nature of man." James was the perfect person to rectify the situation, a scholar "whose scientific training fits him fully to realize the force of all the natural history arguments, whilst his concomitant familiarity with writers of a more introspective kind preserves him from certain crudities of reasoning which are extremely common in men of the laboratory pure and simple."[15] This was his middle way—his psychology was philosophical but not exclusively so; it was scientific without being crudely experimental. And while it represented a break from efforts to buttress Christian doctrine, such as those presented by Bowen, it was not materialism. Eliot shared about the same admixture of skepticism about Christianity and hope for a spiritual replacement, and he supported James in his teaching and bids for promotion. But other observers, students, and faculty, and especially individuals who lacked Eliot's liberal sensibilities, were not sure what to make of James's new notions. Divinity school students thought the new psychology was "blank materialism," a reduction of the self to nervous and chemical discharges; on the other hand, Young Turk intellectuals thought the new psychology was not scientific enough, a metaphysical subterfuge, philosophy leaking in through the back door. James did not know it, but these responses foreshadowed the cascade of confused reactions he would get from future critics and commentators, including religious ones.[16] The psychological theories and experiments were hard to figure out: what did the new science mean?

It meant, first of all, that the mind and experience were relocated, moved from the head into the body's network of reflexes, sensations, and perceptions. Though James joked that the new psychology drew all its insights from the twitching legs of decapitated frogs, in reality the sciences of mind had been decapitated, and James was helping perform the surgery. (Psychologists, James sometimes quipped, refused to accept data from subjects who had their heads intact.) Like the German masters, James viewed experience as being located not in the brain but in the entire nervous and muscular system, in the automatic stimulus-response pattern known as the reflex arc. James recognized this as the crucial insight of the new psychology. The "only *essential* point in which 'the new psychology' is an advance upon the old, is, it seems to me, the very general, and by this time very familiar notion, that all our activity belongs at bottom to the type of reflex action, and that all our consciousness accompanies a chain of events of which the first was an incoming current in some sensory nerve, and of which the last will be a discharge into some muscle, blood-vessel, or gland." Psychological events were made up of innumerable reflex actions. James contrasted this newer approach with older models. "For the Phrenologist, brain-spots represent *faculties*—for the [physiological psychologist], elementary processes, sensory & motor," James wrote in lecture notes. "Such faculties as conscientiousness, self-esteem, causality, hope, philoprogenitiveness, designate the entire man in a particular attitude of his being and are built up of many elementary processes." Even when James was discussing the brain and its activity, he contextualized the brain in its larger neurophysiological systems. The organs of the phrenologist, he continued, "are not elements of mind, but [the] entire mind working in [a] special way." "Each faculty involved all elementary processes"—and because this was the case, "psychological analysis does not deny [the] supreme importance of particular localities for expression of [the] faculty but it shows how each faculty is built of images, motor and sensory, combining in peculiar proportions, and it assumes that the elementary functions of the brain are the production of these images." If there were specific locations in the brain for specific human capacities, those locations were only collecting points for these larger flows and tides of consciousness.[17]

These were intellectual changes worked out in universities and experimental laboratories, but they were, of course, related to broader trends in American culture. In the final quarter of the nineteenth century, nervous and muscular health, not head shape or size, became the marker of virtue, knowledge, and sometimes, piety. It is fitting that a Harvard undergraduate, for one, noticed the change. In the antebellum period, the ideal college hero, Harvard's 1893 Phi Beta Kappa speaker claimed, was "a young man of towering forehead" with pale cheeks, bad digestion, and hair "carefully brushed backwards and upwards to give the full effect to his remarkable phrenological development." The most revealing sign of intense inner striving, moral and intellectual, was that towering forehead, fashionably displayed. Underneath that forehead, and supporting it, was a body that withered and decayed as personal energies were directed to the skull and its faculties. "He was self-conscious, introspective, and indulged in moods, as became a child of genius. He had yearnings and aspirations; and not infrequently mistook physical lassitude for intellectuality and the gnawings of dyspepsia for spiritual cravings." Physically strong men were disparaged by the public, who assumed that they were brutal, immoral, and irreligious. But by the 1890s, times had changed. "Better physiology, coinciding with some changes in popular ideals," now led people to believe that "morbid, or even merely feeble conditions of body tend to generate delusions, selfishness, and susceptibility to the worst impulses." In general, the stronger the body, the better one's moral and religious aptitudes. The result was that the ideal college hero was no longer the dyspeptic, pale lover of Goethe but the baseball or football player, the person who developed, through physical fitness, such things as "courage, coolness, steadiness of nerve, quickness of apprehension, resourcefulness, self-knowledge, self-reliance." All these qualities and others were now located (and produced) not in the brain but in the entire neuromuscular self. These ideas undergirded a remarkable turn in American culture to regimens of nervous health, muscle-culture, and athletics, at Harvard and elsewhere.[18]

Basic knowledge about such things, about how nerves and muscles worked in the body, was possible only with careful physiological probings conducted in experimental laboratories. James knew that American psychologists would have to copy German models here. German successes in experimentally studying our inner lives had excited "an array of younger experimental psychologists, bent on studying the *elements* of the mental life, dissecting them out from the gross results in which they are embedded, and as far as possible reducing them to quantitative scales." The results of these studies (which would come in good time) led to judgments about human life and virtue that would be more certain. "What generous divination, and that superiority in virtue which was thought by Cicero to give a man the best insight into nature, have failed to do, [scientists'] spying and scraping, their deadly tenacity and almost diabolical cunning, will doubtless some day bring about." The matters under scrutiny included the study of the "laws of correlation between sensations and the outward stimuli by which they are aroused"; brain physiology; "the analysis of space-perception into its sensational elements"; "the measurement of the *duration* of the simplest mental processes"; and the way "simple mental states *influence each other,* call each other up, or inhibit each other's reproduction." In some of these fields, James admitted, "the results have as yet borne little theoretic fruit commensurate with the great labor expended in their acquisition." Still, "facts are facts, and if we only get enough of them they are sure to combine. New ground will from year to year be broken, and theoretic results will grow."[19]

For a time, James tried his hand at experimentation, hoping these hopes, dutifully accumulating facts in prescribed ways. At first he used the medical school laboratory of H. P. Bowditch for experiments and classroom demonstrations; but in the fall of 1876, Eliot gave him money to set up an improvised psychophysical laboratory in Lawrence Hall. It was the first psychological laboratory in America, and a humble beginning to be sure. Looking back on it, Stanley Hall recalled that "in a tiny room under the stairway of the Agassiz Museum [James] had a metronome, a device for whirling a frog, a horopter chart and one or two bits of apparatus." (Hall undoubtedly diminished James's accomplishments to magnify his own later work as a laboratory builder.) James probably acquired other equipment over time and used either this laboratory or Bowditch's to do dissections and experiments on vision, vertigo, and the reflex arc. It was in the Lawrence Hall laboratory that he experimented on the "sense of dizziness" in 1880–1881, producing an article published in the *American Journal of Otology.* He was here interested in the sense of dizziness in deaf mutes, and his control group, about two hundred students and instructors at Harvard, were "whirled rapidly around with the head in different positions." (One wishes he had saved pictures.) Earlier he had completed similar studies on frogs, whirling them in similar ways in the cramped psychological laboratory in Lawrence Hall. After being appointed professor of psychology in 1889 (he was previously professor of philosophy), and after hearing the plans for an imposing psychological laboratory at nearby Clark University, James raised forty-three hundred dollars for laboratory equipment. Then in the fall of 1891, he moved the psychology laboratory into a larger space in Dane Hall. At this point he recruited an aggressive researcher and student of Wilhelm Wundt, "the ablest experimental psychologist in Germany," Hugo Munsterberg, to lead the experimental effort at Harvard. When Munsterberg came, he took over most laboratory duties from James.[20]

Though James worked hard to build, staff, and support this laboratory at Harvard, he found experimental work uncongenial. He supervised student laboratory projects on perception, attention, memory, and imagination, and used laboratories for classroom demonstrations and instruction (e.g., in dissection). But he never contributed important experimental results. As Perry has written, for physical reasons James could not endure extended hours in a laboratory: he had painful eye fatigue and a recurring lower back condition that prevented him from standing for long periods. Moreover, Perry wrote, he had a "non-mathematical cast of mind" that prevented him from being interested in quantitative methods; and he was too impatient to "organize experiments and carry them on through years of sustained diligence." But there was another reason for James's lack of interest in experimentation. Though for professional reasons he masked his scientific doubts with prophetic statements about psychology's great promise, he never was able to shake his skepticism about a fully scientific psychology. In the years after the *Principles,* this skepticism grew. "It is indeed strange to hear people talk triumphantly of 'the New Psychology,' and write 'Histories of Psychology,' when into the real elements and forces which the word covers not the first glimpse of clear insight exists," he wrote in 1892. "A string of raw facts; a little gossip and wrangle about opinions; a little classification and generalization on the mere descriptive level; a strong prejudice that we have states of mind, and that our brain conditions them: but not a single law in the sense in which physics shows us laws, not a single proposition from which any consequence can causally be deduced. This is no science, it is only the hope of a science."[21] There was a part of James that was dubious about psychology. Its insights were insignificant, its procedures tedious.

A HEAVY CARGO OF FACTS

While James tired of the painstaking processes involved in experiments on human sensation and perception, his graduate students, like successful graduate students everywhere, were willing to toil. G. Stanley Hall was a toiler.

Hall once claimed that he devoted all his time in graduate school to a frog's leg. (For an experimentalist of Hall's stripe, this constituted boasting.) Like most self-serving exaggerations, this one mixed truth and wishful thinking. In fact, Harvard laboratories were rudimentary and the curriculum in philosophy involved exercises that Hall thought were onerously nonexperimental.[22] But in spare moments, Hall experimented. He conducted experiments on frog nerves and color vision. He formulated a theory about color vision and tested it with several simple experiments. He examined how visual stimuli were registered by the most elementary sensory bodies, the cones in the retina, and he devised several experiments to test perception, using high school boys as subjects. In another set of experiments, Hall was interested in the perceptive abilities of a woman who had been blind, deaf, and mute since the age of twenty-six months. Laura Bridgman had lost all her senses except touch during a childhood attack of scarlet fever. After testing her ability to sense sound vibrations, odors, and the spaces around her, Hall learned that her "muscular sense" and sense of touch compensated in remarkable ways for her defective senses. Her sense of touch was two or three times more sensitive than usual; she could estimate people's ages by feeling the wrinkles around their eyes; she could read their emotions by touching their faces. Hall used all his early experiments to understand better the problems of sensation and perception—and he was specifically interested in the philosophical problem, approached inadequately by speculative thinkers such as Hegel, of how subjective thoughts and feelings were linked to the objective world of extended matter.[23] He was concerned with this same issue in his dissertation.

Hall's dissertation was a careful, philosophical reflection on the experimental literature on what was called the "muscular sense." The muscular sense was composed of sensations of motion transmitted by terminal nerves in muscular tissue, and sensations of nervous energy flowing outward from the nervous system to the motor nerves. Hall thought that both aspects of the muscular sense, the external excitation and the internal movement of nervous energies (which he associated with thoughts), were identical. He pointed to different psychologists who posited the existence of special sensitive fibers in the muscles, places where external excitations and inner, nervous forces united in one substance. Locating this substance, or some other tissue that represented a collapsing point between external stimuli and internal states, was a dream of Hall's; he had been obsessed with this problem since reading Hegel. But research on so-called sensitive fibers in the muscles was contested. In a

Harvard laboratory, Hall himself tried to replicate a study that pointed to the existence of these sensitive fibers, stimulating excised sections of frog muscle tissue in experiments that ultimately yielded inconclusive results. Undeterred, Hall pointed in his dissertation to other evidence. He drew from contemporary evolutionary thinkers such as Spencer, who argued that consciousness began in muscle tissue and moved from there into the nervous system. "Psychical life, which we may conceive as beginning in muscular substance," Hall wrote in the published version of his dissertation, "would retire from muscle to nerve and from nerve fibres to nerve-cells, or rather ascend and unfold in these more special organs." Hall admitted that this causal sequence was unproven—for, he said, "we cannot see more than an analogy between the movement of thought and material motion." Still, Hall thought the analogy was enough to reveal the inadequacies of two competing notions: that inner ideas produced outer (embodied) actions, and that ideas and actions, spirit and body, were entirely separate. The first notion was the mistake made by many idealists; the second was the mistake made by (religious and nonreligious) "dogmatic dualists." The point Hall emphasized was that mind and matter were indistinguishable in human nature, and therefore that knowledge and truth were worked out in the whole organism, body and mind. This led him to the conclusion that "all possible truth is practical"—in other words, that "the active part of our nature is not only an essential part of cognition itself, but it always has a voice in determining what shall be believed and what rejected."[24] Our thinking and believing took place in muscular activities. This insight profoundly influenced American culture, and religious Americans in particular.

Hall's dissertation illustrates well how young psychologists wanted to use psychological experimentation to answer metaphysical questions about mind and matter. This was the source of Hall's early fascination with the new psychology, and it also was the reason he gave—in early articles in *Harper's* and *The Nation*, and in liberal Protestant magazines such as the *Christian Register*—for the importance of the new psychology. Experimentation was the key, and after leaving Harvard in 1878, now the first PhD in psychology in America, he turned determinedly to experimentation. He went to Germany for two additional years of study and laboratory work, where he was a student of Wundt's and became acquainted with Hermann von Helmholtz, and where he worked on several experimental problems with the physiologist Du Bois Reymond and others. When appointed to a position at Johns Hopkins in 1882, he organized a laboratory that inspired the development of other psychological laboratories in America. During this time Hall himself produced a number of studies—on nerves and muscles, on the reflex arc and reaction times, and on optical illusions, tactile sensations, muscle fatigue, attention, hypnosis, and childhood development. In 1888 Hall helped establish Clark University, where he would become a major force shaping experimental psychology in America. Graduates of his psychology department went on to establish psychology laboratories at many other American universities. The growth of the new science was dramatic: in 1888 there was one psychological laboratory, James's laboratory at Harvard; six years later there were at least twenty-six, many of them staffed by Hall's former students.[25]

The explosion of the new psychology was a dramatic event in American culture, representing an enormous outlay of financial and institutional resources, and Hall was often called upon to explain it. By 1887 the large-circulation Christian periodical the *Christian Union* pointed to his importance, declaring that "this modern departure from the traditional paths of the teaching of the science of the mind that is taking so strong a hold in this country, is due, in no small degree, to the energies of Professor G. Stanley Hall."[26]

Hall was often asked how the new psychology might improve the lives of ordinary Americans. At ministerial meetings, liberal clubs, and lyceum circuit gatherings, he answered this and other questions and spoke about brain physiology, nervous tissue, and advances in experimentation. These might not seem like electrifying topics, but in fact the new psychology was au courant and Hall was one of the most sought-after and highly paid scientific lecturers in his day.[27] Often he began by pointing out that new experimental methods illuminated issues that philosophers and metaphysicians had not been able to advance. Fatigue, forgetfulness, self-control, moral development, and the meanings of life and religion—all these things were being made plain by a new science that dealt with the facts "of sense and the inner life under conditions controlled in the laboratory, with statistics based on large numbers." There were matters of taste in philosophy, and matters of creed and inclination in other disciplines, but in psychology knowledge was built up slowly from the most elementary facts of sensation and perception. Dramatizing this fact in *Harper's,* Hall reproduced pictures of several different laboratory experiments on sensation (figure 5). Because the skin was the "boundary between the self and the external world" and the genesis of all other senses, careful studies of its properties told researchers a lot about how human beings perceived their environment,

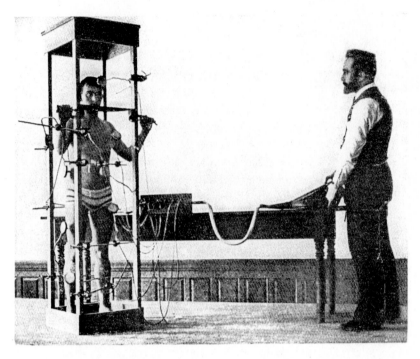

Figure 5.   Experimentally probing the senses and the soul. From G. Stanley Hall, "The New Psychology," *Harper's Monthly,* 1901.

focused attention, and discriminated among stimuli. These studies measured carefully the basic units of the self, the stimulus-response patterns known as reflex arcs. By building the store of knowledge of these stimulus-response patterns, and reflecting on how they might combine in associative patterns and other higher-order mental processes such as thinking, willing, and feeling, psychologists were developing certain knowledge about human nature. "Beginning with touch," Hall thought, "the experimental method has slowly come to include almost every kind of psychic activity. Imagination, sentiment, reason, volition, and all the rest are taken into the laboratory, and its methods have taught us a sharpness and refinement of introspection and self-knowledge which make these methods almost comparable with a microscope for the soul."[28] Could the very soul be probed with these ungainly contraptions?

Hall thought it could. There were different methods of seeing deeply into the self. One method was analyzing automatic reactions to certain words and stimuli. On one occasion, Hall asked a volunteer to perform a word-association test. Hall said one word, and his volunteer indicated what immediately came to mind. "So I said, 'boy,' and he said, 'girl,' and then I said, 'cup,' and he said, 'mug,' and the time was measured. . . . Finally I unfortunately said, 'glass,' thinking he would say 'window,'" Hall remembered. "He said, 'beer.'" Hall and his audience laughed not just at the unexpected turn of events but at how a psychological experiment revealed preoccupations that most people kept hidden. Conducting this experiment on people enabled psychologists to draw up "association tables," Hall said, maps of inner networks of habitual thought processes and feelings. And there were other ways of experimentally probing the obscure parts of the self. Because the logic of the reflex arc meant that any inner state, any feeling or thought, had to be expressed in muscular states, Hall thought it was possible to infer inner states from outer postures, gestures, and muscular tension. In other contexts, Hall talked about advances in physiological studies of nervous fatigue, pointing out that experiments done in his laboratory made him think that "a far greater number of diseases originate in fatigue than doctors have supposed before this." He recommended alternating regiments of rest, recreation, and exercise, as we will see.[29] Other psychologists agreed. Hall often spoke as well about how psychological studies on perception, attention, and learning related to contemporary work in child development, educational methods, religious formation, habits, character, morality, and hygiene.

In the late 1870s and 1880s, Hall emerged as the key experimentalist and spokesperson for scientific psychology. He was full of faith in laboratory work and ever ready to elaborate on the practical benefits of experimental results in the areas of health, hygiene, and morals. He began to fault James for pursuing experimentation fitfully, and their correspondence became tinged with misapprehension and ambivalence. Between 1878 and 1880, Hall wrote from Germany at length about his friendships with experimentalists and the results of his laboratory work. James responded graciously; he too wished he could "pump the German founts of wisdom." At the end of 1879, Hall wrote critically of speculative psychologists. James responded that a "*rounded* mental character" was important, and that this notion "would be forgotten if the laboratory blackguards all had their way." Then again, in January of 1880, James insisted to Hall that all great philosophers had a "personal unitary, all-fusing point of view," by which he meant that great thinkers were able to relate scientific results to deep philosophical problems. "How men who are neither gentlemen nor men of the world, but live swathed in the thick atmosphere of a particular technical calling, writing for each other and quarreling with each other, and senseless clods to all outside, can claim to give voice to the spirit of Universal Being is more than I can understand." Many new psychologists, James claimed, were "mere cads, or university blackguards." Though Hall agreed that the detached laboratory worker was not the ideal, he also boasted that he was fully *"aufgegangen* [merged, or ascended] in empiricism"—adding quite pointedly that he was worried James had given up on the very procedures that gave psychologists epistemological certainty. "What alarms me most is the fear which has somehow arisen within me that you are going the other way," Hall wrote. Was James becoming a metaphysician or theologian, someone like Palmer or Bowen? James responded good-naturedly by reasserting his empirical orientation and reporting that he was "greatly amused" by Hall's assertions, though in fact he was deeply irritated. Privately, Hall continued to talk of James as an armchair psychologist.

At the opening of Emerson Hall in 1905, the new philosophy building at Harvard, Hall and James were both in attendance, and Hall unaccountably kept up the invidious language. Hall admonished the audience that "too long acquaintance with the breezy altitudes of philosophy at the same time predisposes and disqualifies for this task because it tends to a nimbleness impossible for a mind which carries a heavy cargo of facts." Hall had overcome his high-altitude yearnings for something metaphysical; James continued to indulge his. But there is no doubt that Hall's speech was at least partly bravado and bluster: he was performing, he was reproducing the hardheaded sentiments required of science builders. In time, even for Hall, metaphysical preoccupations leaked back in.[30]

## THE MEANINGS OF PSYCHOLOGY

Hall's ascendant experimental career must have signaled to James that the science he was helping create was slipping out of his control. The problem was not that Hall was inattentive to the religious or moral dimensions of the new psychology. In his own way, he reflected extensively on the relations between science, morality, and Christianity—especially later in life, as we will see. The problem for James was instead that Hall used the new psychology to buttress a view of the cosmos as a great material-spiritual monism, a "block universe" of ironclad cause and effect. For obvious personal reasons, James found this revolting. James had always known that the new psychology was freighted with these unseemly possibilities, that some might use it to buttress deterministic worldviews, and that therefore its meanings had to be monitored carefully. This was precisely why Hall's views provoked and challenged him. Hall's ascendancy was a reason to redouble efforts to watch the new science and control both what it meant and how it was viewed by ordinary Americans.

Worried that the general public was becoming "the most promising of all preys for systematic mystification and pedantification on the part of the paedogogic authorities who write books for them"; insisting, at different times, that new knowledge should be accessible to everyone, that, as he once said to a friend, higher education should minister to "the very broad and miscellaneous demands of human beings for the instruction they want"; and mortified that professional psychologists were either unconcerned about the public or busy reducing the public's fondest hopes and wishes to automatic physiological processes, James turned energetically in the late 1870s and 1880s to delivering public talks that set straight the meaning of scientific psychology.

He began even before Hall's ascendant career irritated him. When Hall was still James's student and James was still whirling dissected frogs in Lawrence Hall, James gave public lectures titled "Recent Investigations on the Brain" in a series of public lectures sponsored by Harvard's Natural History Society. (A young "muscular Christian" named Theodore Roosevelt also was a member.) According to the *Boston Daily Advertiser* of March 2, 1877, James concluded by "deprecating any anxiety about materialistic consequences. If the spiritualistic faith of today finds central physiology a stumbling block, that of tomorrow will be all the stouter for successful contact with it. The human mind always has been and always will be able to interpret facts in accordance with its moral interests." James maintained that human agents were in control: humans organized facts, hypothesized theories, created sciences. It comes as no surprise that James thought the trick to making science friendly to spiritual conceptions was ensuring human freedom, something James did in different ways, using different devices, in this lecture and in others given in the late 1870s and 1880s.

Skepticism about cherished scientific certainties served as a useful starting point. "In these recent days we hear a great deal of the marvelous achievements of science," James said; we see how "physiologists by the deep insight they have been acquiring into the nervous system and the brain, have to a great extent banished the mystery which used to hang about the action of the mind, and constituted a new psychology which explodes and renders obsolete the old views of mental action— all based on a priori speculation and metaphysics." These were the same folks who thought, on the one hand, that authentic knowledge came from probing the sciatic nerves of decapitated frogs, and that, "on the other hand, any doctrine chiefly vouched for by the feelings of human beings—with heads on their shoulders—must be benighted and superstitious." Science, James argued, was a cold and abstract construct, a partial view that obscured the dynamic role of the choosing self. He could not believe that consciousness was epiphenomenal. And he promised his audience that he would prove it to them—or at least persuasively suggest it. They would all leave his lectures, he promised, "strengthened in the natural faith that your delights and sorrows, your loves and hates, your aspirations and efforts are real combatants in life's arena, and not impotent, paralytic spectators of the game."[31] James insisted that all of these things helped make the world.

It was precisely these human sorrows, loves, and aspirations that James tried to protect by arguing for a world of "chance" in another impassioned lecture during this period, one presented to Harvard Divinity School students sometime in 1884. Hoping to help students reconcile their scientific and religious commitments, James pointed again to the contingent nature of science, arguing that science was merely one way of rationally shaping the raw data of experience. James suspected that certain assumptions guided scientists as they pursued facts, and he wondered out loud about several of them, including especially uniformity and causation. What is the principle of causation, he asked, but "an empty name covering simply a demand that the sequence of events shall some day manifest a deeper kind of belonging of one thing with another than the mere arbitrary juxtaposition which now phenomenally appears? . . . It is as much an altar to an unknown god as the one that Saint Paul found at Athens." The principle of uniformity in nature was the same thing—merely a gesture toward the unknown, a postulate, a particular way of organizing incoming facts. Though these assumptions made contemporary scientific progress possible, they also produced, when followed to logical conclusions, worrisome philosophical positions such as determinism.

Here, finally, was James's main target. He suggested as an alternative to determinism not "freedom" or "indeterminism" but another word that was more risky and unstable: chance. Chance was the bête noire of science, a word that meant the universe was uncontrollable, in disarray, spinning beyond the ambit of scientific devices. This was precisely the reason James liked it. He used it to hypothesize that the world was *radically* contingent: the word *chance* was "a word of *impotence,* and is therefore the only sincere word we can use, if, in granting freedom to certain things, we grant it honestly, and really risk the game." But James did not want or need to dissolve bedrock scientific notions—in many ways his career depended on them. Instead his strategy was to create the possibility of an open-ended world, to help audience members suspend belief in causation long enough that they might venture a human hypothesis of freedom—as he had. "The most I hope is to induce some of you to follow my own example in assuming [free will] true, and acting as if it were true," he admitted honestly. Our first act of freedom, he said, "if we are free, ought in all inward propriety to be to affirm that we are free." The world was "plastic," apt to be shaped by the presuppositions and actions with which we responded to it.[32]

There was something in James's approach—a vulnerability, an energy, an insistence that subjective beliefs and choices mattered—that in the nineteenth century's scientific culture made his work seem subversive and appealing. His students picked up on this immediately. When confronted with venerable scientific laws such as the conservation of energy, one student recalled, James responded in a characteristic way: "What was the law of conservation of energy among friends?" This same student remembered that "it was when fighting for fair play to human and moral values as standards of truth that James became most vehemently eloquent and impressed most deeply his student audiences."

> I particularly remember his impassioned battling, on experimental grounds, for the freedom of the will in an address on *The Dilemma of Determinism*, and another—most moving of all—on *Is Life Worth Living*, delivered on a hot June evening in tiny, crowded Holden Chapel. As James stood there in the cramped space, close in front of his audience, reading with a sort of tumultuous rush from his nervous manuscript, perspiration streaming from his forehead, one felt almost palpably the tense absorption of the student group as he bared his own fighting faith in life's worthwhileness—closing, as his admonition to the fainthearted, with Henry IV's greeting to the tardy Crillon, after a great victory: "Hang yourself, brave Crillon! We fought at Arques, and you were not there."

James's rushing nervous energies, intense declamations, and streaming beads of perspiration exhibited unmistakably his fighting insistence that his subjective commitments mattered, that *his* life was worth living, and that he, unlike the French military captain Crillon, would not miss a chance at heroism. He would defeat the ironclad "block universes" of theology and especially science by enacting assiduously his own choices. It may be apocryphal, but the most illuminating story about James's appreciation for subjectivity comes from the American writer Gertrude Stein, a one-time student of James who made famous the following anecdote. Stein had spent several nights at the opera before her final exam, arriving exhausted on test day. She wrote in her exam book only this—"I am so sorry, but really I do not feel like an examination paper in philosophy to-day." The next morning James wrote in a note that he understood completely, and that he had awarded her (she said) "the highest mark in the course."[33] In calling attention to the irresistible power of her subjective states, had she mastered James's most important lesson?

Certainly James's ideas allured more than just students. In fact clergymen and other religious Americans became acutely interested in James's formulations, even before he captivated them with the *Varieties* in 1902, no doubt because the vistas he brought into view imagined God just beyond the observable horizon. "Among all the healthy symptoms that characterize this age, I know no sounder one than the eagerness which theologians show to assimilate the results of science," James told Unitarian ministers in 1881. "One runs a better chance of being listened to to-day if one can quote Darwin and Helmholtz than if one can only quote Schleiermacher or Coleridge." Probably James's sense for such things was skewed by his association with Cambridge liberals, but there is no question that wider audiences wanted to know how to reconcile Christian revelation and psychologies of reflex action. Among these Unitarians, James did just this, pointing out that "the physiological view of mentality, so far from invalidating, can but give aid and comfort to the theistic attitude of mind." He began with a crucial modern doctrine that "all educated people" knew about, one that was "so familiar to you that I hardly need define it." This doctrine was not the atonement or the nature of Christ or the problem of faith and works. It was the idea of "reflex action," the basic three-stage stimulus response event made up of sensation, reflection, and muscular reaction. This meant that behavior was the aim and end of all philosophy, and that the most "rational" thoughts also produced the most satisfying responses to the environment, the most satisfying behaviors. If a belief, attitude, or thought (e.g., theism) produced satisfying behaviors, that belief was rational and true. The mind accorded with reality, and "God may be called the normal object of the mind's belief"—therefore belief in God was rational and justified. Belief in God produced satisfying and moral outcomes for real people in the world.[34]

There is a persistent doubleness in James's writing and speeches of the 1880s and 1890s. As he reassured Americans that the new psychology was compatible with theism, he was at work developing a psychology textbook that reduced mental and spiritual states to physiological ones. As he composed specialized psychological clarifications, he embellished them with theistic proofs. He found it very hard, and usually undesirable, to speak about such things as the reflex arc without caveats about willpower and freedom. Though I have argued that this doubleness arose because James felt a pressing need to control the new science's meanings, others who observed James in this period were puzzled by his inconsistencies. When James published his *Principles*, his friend Charles Peirce captured the paradoxical nature of James's undertaking in a phrase that is as confusing as James's book, arguing that the *Principles* "was materialistic to the core— that is to say, in a methodical sense, but not religiously, since [James] does not deny a separable soul nor a future life." James, too, appears to have been confounded by the book, which he had intended as a statement of scientific psychology but which he came to regard as a "loathsome, distended, tumefied, bloated, dropsical mass, testifying to nothing but two facts: 1st, that there is no such thing as a *science* of psychology, and 2nd, that W. J. is an incapable." Other commentators, religious or otherwise, were not always sure what to make of James or the new science.[35] Looking closely at one of his theories will help clarify the paradoxes of James's project and help explain how these ideas were received in American religious cultures, a subject I analyze at the end of this chapter and in later chapters of this book.

## JAMES'S THEORY OF EMOTIONS

The doubleness of James's psychology is captured perfectly in one of his most controversial theories, a theory of emotions that seemed to reduce inner states to physiological ones, but one that also built *choice* into the reflex arc.

James formulated his theory of emotions long before he wrote *The Principles of Psychology*. The basic ideas are clear in "What Is an Emotion?" (1884) and implied in the articles "The Feeling of Effort" (1880) and "What the Will Effects" (1888). The latter article put these issues to a wider audience in *Scribner's* magazine, and James was surprised at how many people "had read it and been struck by it"; it had elicited more responses from readers, he once said, than "all my other articles put together." There was a reason these ideas generated controversy: they seemed to reduce the inner, feeling self to mechanical, physiological processes. In this *Scribner's* article he began with the basic unit of the self, the reflex arc, and pointed out that human beings "are an organized machinery for muscular explosion, placed in an environment full of things which pull and clamp the triggers of the machinery in various preappointed ways." These involuntary reflex arc processes left behind memories, which in various combinations might incite new neuromuscular discharges, which then could reinforce or inhibit one another. The process was mechanistic, but James did suggest a voluntary element here. The mind chose among the reflex possibilities presented to it. James thought, however, that even in the voluntary part of the process, ideas and feelings were generated "by thinking of how they themselves are going to feel [in the body]." It was a memory of what your body felt like in the past—say one time when you wept—that caused you to feel that way again. James guessed that this had some kind of physiological explanation—that the "brain-centres for imagining the contraction of our voluntary muscles, etc., must be connected with the motor-nerves" in a particular way.[36] The end result of James's theory of ideomotor action was a collapsing of mind and body: every inner state, every idea or feeling, issued or had its origin in some kind of bodily action—muscular contractions, neuronal discharges, physiological changes.

The most complete statement of James's theory is in the chapter "Emotions" in the *Principles*. Here he discusses why his theory is an improvement on others, complaining that too many people regarded emotions as "eternal and sacred psychic entities" without causes and effects. James was sure that the "beauty of all truly scientific work is to get to ever deeper levels" of explanation, and in this case he thought he had found the way to a truly scientific view. This way was the same way that psychologists took when making any aspect of their work scientific: they related mental phenomena to bodily processes. James knew his idea here was "pretty sure to meet with immediate disbelief." He explained it carefully. "Commonsense says, we lose our fortune, are sorry and weep, we meet a bear, are frightened and run; we are insulted by a rival, are angry and strike. The hypothesis here to be defended says that this order of sequence is incorrect, that the one mental state is not immediately induced by the other, that the bodily manifestations must first be interposed between, and that the more rational statement is that we feel sorry because we cry, angry because we strike, afraid because we tremble, and not that we cry, strike, or tremble because we are sorry, angry, or fearful, as the case may be." James thought that the body registered the perception first, by "*a sort of immediate physical influence, antecedent to the arousal of an emotion or emotional idea.*" He offered different proofs. First of all, he pointed out that, if bodily states did not directly register our perceptions, perceptions would be "purely cognitive in form, pale, colorless, destitute of emotional warmth." We would, he said, "see the bear and judge it best to run," but we would not actually feel afraid. Second, he gave examples of immediate and involuntary bodily responses to external stimuli. "If we abruptly see a dark moving form in the woods, our heart stops beating, and we catch our breath instantly and before any particular idea of danger can arise." If we listen to music, look at art, or read poetry, we might unexpectedly experience a "cutaneous shiver" coursing through our bodies. In each of these cases, the outer perception is registered immediately in the body. The inner emotion is epiphenomenal. Lastly, James asked readers to do a thought experiment and think of some strong emotion while excluding from consciousness any feelings of its bodily symptoms. The result, James thought, would be that "nothing [was] left behind, no 'mind-stuff' out of which the emotion can be constituted, and that a cold and neutral state of intellectual perception is all that remains."[37]

James knew some commentators would see as materialistic any argument that affections were constituted by "bodily changes." The idea already had met some resistance on these grounds. But in the *Principles* he insisted that the theory was not necessarily materialistic: it was "neither more nor less materialistic than any other view which says that our emotions are conditioned by nervous processes." These were sensational, bodily processes, it was true; but this did not mean there was "something peculiarly base about them." For "our emotions must always be *inwardly* what they are, whatever be the physiological ground of their apparition. If they are deep, pure, worthy, spiritual facts on any conceivable theory of their physiological source, they remain no less deep, pure, spiritual." It was "just as logical to use the present theory of the emotions for proving that sensational processes need not be vile and material," James continued, "as to use their vileness and materiality as a proof that such a theory cannot be true."

Though obscured in difficult writing, there was in this phrase a revealing turn to James's argument. James was not claiming that "vile," material things determined inner outcomes; he was saying that the truths of inner spiritual realities were material realities as well. He was making the outer self, the profane self, sacred—not making the sacred, inner self profane.[38] This kind of sensibility was exactly the sensibility that religious liberals in this period embraced: a spiritualized body, not a material soul.

There was one additional way in which James, while admitting that inner states were "conditioned" always by the body, insisted that human beings remained spiritual and, by implication, free. This was in an important corollary to his theory of emotions, added to the text in the abridged revision of the *Principles*, where he drew out some of the practical implications of his theory. Here he said quite simply that, if his theory of emotions was true, a necessary corollary was "that any voluntary and cold-blooded arousal of the so-called manifestations of a special emotion should give us the emotion itself." Voluntarily changing the body could yield particular inner emotions and dispositions. James put it this way:

> There is no more valuable precept in moral education than this, as all who have experience know: if we wish to conquer undesirable emotional tendencies in ourselves, we must assiduously, and in the first instance cold-bloodedly, go through the *outward movements* of those contrary dispositions which we prefer to cultivate. The reward of persistency will infallibly come, in the fading out of the sullenness or depression, and the advent of real cheerfulness and kindliness in their stead. Smooth the brow, brighten the eye, contract the dorsal rather than the ventral aspect of the frame, and speak in a major key, pass the genial compliment, and your heart must be frigid indeed if it do not gradually thaw!

So one implication of James's theory was that it became easier to understand and control inner states: we did it by controlling our bodies. We developed our inner selves by shaping our outer selves.[39] This message James conveyed quite effectively to popular writers, mental hygienists, Protestant moralists, and liberal pastors. All of them were convinced that, notwithstanding the lurking materialistic possibilities, James's notions, and perhaps the notions of other new psychologists, could be used to understand better and control our inner lives and outer behaviors.

## NEW PSYCHOLOGIES, NEW THEOLOGIES

James's work elicited psychological conversation on a large scale. In the 1890s in particular, after James published his remarkably popular text, psychologists and others reviewed his book for theological journals, and theologians weighed in on the meaning of a psychologically inflected religiousness. Was the new psychology a dangerous materialism—or did it provide new, scientific ways to test the truths of revelation and experience? There was a range of responses.

Some objected to the new psychology with what was, for anyone familiar with the history of American science and religion, an utterly predictable complaint: the new science, like older ones, reduced spirit to matter. This objection came from both conservatives and liberals. Conservatives dismissed the new psychology as the latest form of materialism, while liberals, seeing the problem essentially as James had, worried that the new science obliterated moral choice. "The currents of modern psychology have ... been setting strongly in the direction of materialism," one writer for the *Presbyterian and Reformed Review* wrote. "In its origin mind is the product of material particles organized in the form of brain cells, while its processes are the result of molecular movement in the brain." The reduction of mind to matter destroyed freedom and moral responsibility, an intellectual move that left people in a quandary that, as even Huxley admitted, "may paralyze the energies and destroy the beauty of a life." Others, such as the Presbyterian pastor and Hanover College president Daniel Fisher, thought experimental data supported reflex action in animals—but not in human beings. "As the scale of existence is ascended," he wrote, human behavior is "more under the control of the will." These were the arguments of moderates, but they came easily to liberals too, who, despite their modernist impulses, were worried above all that science might undercut morality and the freedoms it depended upon. Reviewing this literature for the *Universalist Quarterly*, the liberal minister William Jewett Tucker made a fervent but uncritical accusation that the reduction of mind to matter was "suicidal": "Without freedom to choose between right and wrong, virtue and vice, moral action and moral character would be impossible." The result was apathy, immorality, and irreligion. The criticism here has a familiar tone to it: liberals used the same language against another "deterministic" system—Calvinism. Following his mentor Francis Bowen (that inveterate Christian opponent of Darwin, James, and other heretics), Tucker pointed out that consciousness itself testified to our freedom.[40]

But if some were so paralyzed by the fearful moral implications of the new psychology that they avoided it altogether, others were so fortified by James's reassurances that they were able to probe more judiciously its nature and meaning. Perhaps the new psychology was materialistic only in certain instances or procedures. Perhaps it was materialistic, for example, only methodologically. Another writer for the *Presbyterian and Reformed Review* pointed out that physiological psychologists were not denying freedom but bracketing the question altogether because of methodological constraints built into their science. Drawing heavily on James, this writer explained that psychology "is a phenomenal or empirical science" and, as such, "deals with states of consciousness . . . without inquiring into their ultimate ground or meaning." Every science did this—every science renounced "ultimate solutions," carefully circumscribing their procedures in order to arrive at more measured results. Every science eschewed metaphysical and "speculative" questions. But there were problems with this approach, too. While it was useful to "set apart certain psycho-physical phenomena"—sensation, perception, reflex actions, and memory—there were aspects of the mind that could not be grasped using such a method. And there were times when methodological materialisms made materialist conclusions more likely. In many cases, for example, the will "is represented as, psychologically considered, only a complex of sensations"; and yet in reality there *is initiative*, there is "selective and preferential energy" in the will. In this case, materialist models led to a presumption in favor of materialism. This writer could quote an authority as powerful as the Harvard experimental psychologist Hugo Munsterberg, who, in a popular article written a few years prior, conceded that psychologists operated with artificial notions, including the notion of the will. "The will analyzed by the psychologist is not the real will," this commentator wrote, "but is an artificial abstraction from it containing only its sensational elements." The real will was "not describable and explainable." The professor of logic and ethics at Columbia and future psychical researcher James Hyslop also warned believers that the methodological materialism of the new psychology could lead to agnosticism or more thoroughgoing materialist positions.[41]

James had tried to hold the line on this. In his *Principles* he had claimed that metaphysics and general framing questions could be bracketed out—that, in fact, creating a truly scientific account of the self depended on such bracketing. Other psychologists observing this situation, however, some of them personal friends, let James know they were infuriated by this unwarranted circumscription of reflections on mind. In his review of James's text, the liberal Congregationalist and Yale University psychologist George Trumbull Ladd (1842–1921) argued that psychology could not easily be separated from philosophical and metaphysical concerns. Ladd, a fanatical worker who found personal relationships an almost impenetrable problem, was in many ways quite similar to James: both had written a standard psychology text (James taught with Ladd's book before his appeared), and both were troubled by imperialistic scientists and recurring nervous ailments. But Ladd was committed to Christianity in a way that James was not, and he was more irritated by intellectuals who thought that being scientific involved first of all obliterating Christian or metaphysical commitments.

And so, when James insisted that the "simplest psycho-physic formula" was "the ascertainment of a blank unmediated correspondence, term for term, of the succession of states of consciousness with the succession of total brain-processes," Ladd was provoked. He saw James's position here as not only "a most astonishing abbreviation of the rights of a psychologist" but also a fundamentally disingenuous position; James himself knew that it was impossible to proceed without *some* kind of metaphysical or philosophical assumptions. Why not make these assumptions part of the discussion? Several other commentators, liberal and conservative, Protestant and Catholic, made the same criticism of new psychologists.[42] Ladd also wondered why categories like "brain" were better than "mind" and "soul." The "postulated being which is to serve as the subject of thoughts and feelings, and so to explain them, is no more 'cantankerously' or dangerously metaphysical than the being which is to serve as the subject of conjectural 'explosions,' 'central adjustments,' 'overlappings' of processes, etc." In conclusion Ladd pointed again to the "explanatory value of the metaphysical postulate of the soul" or mind, which he felt did a better job of capturing the "progressive manifestation in consciousness of the life of a real being, which, although taking its start and direction from the action of the physical elements in the body, proceeds to unfold powers that are *sui generis*, according to laws of its own."[43] Wasn't "soul" still a better category for our powers?

James's response illustrates his profound ambivalence about these matters. Admitting that "many of [Ladd's] thrusts strike home"; wondering, apparently without irony, how his *Principles* might have "given my critic so false an impression of my beliefs"; and promising that a less ambiguous presentation of his general position appeared in his recently published shorter version of the textbook, James offered three reasons to exclude metaphysics from psychology. First, he argued that the public wanted a practical, not speculative, science. "All natural sciences aim at practical prediction and control, and in none of them is this more the case than in psychology to-day. We live surrounded by an enormous body of persons who are most definitely interested in the control of states of mind, and incessantly craving for a sort of psychological science which will teach them how to *act*. What every educator, every jail-warden, every doctor, every clergyman, every asylum-superintendent, asks of psychology is practical rules. Such men and women did not care about philosophical issues." Second, James, like other new psychologists, wanted to preserve the integrity of induction and experimentation. The patient accumulation of experimental facts should drive the new science, and experimenters, moreover, should not be distracted with metaphysical disputes. Once the experimental pursuit of correlations between brain and mental states matured, the "whole body of its conclusions will fall prey to philosophical reflection." Philosophical reflection was useful, but for now, philosophers should not meddle. Third and finally, James excluded metaphysics in the *Principles* as a way of trying to shape a fully scientific discipline. "I wished by treating Psychology *like* a natural science, to help her to become one," he explained. Though psychology was not a science yet, there was "real material enough to justify one in the hope that with judgment and good will on the part of those interested, its study may be so organized even now as to become worthy of the name of natural science at no very distant day."[44]

But what James gave with one hand he took away with the other. Right now, he admitted, psychology was a dreadful mess, just a "mass of phenomenal description, gossip, and myth," a "mere fragment of truth." The conclusion is inescapable that James was proposing a methodological framework for psychology that even he had trouble believing in. In fact he had already admitted that his emotions theory in particular was hard to accept. Could emotions, consciousness—anything—be reduced to bodily states? "The best thing I can say for it," James said once about the emotions theory, "is, that in writing it, I have almost persuaded *myself* that it may be true."[45] Almost.

Though the problems of determinism and methodology continued to exercise some believers, others had no qualms about using psychology to buttress liberal religious positions. As in the earlier period, liberals developed different psychological apologetics. Some thought the new psychology would help Christians fashion new proofs of God's existence or new ways of thinking about essential doctrines. George Ladd, working tirelessly to mediate between old doctrines and new sciences, argued in the key progressive theological journal the *Andover Review* that psychology was having a "profound" influence in the "modification of theological opinion," helping Christians better understand faith, knowledge, and the status of the "Christian consciousness" as a proof of Christian truth. Analysis of the Christian consciousness was in fact a key preoccupation among liberals like Ladd. In a number of different conversations about intuition, instinct, and religious feelings liberals turned to experience as the source of immediate and certain knowledge. Progressive evangelicals associated with Andover Seminary argued about how precisely to understand the immediate intuitions given in consciousness, but they agreed that something called the Christian consciousness could function as the "organ and criterion of truth." Their arguments were tested and expanded later by psychologists who said that, because the contents of our consciousness accurately pointed to objective realities, and because consciousness seemed universally filled with religious notions, duties, and feelings, therefore God (and Christ) were objective entities. Others said the same evidence showed that religious faith was rational and even healthy, insisting that, because faith was an essential and universal part of human nature, belief was useful and justified.[46] While avowed Christians such as George Ladd resisted the universalist implications of these notions, calling for analyses of *Christian* experiences as the highest sources of truth, others considered Ladd's sectarianism bad form. Many were content to show that psychology demonstrated that any kind of faith was rational and useful. These were some of the apologetic aims of liberals borrowing from new psychologists.

Interest in relating Christianity to the new psychology was widespread, and even hardheaded lab men could be enticed to think about how their work influenced religious conceptions. Though he continued to insist on the primacy of experimental work, a middle-aged Stanley Hall also could not resist pointing to ways that the new science would reform religion. "The new psychology, which brings simply a new method and a new standpoint to philosophy, is I believe Christian to its root and centre; and its final mission in the world is not merely to trace petty harmonies and small adjustments between science and religion, but to flood and transfuse the new and vaster conceptions of the universe and of man's place in it . . . with the old Scriptural sense of unity, rationality, and love beneath and above all, with all its wide consequences." Hall believed that the new psychology identified the actions of an immanent, rational, loving spirit in matter. In this, Hall was like other progressives who wanted to exchange cold, mechanical languages for salvation for more natural and organic ways of thinking. Psychology helped people imagine the self as spiritual and divine, as a spiritual unity, and it probed the possible ways that God impressed himself upon us in embodied experience. Hall and some liberal theologians thought Christians needed a new psychology as a prolegomenon to a new theology.[47]

It is fair to say that Hall's vision of a new theology was more critical than affirmative, for if one thing is clear in Hall's religious writings, it is that older ways of believing, especially in America, had to be improved. "We must not forget," Hall said once to a public audience, that in America, "where the very depth and strength of religious instincts makes us too satisfied with narrow and inadequate mental expressions of them, that the first step towards securing an adequate theoretic training of those sentiments . . . is to rescue the higher mythopoeic faculties from the present degradation to which prejudice and crass theories have brought them. That deeper psychologic insights, in directions to which attention in this field is already turning, are to effect a complete atonement between modern culture and religious sentiments and verities is now becoming more and more apparent." In other words, psychology would separate the true from the false in religion, marking "crass theories" and other false doctrines for obliteration and rescuing our "higher" religious sentiments from obscurity. Elsewhere Hall described the function of the new psychology with respect to religion as "draining the marshes and letting in the light." God's work in this age was to restore religion's essential meanings and power. "We believe that psychology has before it a great future in rescuing the

Bible and religion to the respect of all men, scientific as well as others, and that it is in the end to transfuse the world with the old reverence, faith, and devotion." Late in life, Hall attempted to "rescue the Bible" and Christianity from superstitious accretion in his six-hundred-page *Jesus, the Christ, in the Light of Psychology* (1917). In it, Hall explained that he intended to add "a few psychological remarks" to the "resume of modern German higher criticism concerning the source material" of the New Testament. This he did by analyzing the developmental stages of Jesus's life and isolating and rooting out the pathological implications of Christianity. Hall overflowed with prophetic enthusiasm. In his mind, the new psychology was a purifying fire that produced indubitable judgments on philosophical problems, certain guidelines for aesthetic and moral questions, and clarity on religious doctrines and questions.[48]

(Understanding precisely what beliefs Hall's critical project left him with is a confounding problem. He could both reduce Christian doctrines to psychological artifacts and claim to believe in them; he could point to divine or "imponderable" forces in the world but also identify spirit with matter; he could critique American Christianity as harmful and unseemly but affirm earnestly that [pure] Christianity was the most useful thing in the world; and he could debunk mediums and spiritualists while preserving one medium's message—a comforting report from his dead wife—next to his wedding announcement for thirty years after her death. Perhaps it was not always clear in his own mind how much of the old to obliterate and how much to retain.)[49]

A large number of other Christians embraced the innovations of the new psychology because, like Hall and Ladd, they saw promising new theological and practical possibilities. Writers in almost all liberal denominations praised the new science as being far more precise and useful than older psychologies. A writer for the *Methodist Review* pointed out that the images of sin and self provided by the new psychology were far superior to the old: "It is not enough for him to know sin as it is portrayed in systems of theology; he must know it as it appears in each individual." Knowing this, and using the science to grasp better a "sure and accurate knowledge of human motives and conditions" might give preachers "mastery over individuals and congregations not otherwise possible." He thought psychology was assembling facts and laws that might help pastors predict how individuals and congregations might act. "The pastor has to deal with individuals who are affected by hopes and fears, passions and aspirations, joys and sorrows. He should be able to estimate each and all of these in their relation to the divine life and the development of the Christian personality. He should know how to repress, guide, develop, or employ these traits for the good of the individual in whom they are found, and for the welfare of the kingdom of God."[50]

Writing in the *Baptist Quarterly Review*, C. L. Herrick drew on some of these insights to speculate about how the new psychology might help Christians develop the proper thought patterns and habits. Borrowing psychological language (from James, probably), Herrick argued that both external sensations and internal ideas were the "immediate parents of voluntary acts," and that the greatest attention should be paid not just to the external environment but also to the "mental pictures which flit through the mind." The grooved patterns in the mind that these pictures created could easily be transformed into actions. "You must cherish the image of a sinful pleasure or violent act only at your constant hazard," for a "specific evil act [imagined], or one like it, may suddenly spring out of the mirror of the mind as a dread fact of your own present existence." So the "concepts of our musing hours," the "visions of wayward fancy," were not "phantoms of a harmless dream but the real actors in our own possible future." How should we watch and guard these inner "avenues of the soul"?[51]

.　　.　　.

Hall and James represent two different trajectories among psychologists who also were interested in religion. Hall was more of a deist who delighted in exploring experimentally the endlessly complicated and beautiful arrangements of nature and human nature designed by the Creator. But as Hall developed this system and reposed serenely in the midst of it, James wiggled uncomfortably in its ironclad spaces. To him, this was another "block universe" that obliterated creativity and freedom. Nevertheless, their differences on these matters should not distract us from the one crucial preoccupation that they shared. Though their systems were different, both thinkers offered ways of reconciling faith commitments and psychological ones. Both supposed that imponderable (spiritual) energies or principles haunted the mechanical body and natural world. And, more important still, both pointed to ways that new psychological knowledge could help believers understand, probe, and even measure confounding inner things like emotions, religious instincts, and spiritual growth. Their insights would be borrowed again and again by Americans hoping to figure out how faith worked in an at least partly physiological self.

# 3   Nervous Energies

Except in the minds of the most materialistic scientists, a fully stimulus-response self never came into existence. For everyone else, including, as we have seen, James and Hall, the self also incorporated dimly perceived freedoms, unmeasurable choices, transcendent elements, and unpredictable states that came and quickly evaporated. These inscrutable parts of the self had always existed, but interest in them quickened when physiological accounts of the self were tested and made operational in European and American universities. The inscrutable parts of the self that are best known, such as the unconscious, have been analyzed elsewhere; and in any case, the unconscious became popular in American culture only in the early decades of the twentieth century. Other mediating categories represented the inscrutable self much earlier, including, especially, nervous energies. These were imagined differently in different ages, and though some insisted that this category too was fully physiological, its association with the deepest, most vital parts of the self meant that it was identified with universal, sometimes metaphysical, powers that undergirded life, faith, or moral laws. American believers in particular were fascinated by this category, and they embraced it not just because it suggested nonmaterial forces in the self; they embraced it also because the science of how these forces were transmitted and husbanded promised better ways of living religiously and morally in the modern world.[1]

## IMAGINING ENERGIES

What exactly were the mysterious energies and forces that animated the human body? Scientists speculated for centuries about this question, wondering precisely how nerves carried messages through the body and caused muscles to contract. Agents considered responsible for transmitting messages in the nervous system varied, ranging from "animal spirits" or "fluids," according to the Greeks, to oscillations of the ether, explosions, or electrical powers. When discovered as a property of physical and biological life, electricity was thought of as a subtle and pervasive fluid, and many thinkers during the Enlightenment and afterward identified this fluid with nervous function. Toward the end of the eighteenth century in particular, a number of distinguished anatomists studying electric fish popularized the notion that a kind of electricity animated human nervous systems. A great deal of research on neuromuscular electrophysiology was done in the eighteenth century by the Italian anatomist and physician Luigi Galvani (1737–1798), who believed that his experiments on frogs demonstrated that the "animal spirits" spoken of by the Greeks were embodied in a kind of electrical fluid. Galvani thought it was likely that "the electrical fluid is prepared by the force of the brain, being extracted from the blood, that it enters the nerves, and that it runs through them internally." The excitement stirred by Galvani's experiments stemmed from hopes that he was penetrating one of life's great mysteries. Did the substance he was exploring, electricity, have something to do with the sources of life itself? A number of scientists and philosophers, including in particular German romantic and *Naturphilosophie* figures, believed it did. Physiological psychologists like those Hall had studied with in Germany were deeply influenced by this way of thinking. They too tended to reject materialism in favor of philosophical systems that reduced mind and matter to living forces penetrating all things. These mysterious living energies vibrated with the same rhythms in nature and human nature. In some sense at least, these were spirits in the body.[2]

Among individuals inclined to such beliefs, new studies about nervous systems and functions excited the imagination. Some thought they had discovered the secrets of nervous forces and how to use them to strengthen and heal. Though dismissed by scientists as arrogant and opportunistic, the Viennese physician Franz Anton Mesmer (1734–1815) acquired a huge following, creative imitators, and a lucrative healing enterprise peddling new ways of understanding and manipulating life's vital energies. Mesmer's success shows something of the depth of popular interest. Arguing that an invisible energy or "animal magnetism" was the medium through which passed sensations of all kinds (light, heat, electricity), he described a complicated vital economy of forces in the self, an equilibrium that had to be maintained for good health. "There exists a mutual influence between celestial bodies, the earth, and animated bodies," he pointed out, an influence operating because of a "fluid which is universally widespread and pervasive in a manner which allows for no void, subtly permits no comparison, and is of a nature which is susceptible to receive, propagate, and communicate all impressions of movement." His was an imperialistic project, subsuming all operations of mind and body into one system—his own. "There is," he said, "only one illness and one healing." When applied to the body, magnetic powers and artificial electricity might help, but their effects resulted from the vital source undergirding them. Really, animal magnetism was the source of immediate cures of "illness of the nerves and . . . all others."[3]

Popular speculations about the nature or uses of these vital forces did not end with Mesmer, despite Mesmer's assurances that they would. In the eighteenth and nineteenth centuries, a multitude of clinical and popular movements imagined nervous forces in different ways, including those movements loosely categorized under the names "Mind Cure" and "New Thought." To most New Thought practitioners, Mind was "the only power in heaven or earth or hell," as the American publisher and writer Elizabeth Towne wrote in 1904, and it therefore animated and often determined the forms matter took. Many with this mind-set speculated about how neurophysiological mechanisms, as connecting points between mental and physical phenomena, lured and pooled mental forces. Did such forces external to the self manifest themselves in the electrical impulses of the nervous system? Was the nervous system sensitive enough to register someone else's magnetic, mental, or divine transmissions? "It will be realized that at its origin the nervous mechanism is simply a device through which the great forces of the universe are brought to play upon the muscles of a living body, and cause the body to live and move. That the movements thus dictated to an otherwise inert mass, are such as to bring about steady development, and evolution to something finer and higher, bespeaks with an authority of fact a guiding force or a master hand that should prove a valuable supplement to faith." This New Thought believer illustrates something of the wonder that people felt about nervous forces: a divine hand marshaled and distributed them. Nerves, too, were approached with wonder. "Nerves are hollow tubes in which lie a sort of delicate jelly which is the medium of thought transmission," Towne wrote. "This almost fluid substance is the most delicate matter in creation." Nerves were places where mind became more fixed in matter, in this case in mysterious neurophysiological channels. "The nervous system is so wonderful in its present power for good or ill," another New Thought writer exclaimed; "it is not surprising that it is looked upon with awe."[4]

Though by the latter half of the nineteenth century the medical establishment ridiculed such fanciful notions, doctors too were keenly interested in human vital forces. They too tended to judge the health of any organism by its levels of nervous energy. Though not the first to talk about nervous forces or their chronic depletion, the New York neurologist George Beard (1839–1883) made these matters into a topic of American national debate. The son of a Congregational minister, Beard suffered as a young man from depressing religious and vocational uncertainties that led precisely to the kinds of nervous ailments he later saw with alarming frequency in other Americans. (That his two brothers had journeyed down expected paths, both into the ministry, made him feel worse, and he chastised himself in his journal for religious indifference. But apparently he had other tastes—for instance, for tobacco and champagne—that also propelled him in uncharted directions.) After nervous recovery and medical school at Yale, Beard turned with zeal to writing popular books for those suffering from psychological ailments. His diagnosis of the American condition, one built on metaphors of civilization and decadence, was that the emotional and physical trials involved in urban life were sapping people's "nerve force." (The idea that advancing civilization caused mental illness was not a new one, even if nineteenth-century doctors took to it with particular enthusiasm.)[5] In his widely read 1881 book, *American Nervousness*, Beard did not precisely define the nature of this "nerve force," though he used two metaphors to describe it, one linked to the *Naturphilosophie* tradition, the other to contemporary business idioms. In the first, he talked of vital forces as a kind of electricity moving in electric circuits. (The metaphor drew from contemporary scientific developments as well: in 1879, Beard's friend Thomas Edison invented an electric lightbulb that could burn for up to forty hours.) "[When] new functions are interposed in the circuit, as modern civilization is constantly requiring us to do, there comes a period, sooner or later[,] . . . when the amount of force is insufficient to keep all the lamps burning; those that are weakest go out entirely, or as more frequently happens, burn faint and feebly—they do not expire; but give an insufficient and unstable light—this is the philosophy of modern nervousness." The harsh, jarring sounds of machines, cramped living and working conditions, the fast pace of electronic communications, the rapid development of new ideas and technologies, the "friction and unrest" of American capitalism, the speed of the locomotive and steam-powered engines—all these things drained our power circuits.[6]

William James too was persuaded of the existence of nervous energies and believed that better utilizing them might help Americans overcome spiritual problems. Like others, he thought the individual had a finite fund of "stored-up reserves of energy"—energy in a "strata of combustible or explosible material" deep in the self. He was sure that most did not use this fund of energy, certain that, in his words, "men habitually use only a small part of the powers which they actually possess and which they might use under appropriate conditions." The result was nervous disorder, fatigue, and mental collapse. Because nervous energies were connected to both mind and body, there was a complex economy of forces in the self that involved nerves, muscles, and the mind. "When I speak of human energizing in general, the reader must therefore understand that sum-total of activities, some outer and some inner, some muscular, some emotional, some moral, some spiritual, of whose waxing and waning in himself he is at all times so well aware." Outer and inner, muscular and spiritual—in James's mind, nervous energies were both physical and metaphysical. They slipped back and forth from body to spirit. James recommended different ways to keep nervous energy levels at "an appreciable maximum." Strong emotions (negative and positive), persuasive ideas, pressures to perform, religious enthusiasms, drugs, "crowd contagion," and bodily exercise could all help us "to make an extra effort of will," a process that opened deeper energy levels. "The normal opener of deeper and deeper levels of energy is the will," James argued. On this matter, for one, James was consistent: one's inner intensity was linked to outer acts and behaviors. He pointed out that things like exercise and ascetic practices (such as Yoga) might tap nervous energies. "The best practical knowers of the human soul have invented the thing known as methodical ascetic discipline to keep the deeper levels constantly in reach. Beginning with easy tasks, passing to harder ones, and exercising day by day, it is, I believe, admitted that disciplines of asceticism can reach very high levels of freedom and power of will." Fasting, breathing, and bodily postures and exercises all stirred deeper levels of will and power. James recommended a wide range of exercises as a way of solving nervous disorders. The will was a crucial category, and I return to it in the next chapter.[7]

James's reflections here were only the beginning, for other religious liberals worked even harder to prove, in the words of one progressive theologian, the existence of "a spiritual potency and tendency in the nature of things." In the 1870s and 1880s, scientific psychologists like Hall and liberal theologians like Newman Smyth (1843–1925), a pastor and writer who borrowed a passion for religious feelings from the great German liberal Protestant Freidrich Schleiermacher, complained that "atomistic" British psychologies were materialistic and should be exchanged for more "organic sciences" that sought to "apprehend nature and mind in their forces and growth." Smyth's bookishness and extreme nearsightedness sometimes made him seem cold and detached; but in fact he was engaged passionately in the issues of the day, boldly encouraging inchoate liberals in the pews and coaxing others, ready or not, into new formulations. Any successes he had in these matters evidently had less to do with his rhetorical abilities—his "voice is not good," one observer noted, "his enunciation or articulation not very clear, his bodily movement somewhat awkward, and his whole manner heavy and unattractive"—than with his affecting belief in unseen, spiritual aid and, just as important, an intellectual power and adroitness. He was clever. Around the time of Smyth's contested elevation to a professorship at Andover Seminary, one observer noted that he heard "him preach once on 'election.'" Smyth was trying to move his congregation from thinking about God's sovereignty to trusting in their own abilities to choose, think, and develop religious feelings. "In his treatment ['election'] became 'selection,' which he declared differed in only one letter."[8] More evidence of the liberal distaste for determinism.

Smyth continued to call attention to human abilities and possibilities, and he, like earlier generations of liberals, turned for help to new psychologies. "Certainly, if we have once gained this conception, however vaguely, that man comes to himself in the midst of the powers of the universe, and is in all his manifold, conscious life himself a pulsating centre of forces, a being of wonderful receptivities and activities, himself the most living being in the whole world except God, we shall hardly remain satisfied with the inventory of man's faculties and primitive beliefs so confidently repeated to us by the Scotch intuitional philosophy as the . . . final account of our consciousness." The vision of the self that Smyth saw in scientific psychology was a living, active, purposive whole. The mind was not a machine that processed images, but an organ with a "hidden root beneath consciousness in the deep things of God, vibrating with manifold influences, and tremulous with the Light in which its life blossoms forth." Scientific psychologists, he thought, were turning from rationalistic inventories of mental capacities to glimpses of something vibrating deep within us, something "at work beneath consciousness, at the root of all our thinking," a supernatural force "by which we are shaped and swayed." For this spiritualized psychological monism, Smyth drew on the German theologian Isaac A. Dorner (1809–1884), a man that Smyth, Hall, and other American liberals had studied with in Germany, and one who was an inspiration to anyone trying to mediate between scientific and religious views of the world. Dorner had insisted that "we think God through God." Smyth repeated him—"Were there no God active and potential in the human mind, no man ever would have thought of him." Theology had to learn new techniques for seeing spirit in the mind and world. "Theology cannot remain content with repeating the old phrases for faith when science offers a richer natural language for the expression of spiritual truth."[9] Though Smyth and other Christian romantics identified the vital parts of the self less with nervous energies and more with emotions, the logic of their approach was similar to the approaches used by other liberals. There was an economy of forces in the self that, when carefully studied, might tell us something about the divine and how it worked.

## PROBLEMS OF NERVOUS FATIGUE

But difficult problems arose when the deeper energies of the self went awry or atrophied. And so discourses imagining nervous energies led to other discourses about managing, husbanding, and buttressing them. And as America industrialized, and as physicians and neurologists documented ways that modern civilization disrupted nervous forces, the discourse on the nervous system became more urgent. The mountain of literature scientists produced on this matter amplified American anxieties to a crescendo.

During the nineteenth century, medical scientists and physiologists studied the inner economy of afferent and efferent nervous forces and described in detail the proper functioning of these systems. Study of how nerve cells and fibers worked, and how, in particular, nervous energies were transmitted along nerve cells changed rapidly, and the problem of the exact mechanism of nervous conduction proved to be an enduring puzzle. In popular discourse, the electrical metaphor worked for the entire century and beyond, but in scientific circles it was dispatched when scientists such as the German physician Hermann von Helmholtz, working at midcentury, measured the speed of nerve conduction and found it to be much slower than electricity flowing through a wire. (In the twentieth century, scientists demonstrated that nerve conduction resulted from a physicochemical process, the transfer of ions across the nerve membrane.) In any case, though the precise methods of nerve conduction remained mysterious, most believed that basic stimulus-response patterns undergirded all our sensorimotor activities, from the simplest to the most complex. Reflex action remained the key category. As I have already described, reflex action included everything from the environmental stimulus and its afferent (incoming) sensation to the consummation of that impulse in an efferent, muscular discharge.

Because this was the basic unit of the self, and because all nervous activity was plastic, it was crucial not to disrupt these incoming and outgoing circuits. In infants and children, these circuits were developed as children moved about, tried to talk, engaged in play, and developed their entire muscular systems. Children encountered stimuli and naturally expressed recognition, joy, or some other appropriate emotion. Their nervous transmissions were therefore reinforced and strengthened. But adults did not always manage nervous impulses properly. They worked too long on monotonous tasks, they did not eat or rest properly, their lives were specialized and routine. They did too much intellectual work and too little muscular exercise, and therefore they atrophied crucial nervous capacities. They also experienced sensations and emotions that they then repressed. Adults needed to manage more carefully the economy of nervous forces in the self.[10]

Ignorance about such issues and about nervous health in general could lead to a number of mental and spiritual health catastrophes. Physicians and psychologists responded with a sense of urgency. Because they knew how the reflex arc worked—because they knew, for example, that environmental stimuli and motor responses always were closely related—these experts insisted that individuals preserve the integrity of inner and outer processes. If you felt something, you needed to act on it. "Every time a resolve or a fine glow of feeling evaporates without bearing practical fruit is worse than a chance lost," James once wrote. "It works so as positively to hinder future resolutions and emotions from taking the normal path of discharge. There is no more contemptible type of human character than that of the nerveless sentimentalist and dreamer, who spends his life in a weltering sea of sensibility and emotion, but who never does a manly concrete deed." The gendered language adds a complication that I address in the next chapter; here I merely draw attention to the scientific belief that disrupting the circuit of nervous energies as they pulsed from inner to outer eventually obliterated our ability to feel deeply and act effectively. The "whole neural organism," William James once reminded his students, "is, physiologically considered, but a machine for converting stimuli into reactions." James popularized this notion in dramatic fashion in his already discussed emotions theory, which essentially said that our inner health is a product of our outer actions and how we use these actions to coordinate or strengthen our nervous lives. And when James looked carefully into his audience and at revealing signs all around him, he discovered alarming evidence that Americans were becoming nervously unhealthy. American manners, movements, and gestures, he said, were characterized by "over-tension and jerkiness and breathlessness and intensity and agony of expression." Americans smiled, frowned, and fidgeted nervously. Was this the source of the problems of our inner lives? Was outer busyness and agitation making us nervous, edgy, and even spiritually depleted? "The general over-contraction [of the muscles] may be small when measured in foot-pounds," he worried, "but its importance is immense on account of its *effects on the over-contracted person's spiritual life.*"[11]

There was something alarming about all these twitches, frowns, and nervous agitations. Was America mentally and spiritually sick? Many others saw these symptoms as unassailable evidence of an American inner dis-ease, and one in particular, George Beard, popularized a name for the underlying condition: neurasthenia. Neurasthenia itself represented an elastic set of symptoms, including exhaustion, obsessions, irritability, and mysterious neuralgias and fears, and Beard thought the condition was caused by the city's cacophonous sounds and unceasing agitations. Nineteenth-century civilization made people sick. "Civilization is the one constant factor without which there can be little or no nervousness, and under which in its modern form nervousness in its many varieties must arise inevitably." Assuming that individual human beings operated with a finite amount of nervous energy, and using electrical metaphors, Beard warned that civilization demanded more nervous output than the "charge" on our internal batteries. In making his case, Beard pointed to a list of causes of neurasthenia that included everything that produced a jarring sound or stressful condition—industrial machinery, loud noises, the telegraph, long work hours, doing two things at once, and so on. There were other ways to squander nervous energies as well, including excessive sexual activity and masturbation. In these activities nervous forces were drained off without producing something higher or better. (Sexual activity for procreation was an example of a nervous investment that delivered healthy returns and even peace and "finer and spiritual things.") The key problem was expending nervous forces in unfocused or illicit ways, a vice that led to dissipation. Dissipation in turn could lead to "decadence"—the total breakdown of nerve centers in the self and a corresponding decay of our civilization. These were urgent reasons to watch carefully how you spent your time and attention.

But if some Americans were lucky or perhaps wealthy enough to escape the dissipating noises and commotions of modern life, there were other threats to nervous health that were more difficult to avoid. A growing number of observers worried that modern life required an unnatural repression of the inner self. In America, Beard reflected, "it is not polite either to laugh or to cry in public; the emotions which would lead us to do either the one or the other, thus turn in on the brain and expend themselves on its substance; the relief which should come from the movements of muscles in laughter and from the escape of tears in crying is denied us." This was James's concern as well: Social codes prevented us from expressing emotions. And so the vital force that would have been expended in physical action turned back and savaged the inner self. "Nature will not, however, be robbed," Beard cautioned. "Her loss must be paid and the force which might be expended in muscular actions of the face in laughter and on the whole body in various movements reverberates on the brain and dies away in the cerebral cells." Discourses on nervous health undergirded a host of reforms in this period, including programs to make cities quieter, women's fashions less constraining, and natural environments more accessible. They also undergirded new ways of thinking religiously about temptation, belief, and morality.[12]

There were a variety of possible remedies for neurasthenic illnesses, though at a deep level the precise mechanisms of nervous disorder and cure remained mysterious. Beard's prescriptions changed over time as he revised his ideas about the disease and its provenance, but they included, at different times, electric shock, phosphorus, strychnine, arsenic, and muscular exercise. He and other neurologists advised some to work (men, mostly), others to rest (women). Others, including William James, thought that religious faith, when rightly conceived, would cure nervous disease.

Religious Americans, like others, were concerned about the problems of nervous fatigue, and they incorporated physiological discourses into their advice on faith and morality. Some went to great lengths to educate believers about fagged nerve cells, how nerves worked, and the etiology of nervous disorders. They sometimes included in their religious tracts sketches of the body, the nervous system, or depleted nerve cells.

One individual who closely followed the scientific literature was the popular writer, muscular Christian, and president of Oberlin College

H. C. King (1858–1934), who wrote extensively about these matters and urgently reminded Christians that "much of the dissatisfaction of the moral and spiritual life results from a wholly unnecessary and senseless disregard of bodily conditions." The problem of nervous fatigue was not his only concern, but it was a crucial one, for it produced undesirable physiological, psychological, and moral consequences. "The importance of surplus nervous energy is emphasized by all specialists," King wrote, warning that nervous fatigue was a "sign that the reserve stock is being drawn upon, that one has begun to consume his principal. To continue work in spite of warnings of weariness is simply to drug the watchman of the treasury." This had clear physiological manifestations—namely, nerve cells shrank. "Direct experiment in electrical stimulation of the nerve-cells of frogs and cats shows a 'remarkable shrinking of the nerve-cells, particularly of the nuclei.' After five hours continuous work, the cell nucleus is only half its normal size, and twenty-four hours of rest are necessary for complete restoration to its normal state." And these forms of depletion had psychological and spiritual effects as well, for the result of nerve fatigue was memory loss, irritability, sleeplessness, depression, and inability to resist temptation. Nervous fatigue was "intellectually and morally dangerous," King warned, sometimes leading to morally profligate behavior or religious indifference. Our powers of self control were "directly proportioned to the amount of surplus nervous energy."[13]

A deeply religious man, certain of himself and Christian truth, a man who wrote faithfully and intelligently on everything from scientific psychology to Jonathan Edwards, King probably was the least nervous of all the liberal believers I have examined thus far. (He also was a beloved president of Oberlin College for twenty-five years, where, even though his chapel talks could be "rather stiff scientific" lectures on "the psychological principles underlying conduct"—"as unsparing as surgery," his friend Washington Gladden once quipped—they concluded inevitably with rousing ovations of the kind that only beloved college presidents receive.)[14]

But if King was motivated by optimism about the next generation and certainty in religious matters, there were others who, like Beard, were uncomfortable and uncertain because of youthful problems that left a residual uneasiness. Though I will not multiply examples, there are one or two that are important. For example, the psychologist of religion George Coe (1862–1951) had, as a boy, hoped for a Methodist conversion experience that never materialized; as a man, he saw clearly that these psychological pressures and other forms of nervous agitation led not to the deep pleasures of religious contentment but to an intractable type of religious morbidity.

> For our purposes the essential characteristic of a fatigued nerve is its increased irritability; it reacts to less than the normal stimulus, and hence more or less spasmodically. For example, in a state of fatigue one is more likely to start at small noises; furthermore, one's reaction is likely to be ill-directed, uncertain, prolonged. Let the same cause produce its natural effects in the workings of the intellect, the feelings, and the will, and we shall have, among other things, an important group of morbid moral and religious states. The following may be enumerated as examples: worry, despondency, bad temper, emotionalism of various kinds, oversensitiveness, lack of decision in small matters, morbid introspection, hyperconscientiousness, increased susceptibility to temptations of appetite and sex.

Nervous or psychological irritability led to religious irritability; psychological upset contributed to religious upset; generalized anxiety led to morbid religious states. Henry Ward Beecher, King, Coe, and other liberals were obsessed with diagnosing and curing these morbid states and related forms of religious "hyperconscientiousness." Coe reviewed cases he had encountered in his research—a woman "tortured by uncertainty as to what she was created for"; a "very nervous and very religious" girl who "became a mental and physical wreck with the delusion in her head that she had committed the unpardonable sin" (she had not); a young man "continually in a state of unrest and trouble, magnifying . . . perfectly innocent things into sins of the deepest dye." Like King and other religious liberals, Coe was concerned in particular about adolescents, who already were enduring a time of severe nervous strain. Their bodies and minds were changing; this itself taxed their systems. And a young man with a nervous system already "overburdened" was not helped by pastors and parents "multiplying the doubts," "adding blacker hues to the outlook on life," "appealing to his fears," or telling him to "examine his heart frequently. . . . The victim of such teaching may be religious, but he is pretty certain to be spiritually deformed also." The sad result was that "untold spiritual treasure is slipping from our hands" simply because Christians had not thought enough about how the body, the nervous system, and spirituality were linked. Of course, embedded in Coe's prescriptions were clear guidelines for American believers, a cautionary discourse about intemperate (read: evangelical) religious practices. Doctrines concerning damnation and fear-inducing sermons on the fires of hell were off-limits.[15]

But while these believers were sure that deficient nervous energies fed religious doubt, they were just as sure that strong faith cured nervous problems. Using nervousness, anxiety, and worry synonymously, James said explicitly that the "sovereign cure for worry is religious faith"—though of course he, like other liberals, knew that some religions, such as evangelical Calvinism, stoked unhealthy worries rather than soothing them. There were arguments that religion augmented nervous forces, prevented psychological disorders, and quashed worry. "The two greatest religions the world has ever seen, Buddhism and Christianity, are essentially anti-worrying religions," one religious liberal wrote—even if the negations of desire and striving found in Buddhism were less appealing than the affirmations of God's goodness in Christianity. "Replace your doubting, restless, distrustful, faithless, attitude to God, by a trustful and confident faith in God. Take God at his word. Accept and believe His promises and your worries will gradually disappear, and all life will become new." Christ himself had promised many things to those with faith: "all things whatever you pray and ask for, if you believe that you receive them, you shall have them." And fast on the heels of scriptural authorities were scientific ones delivering confident proclamations buttressed by diagrams and tables. Physiological evidence showed that faith cured worry and nervous fatigue. The psychiatrist and popular Chautauqua lecturer William Sadler (1875–1969), for one, could recapitulate scientific studies showing how faith-states led to more regular and slower heart rates, better circulation, and lower blood pressure (see figure 6). He also could draw on many years of observing patients in his clinic, prescribing prayer and other religious exercises and noting patients' progress in nervous and physical functions. Religious liberals tended to be ecumenical, but in his views of "faith generators and fear destroyers" Sadler outdid all of them. "Any and all procedures, practices, superstitions, religious beliefs or systems of healing"—including "idol worship," "oriental sophistry," and even "nominal praying"—seemed to reduce fear and worry and abet physical health as well (see figure 7).[16]

WORK AND PLAY

General literatures on nerves and nervous fatigue were used in specific ways by religious liberals wondering how to find their way in the modern city. Drawing on scientific notions such as those outlined above, these liberals believed that nervous and spiritual fatigue was caused by several different sources. First, civilized morality and social codes, as I noted

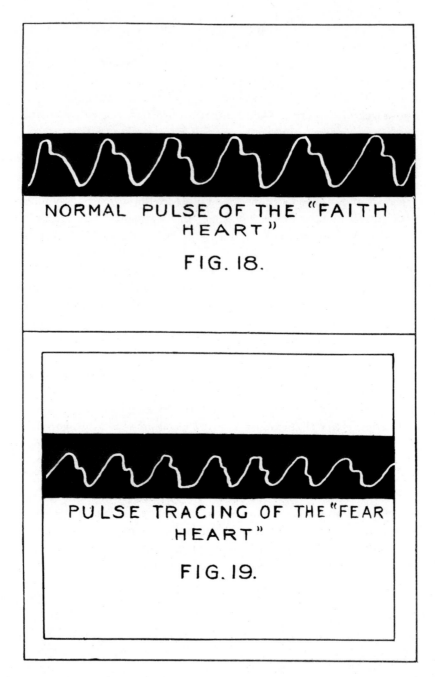

NORMAL PULSE OF THE "FAITH
HEART"

FIG. 18.

PULSE TRACING OF THE "FEAR
HEART"

FIG. 19.

Figure 6.   Faith lowers the heart rate. From William Sadler, *The Physiology of Faith and Fear*, 1920.

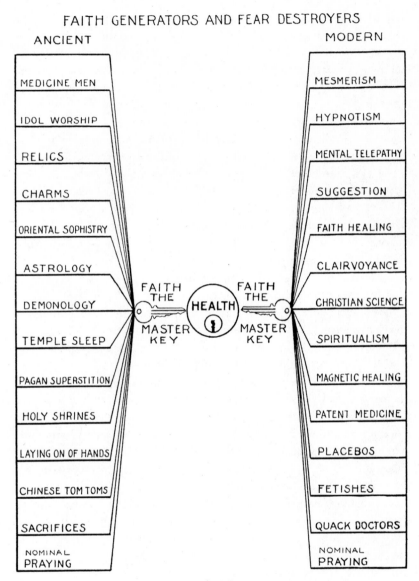

FAITH GENERATORS AND FEAR DESTROYERS

ANCIENT                                              MODERN

| ANCIENT | MODERN |
|---|---|
| MEDICINE MEN | MESMERISM |
| IDOL WORSHIP | HYPNOTISM |
| RELICS | MENTAL TELEPATHY |
| CHARMS | SUGGESTION |
| ORIENTAL SOPHISTRY | FAITH HEALING |
| ASTROLOGY | CLAIRVOYANCE |
| DEMONOLOGY | CHRISTIAN SCIENCE |
| TEMPLE SLEEP | SPIRITUALISM |
| PAGAN SUPERSTITION | MAGNETIC HEALING |
| HOLY SHRINES | PATENT MEDICINE |
| LAYING ON OF HANDS | PLACEBOS |
| CHINESE TOM TOMS | FETISHES |
| SACRIFICES | QUACK DOCTORS |
| NOMINAL PRAYING | NOMINAL PRAYING |

FAITH THE MASTER KEY — HEALTH — FAITH THE MASTER KEY

FIG. 15.

DIAGRAM SHOWING ANCIENT AND MODERN
FAITH GENERATORS AND FEAR DESTROYERS

Figure 7.   All kinds of religious faiths promoted psychological well-being.
From William Sadler, *The Physiology of Faith and Fear*, 1920.

earlier, made it impossible to express emotional states properly. Certain emotions had to be repressed in unhealthy ways, and this led to nervous fatigue. Second, and related to this, was the problem of civilized amusements—the theater, the symphony, the modern novel. These amusements could be problematic because they stimulated inner states without providing proper channels for their expression. Third, religious liberals worried about "stimulants" such as alcohol, tobacco, and sexuality. All these temptations artificially excited the neuromuscular system and drained nervous energies. In laying out these temptations and their remedies, Christians in this era, as in others, developed sophisticated ways of evaluating their participation in the world.

There was one remedy for nervous fatigue that, once it caught on, dramatically changed how religious Americans thought about amusements and other secular pursuits. By the latter half of the nineteenth century, the "rest cure" was so pervasive that even Protestant moralists who had resisted rest as indulgent and unproductive gradually embraced it as healthy and spiritually helpful.

Several pervasive physiological and psychological discourses promoted this change. The first was a clinical literature that authorized rest as the solution to overworked nerves, a literature that began in Europe but was expanded in America by George Beard and another popularizer of nervous diagnoses and their cures, a Philadelphia physician named Silas Weir Mitchell. Mitchell is well known for popularizing the "rest cure" especially for women exhausted by modern life. Since women were viewed as more susceptible to fluctuating, uncontrolled, or intemperate emotions, many neurologists, including Mitchell, thought the rest cure particularly important for them. The rest cure, according to Weir, involved avoiding excess in all things—intellectual overwork, "excitement or perversion" of the sex instinct, excessive grief or shock, emotional intemperance, morbid or excessive subjectivity, and too much religious emotion. The treatment involved isolation, bed rest, massage, a diet rich in nerve-building proteins, and even having physicians or others assist with simple tasks such as eating. The effect of the treatment was to make female patients totally dependent on (male) physicians. "It is not surprising," one historian has written, "that Mitchell's most notable therapeutic failures were women like Charlotte Perkins Gilman and Jane Addams, who rejected both the paternalism inherent in the rest cure and the subordinate role assigned to their sex." But Mitchell's failures point to other problems with his profession, a guild of clinical entrepreneurs who essentially were mystified by nervous forces and how to restore them. Neurologists prescribed work and rest cures in different cases without knowing whether or how they worked. Sometimes they were prescribed at alternating intervals. Though specific regimens differed, the rest cure was widely practiced as a crucial antidote to the deadening routines of work in industrial America.[17]

A second set of discourses recovering the importance of play, especially for children, also pointed to the healing and even saving power of structured leisure and rest. This literature was undergirded by the developmental psychology of scientists like G. Stanley Hall, who did many studies on child development in addition to the experimental work I surveyed in chapter 2. Hall persuaded many that children were overstimulated by the loud, artificial, and often corrupt urban environments they lived in. Several problems had to be addressed. One was simply that urban environments did not provide venues for physical exercise or cooperative, wholesome play. Reformers involved in the American Play Movement enthusiastically constructed urban playgrounds and touted the importance of play in creating healthy, moral citizens. But while these reforms would bring better hygiene and cooperative values to children, social scientists had deeper and more important aims in mind. The play movement would help children and young people better manage nervous and emotional energies. This was so because play helped individuals connect with original, creative instincts and emotions—to fight, struggle, and love—and learn to express these inner states in socially approved ways. The psychological theory here was the recapitulation theory of human development—namely, that each child recapitulated in his life stages the earlier stages of human social evolution. Children and young people, then, were savages who, in order to develop properly, had to express primitive instincts and emotions in play activities; for this, they needed less civilized and artificial environments. If children were not allowed to manifest these primitive, creative instincts, their vital forces and potentials would be repressed and minimized, leaving their inner selves a "spiritual waste . . . desiccated of all meaning." Play helped individuals build the emotionally intense parts of the self. Play also exercised muscular, emotional, and spiritual capacities not activated during work, allowed overworked organs to rest, and called into action unknown nervous reserves.[18]

There also were distinctly religious discourses of rest and passivity developed at the time, including especially discourses of self-surrender in New Thought and other liberal religious traditions. By the 1890s, New Thought leaders such as Ralph Waldo Trine, Orisen Swett Marden, and Annie Payson Call promised power and success to all who mastered the relaxation that came with fully opening to the divine inflow. In *Power through Repose*

(1891), a very popular book even among Protestant clergy, Annie Call helped make rest an accepted part of spiritual health. Rest helped us access divinity. "The greatest act, the only action which we know to be power in itself, is the act of Creation. Behind that action there lies a great Repose. We are part of Creation, we should be moved by its laws. Let us shun everything we see to be in the way of our own best power of action in muscle, nerve, senses, mind, and heart. Who knows the new perception and strength, the increased power for use that is open to us if we will but cease to be an obstruction?"[19] Rest worked because it put people in contact with vital energies that were at the same time supernatural and indigenous to the self. When the self was rightly relaxed, these forces could rush into consciousness, replenishing our energies and righting nervous imbalances. Of course, New Thought authors were not the only ones reflecting on the deeper aspects of the self. More mainstream religious liberals and even psychologists like James suspected that our economies of nervous forces were connected to supernatural energies tapped in rest. James thought that alternating forms of exercise and rest, activity and passivity, drew in nervous energies.

So for the first time, a wide range of believers was willing to embrace rest and leisure as a means of increasing religiousness. At about the same time, and for some of the same reasons, they embraced play and sports. Religious liberals recovering the importance of these activities often turned for support to physiological notions. "All our powers of body and mind depend on activity for their development and for their continued efficiency. But work never employs all our faculties," the social gospel reformer Josiah Strong wrote, "and sometimes very few; while it spurs some it ties up others, and the natural desire to play is simply the impulse to let them loose. Play affords a change of activities; it permits the faculties or muscles which have been at work to rest," and thus "by equalizing and harmonizing our powers it *re-creates* us." Alternating rhythms of work and play kept vital forces flowing properly. If we Americans, Strong surmised, "with our nervous temperament," would "relax somewhat the intensity of our living and obey more often nature's impulse to play, there would be fewer shattered nervous systems, fewer madhouses, fewer deaths from obscure causes."

There might even be fewer unbelievers. Those denied opportunities to play, another expert agreed, "lack not only in physical vitality, but in those larger spiritual qualities of enthusiasm, spontaneity and creative ability." Some thought that play was good practice for worship: both were spontaneous forms of self-expression. Others pointed to a wide range of spiritual attitudes cultivated by organized play, which included especially obedience, focus, and dedication. "The demand of Jesus, touching love of God or neighbor, or regarding enlistment in His cause, is a demand for prompt action of the total self. Possibly no other single virtue has a more varied field of application than the ability for decisive and whole-souled action, which is constantly cultivated in all physical training, and especially in competitive athletic games." The right kinds of play helped people learn to submit themselves to greater ideals, such as fair play, and to the common good, and this, too, would eventually lead to "triumph in a yet more searching test, and [exercise] another set of spiritual muscles." There was no doubt about it; current psychology, one theologian exclaimed, was "giving us wonderful revelations of the function of play in religious mental economy."[20]

## AMUSEMENTS

Commentators used these ideas to fashion a set of specific recommendations regarding amusements. Amusements were legitimate if they helped build an efficient, balanced Christian life. But if believers became preoccupied with them, spending too much money or time on them, or if their content was explicitly immoral or irreligious (as, for example, in the theater), these activities could dissipate the spiritual self rather than build it up. And there were other problems to consider. Though some amusements usefully exercised unused mental capacities and released pent-up emotions, if excited emotions were not translated into productive activities, individuals could be left passionless and passive. "All legitimate amusement increases our effectiveness, our power to serve," Joseph Strong once pointed out. "All amusements which are followed the next day by lassitude or distaste for work," on the other hand, "violate the law of service." When amusements stimulated the inner self without providing some kind of outer (muscular) expression of these inner states, they could consume vital energies rather than replenish them.[21]

Amusements like concerts and the theater were problematic for just this reason: they uncoupled emotions from the neuromuscular self. This was James's complaint in the *Principles*, to which I have already alluded.[22] James was not the only one concerned. "The stage, the dance, the games and things of like nature," the liberal Congregationalist pastor Theodore Munger worried, "consume vitality rather than furnish a channel for it." This was so partly because they "cannot, from their nature, be closely enough ingrafted with daily life." Religious liberals fretted about music in particular. Vida Scudder, a liberal Episcopalian and socialist reformer, wrote in the *Andover Review* that, "more than any other power on earth, music arouses emotion without furnishing any hint of an end to which the emotion shall be directed." Looking back, this might seem an odd concern, but in the context of broader anxiety over how to police the "nerve-wracking" noises of modern technologies, concern about the moral and emotional effects of all sounds should not surprise us. Scudder worried above all that saturating oneself in musical presentations was an "enervating luxury" that "tears in two those delicate threads of association which were intended to bind together with almost automatic precision the impulse with the effort to achieve." Music could break down the subtle economy of forces in the self, severing the chains of sensation and reaction, alienating outer self and inner. The result was an emotionally impotent and physically weak class of Americans. Scudder saw signs of mental weakness especially among regular, upper-class patrons of the arts. "Too highly educated to care for vulgar excitements, or for coarse and primitive emotions, their philosophy is a refined hedonism, their one endeavor to educate the nature to the utmost keenness of perception and of feeling." Unfortunately, the enervating luxuries of music were spread broadly in culture. Even in worship, for example, Americans experienced music as an end in itself, not as a means to make the emotions "efficient and eager ministers to the sluggish will." Music should inspire pious acts or social reform. Scudder despaired of easy solutions. The only way to prevent this kind of nervous depletion was to add to musical performances "a strong intellectual and volitional element"—to use music, in other words, to inspire action. The right kind of music could inspire us to fight for a just cause on the battlefield, but what could be done for music in symphony halls? Could these musical performances somehow be connected to useful actions? Liberal Protestants like Edward Griggs also wondered. "Do you ever listen to beautiful music without a certain exaltation of spirit, a feeling that now you could really achieve the ideal of which you have always dreamed? If you do go home and fail to express that powerful appeal in some form of helpful action, you would distinctly better not have gone to the concert."[23]

Concern over music as a source of excessive emotion was so great that several liberals wrote deliberately about whether and how exactly to use music in worship. Was it stirring up inner states that were then stifled or unexpressed, a process that withered the self? "You go to church on Sunday. The music puts you into a receptive, meditative mood. The minister says something that touches your mind and heart. You go away saying that you feel 'good.' If you put off that good feeling with your Sunday gown or coat for the six days that follow, you would distinctly better not have gone to church. The good feeling was simply so much inspiration to helpful action, and when not embodied in conduct tends to a dissipation of the energies of character." Others shared these concerns, and some, like George Coe, fashioned specific recommendations about using music in church. In *The Spiritual Life* (1900), Coe found that only about one out of seven hymns in the Methodist Episcopal Church's hymnal, for example, dealt with "Christian activity"; the hymns could stir deep and important religious emotions, but they often did this without suggesting proper outlets for these emotions. Like Scudder, Coe suspected that uncoupling emotions and neuromuscular actions in this way was enervating. Though hymns could enrich one's inner life, they also could lead to a deadening subjectivity—or to "a selfish, unsocial and hence unchristian view of life." We need songs, Coe thought, "infusing love . . . into the occupations of hand and of brain." Song should inspire good Christian work in the world. Coe unfolded these cautions into a broader critique of emotional displays and intemperate outbursts in worship. He devoted entire sections of his book to the problem of "sham," shallow emotions and how they were produced especially in evangelical revivals. He and many other religious liberals thought revivals and amusements like music led to the same kind of emotional and spiritual problems: both overstimulated our nervous systems and thus atrophied our inner powers.[24]

Those in the habit of seeing hazards in drama and music did not stop, of course, with these two amusements. On the subject of novel reading, for example, concerned believers continued to try to separate the recreative from the enervating. While the best novels have "raised the tone of morals and manners, championed many a depressed but righteous cause," and "contributed to the redressing of wrongs" and sins, inferior kinds of novels fostered weakness and passivity, the critic George Clarke wrote. Many novels did not activate our "constructive and creative imagination" and appealed only to individuals "deficient in mental energy and creative powers." Much of this inferior literature functioned like intoxicating drinks or opium, deadening daily cares and anxieties instead of solving them. This amounted to an unhealthy and potentially addictive escape. "The effects of the novel-habit are not so conspicuous as those of tippling, and are doubtless less disastrous to mind and body, but it might fairly be urged that habitual debauches of novel-reading work sufficient havoc on the mental faculties to justify a crusade against the evil." The havoc worked on someone so addicted was spelled out clearly by a number of Protestant commentators, including the Christian psychologist George Ladd, who spoke for the solid majority of expert opinion when he insisted that "excessive delight and unceasing practice in telling and hearing tales belong to a condition in which a luxurious imagination, easy morals, and much leisure are combined." Cheap novels filled people with unhealthy and overstimulated emotions that never could be acted upon. On this matter, even William James agreed with Ladd. "Excessive novel-reading and theatre-going will produce true monsters in this line," James worried. "One becomes filled with emotions which habitually pass without prompting to any deed, and so the inertly sentimental condition is kept up." When we "let our emotions evaporate" in this way, "they get into a way of evaporating"; just as "if we often flinch from making an effort, before we know it the effort-making capacity will be gone." The "novel reading habit" destroyed our capacities for real feeling, real action, and upright deeds. "One may shed so many tears over the imaginary characters of novels that one's eyes are dry towards the people who starve, physically or spiritually, in the next street," another religious liberal wrote. "Whenever the beauty of the arts is sought as a mere selfish indulgence and the stimulus from it finds no expression in bettered action, the result is a very refined but most positive deterioration in moral character."[25] Though no historian has investigated this in detail, the physiological literatures I am discussing also influenced the late-nineteenth-century turn away from enervating "sentimental" novels.


## STIMULANTS AND TEMPTATIONS

These were not the only illicit enjoyments that psychologists and physicians helped Americans worry about. There were other temptations that exhausted the self, including especially alcohol, other drugs and "stimulants," and sexual indulgence.

Mental hygienists and medical authorities in this period developed an extensive literature about the bad effects of alcohol. For much of the nineteenth century, in popular literatures ranging from hygiene manuals to religious tracts, alcohol was lumped in with other enervating stimulants, including tobacco, coffee, tea, chocolate, and (too much) sex. (Alcohol was considered a stimulant because it decreased motor control and inhibition and increased vigor. Didn't people who drank wine talk a lot?) It did not take a scientist to see that the effect of excessive stimulation from alcohol consumption was a corresponding reaction, often the next day, that included headache, nausea, and exhaustion. When scientific knowledge about alcohol toxicity and its effects on nervous tissues and bodily organs advanced during the second half of the nineteenth century, experts agreed that alcohol did not just overtax the nervous system; it also quite directly

poisoned it. It was a nerve toxin, an anesthetic that temporarily paralyzed higher cerebral (inhibitory) functions. This could lead to all sorts
of immoralities. Though scientists would not speak with one voice on
this question, their studies, when combined with conventional wisdom,
were enough to alarm reformers who, like the evangelical temperance
crusader Mary Hunt, insisted on total abstinence. Liberal-minded doctors, hygienists, and religious believers, for their part, though chagrined
that enthusiasts like Hunt took things to an extreme, also were uneasy
about alcohol, especially about the alarming amount of spirits and wine
consumed in America. Alcohol appeared to be decreasing our ability to
reason, remain mentally alert, retain our muscular strength, and above
all, remain in control of our desires and impulses. Even if it provided
some medically or socially useful benefit in the short run, alcohol led to
permanent physical, mental, and spiritual decline. It was true that those
who drink alcohol "may tend towards conviviality and good-fellowship,"
one concerned biologist wrote; "but it is no less true that the path of history is strewn with human wreckage directly due to alcohol; that many a
promising career has been drowned in wine; and that indescribable mis-
ery follows in the trail of drunkenness."[26]

Of course, on this matter pastors would not be outdone by concerned
biologists or anyone else. Reinforcing arguments with illustrations of alco-
hol-drenched nerve cells, some even argued that alcohol was *the primary
reason* for America's nervousness (a secondary, and sometimes related,
cause was illicit sexual activity). They followed such pronouncements with
educative digressions on related physiological problems. Assuring Christians that "all vice leaves its record on the nervous system," the Unitarian
educator David Starr Jordon, for example, cautioned that coffee, tea, alcohol, and other stimulants, by borrowing "from our future store of energy,"
give an impression of "joy, of rest, of activity, without giving the fact; one
and all their function is to force the nervous system to lie." The artificial
spike in nervous functioning would end with a precipitous drop in our
energies. Without noting specific spiritual consequences, Jordan warned
ominously that "subjective pains" often followed as a matter of course. The
use of any of these drugs, he continued, repeating commonplaces from the
mental hygiene literature, "brings incapacity, insanity, and death." The
twentieth century would be a complicated one that would tax our nervous
energies to their limits, and only sober men, Jordan thought, would be
able to "bear the strain of its enterprises." Those who used alcohol to "live
too fast," another commentator warned, would "die too soon."[27] Muscular
Christian and YMCA thinkers discussed alcohol within the even broader

contexts of physical fitness and neuromuscular health. I explore these contexts in the next chapter.

Believing with new psychologists that body, mind, and spirit were overlapping entities, liberals like Washington Gladden worried that alcoholic poison might also atrophy our moral and religious powers. Gladden reviewed the "accumulation of weighty evidence" against alcohol in passages on the vitality of athletes, military men, and others, finally concluding that science demonstrated that "strong drink is man's foe. . . . Life from every station and every calling, disease by every destroyer in its vast army, and death itself from every graveyard in the land, unite in the testimony that alcoholic liquors are the deadly foes of the human race, despoiling men of their strength, and joining hands with the dark slayer to do his terrible work." This was bad indeed. Alcohol also injured the moral nature, working to "stimulate the lower appetites and propensities, to aggravate the animalism of the nature, and to paralyze the nobler sentiments." It was "well known that sensuality of the foulest type is nourished by ardent spirits." Alcohol led to other immoral and indecent behaviors. On this matter, Gladden drew on common sense: "Go into any bar-room where a company of men are drinking together, and you will not stay long without hearing the vile jest or the indecent allusion. . . . Intemperance," he knew, "is always the prime minister of lust." Alcohol stirred lusts and deadened higher impulses, beating down, Gladden said, "every sentiment of purity and honor." Might alcohol even destroy our pure and honorable feelings? Certainly it decreased our powers of self-control and willpower, sabotaging our struggles against sin and worldliness.[28]

Critics of scientific temperance glossed anxieties about alcohol as holdovers from an antiquated and repressive orthodoxy; but in fact, late-nineteenth-century temperance movements were fully modern phenomena undergirded by scientific discourses linking alcohol consumption to mental, moral, and cultural decay. The problem was often explicated in the most powerful scientific vocabulary of the day: evolution. Alcohol degraded our nervous capacities, a process that led to declining nervous and physical fitness and, to borrow G. Stanley Hall's urgent phrase, entire "race suicide." (Hall thought the lower birthrates that portended "race suicide" had complicated etiologies; but nervous depletion and alcohol and drug use were part of the problem.)[29] Relying on Lamarckian notions about the inheritance of acquired characteristics, Hall and others insisted not just that alcohol drained our nervous supply but also that this deficient supply would be passed to coming generations. (Lamarckian notions were discredited by the first decade of the twentieth century.) This kind of thinking also informed Josiah Strong when he singled out "intemperance" in his 1885 jeremiad, *Our Country*. He too was worried that Anglo-Saxons, because they were highly civilized and thus highly nervous, were turning to stimulants like alcohol to recover nervous energies—a backward strategy, for though alcohol might spike our energies in the short term, in the long run the result was nervous fatigue. Others, like the liberal pastor Elwood Worcester and the Protestant writer Frances Jewett, produced graphs and charts showing how the effects of alcohol were passed down through generations. The overall effect of alcohol-induced nervous depletion was idiocy, infertility, and the extermination of the family line. Worcester thought alcohol was the principal cause of American nervousness, and he argued that intemperate parents passed nervousness and the alcohol habit to their offspring.[30]

Concerns about alcohol and race fitness drew strength from other discourses about debauched immigrants, effeminate boys and men, and unmarried women. All of these unfortunate degenerates were signs of the crucial problem of the era: loss of virility. Historians have shown the different ways that the discourse on alcohol was related to the "problem" of the intemperate Catholic immigrant; and Gail Bederman recently has examined connections between physiological studies, notions of virility, and gender. But the discourse on alcohol also was related to liberal understandings of another type of stimulant, a particularly threatening stimulant used by Americans addicted to extreme religious experiences. Around the time of the Scopes trial, David Starr Jordan remarked that evangelical revivalism was "simply a form of drunkenness no more worthy of respect than the drunkenness that lies in the gutter!" This was a common sentiment among religious liberals, who often associated dangerous drugs and intoxicating religions. Faith could be an exciting stimulant that aroused the conscience in momentary fits that led quickly to deep depressions. These depressions weakened our nervous and spiritual powers. To find the best path through extremes on both sides, liberals had to seek exacting combinations that involved balancing cautious emotional stimulation and moral relaxation. "The true concept [of Christianity] must minister evenly both to the conscience and the heart, and thus, while it builds up moral character, impart spiritual love and rest," another liberal counseled. This was a carefully balanced prescription: moderate excitement followed by spiritual rest. The "animalizing and selfish tendencies" of atheism and the irritating and depressing consequences of revivalism, he continued, both had to be avoided. More thought had to be given to the mental consequences of frightening doctrines, certain kinds of preaching, and drawn-out emotional meetings. These, too, made their imprint in the very lineaments and sinews of the body. Unfortunately it had not occurred to many Americans that wrongheaded doctrines and practices were tracing a "course along the lines of [one's] nervous system, and depositing there in every organism a transcript of itself."[31]

Is it possible to talk about all of these illicit enjoyments and intemperate excitements without also talking about sex? For religious liberals in this period, the answer was clearly no, for there was little doubt that sexual activity, and especially masturbation, led to all manner of derangements of body and spirit. Repressed Victorians had nothing on nineteenth- and twentieth-century liberals when it came to the literatures of sex and self-control. The difference was that by the early twentieth century these concerns were being sustained by powerful physiological and psychological theories, theories that emphasized how sexual temptations, if indulged, unhinged physiological mechanisms and siphoned off precious nervous forces. We do not usually think of James as particularly prim, and in most ways he was not rigid, but on the matter of chastity he was unbending. "No one need be told how dependent all human social elevation is upon the prevalence of chastity. Hardly any factor measures more than this the difference between civilization and barbarism. Physiologically interpreted, chastity means nothing more than the fact that present solicitations of sense are overpowered by suggestions of aesthetic and moral fitness which the circumstances awaken in the cerebrum." James was in good company on this matter, believing with other experts that adolescents in particular had to turn their sexual energies toward productive channels—to education, exercise, and other activities that would generate strength and power. Over time these energies could build and be passed to succeeding generations. One Protestant advice manual listed the many eminent individuals, professional and clerical, descended from Jonathan Edwards. Another widely circulated book, covered with endorsements by Josiah Strong, Russell H. Conwell, and other influential liberal Protestants, argued not just that unbelief and vice were caused by sexual sin but also that resulting nervous and spiritual weaknesses would be passed (Lamarckian-style) to one's children.[32]

The most impassioned rhetoric on this subject came, of course, from G. Stanley Hall, who had a more rigid personal style and knew from experience the imperiling temptations of masturbation. Here was a problem that, if not arrested, threatened the health and eventually the survival of our civilization. Speaking for disciplines that he helped organize, disciplines such as psychology and child study, Hall worried that sexual temptations spent nervous capital needed to help boys mature into virile and powerful men. How could enervated boys mature into fertile and responsible husbands? "Between the ages of twelve and sixteen . . . the young adolescent receives from nature a new capital of energy," Hall wrote; "and success in life depends upon the care and wisdom with which this energy is husbanded." Adolescence was the moment when young men were flooded with primitive, sexual energies, energies that could replenish and vitalize them. If the energies of young men were handled properly at this stage, their strength would contribute to civilization's advance—to, in Hall's messianic rhetoric, "the salvation and ultimate development and end and aim of creation and of history." Masturbation and other forms of indulgence imperiled this process at its most delicate moment. Masturbation had enduring consequences. (Hall's use of religious and moralistic language, especially when talking about this issue, irritated many observers. Reviewing Hall's ideas on sex in Hall's 1904 classic, *Adolescence*, E. L. Thorndike, a leading American psychologist, warned readers that Hall's discussion of sex was highly unusual. "To realize the material presented," Thorndike wrote, "one must combine his memories of medical text-books, erotic poetry and inspirational preaching." Privately, Thorndike was less diplomatic, complaining to a friend that the book was "chock full of errors, masturbation and Jesus." Hall, he said, "is a mad man.")[33]

Thorndike was only partly right. He was right that fears about masturbation and Jesus haunted Hall's book, but he was mistaken in thinking Hall was mad or marginal. To be sure, there were many others convinced that adolescent passions had to be controlled, and many religious believers in particular whose beliefs on this matter were reinforced by what seemed a clear connection between adolescent successes in suppressing sexual impulses and victories in developing religious ones. The new energies released at adolescence were also energies that built religious sensibilities. Adolescence was a crucial time for religious commitment, and depending on how they were handled, sexual urges could quash these commitments or abet them. Several psychologists noted the prevalence of sexual temptations in youthful accounts of conversion experiences and emotional struggles preceding them. Though he assured readers that he had not in his surveys "sought for revelations of experience on this point," George Coe also could not keep such experiences out of the clinical picture. "A considerable portion of the young men found it necessary to mention such temptations in order to make their religious experiences clear to me. . . . It is perfectly clear that the most serious source of religious difficulty for adolescent males lies precisely in sexual irritability." Pastors and other believers had observed the same thing. "Lust is the most common and serious vice of youth," one pastor confirmed. And others noted the close relationship between sexuality and religiousness—and conversion experiences in particular. The Christian physician Richard Cabot spoke for many other liberals when he pointed out that sexual and religious urges had a single source in our hunger and longing for God. *This* was the foundational urge (not the other way around, as some psychologists, like Freud, insisted). Young people had to be careful not to appease their base desires by pursuing sexual gratifications or worldly ambitions or amusements. Collapsing the physical and the spiritual, Cabot also insisted that nervous irritability and physical infirmities led to impure thoughts, and impure thoughts led to nervous irritability. With sexual issues in particular, temptation might begin in either outer or inner sources, body or mind. Cabot issued important reminders for Christians to think about these problems not merely in terms of medicine or hygiene. The problem with masturbation and other sexual sins was not that they were merely unhealthy or enervating but that they sundered our relationships with God. Spiritual and physical dimensions always had to be considered together. Because they often considered the bodily (ritual) dimensions of worship, Cabot thought Catholics understood this well; Protestants might learn from them.[34]

.   .   .

Liberal religious reasoning on the masturbation question was similar in many ways to reasoning about the other temptations and nervous excitements I have discussed in this chapter. All these activities artificially stimulated the nervous system, a process that led eventually to the depletion of nervous energies. Alcohol, for instance, because it overstimulated higher brain functions, degraded capacities for self-control; masturbation overstimulated sexual organs, drained nervous forces, and caused sexual impotence; and religious revivals overstimulated religious affections, leading to spiritual incapacities and even infidelity. All these excitements spent nervous forces instead of husbanding them. Each kind of nervous excitement posed a greater risk for youth, because youthful physiological and psychological systems were immature. "It is a law of the organism," one expert wrote, "that any function which is over-exerted before the organs producing it are fully matured is certain to lead to the derangement or even extinction of that function."[35] For these reasons, the issue of nervous energies was far from trivial. How young people husbanded their energies would determine how well they later acted when faced with modern trials and temptations. For many religious Americans, young and old, physiological studies provided new ways of understanding and monitoring both the self's vital forces and the moral and spiritual capacities built on them.

# 4    Neuromuscular Christians

The impulse to borrow from physiological discourses was by no means exhausted by believers pondering modern moral problems and nervous and spiritual health. This impulse led also to other, more dramatic transformations, producing, in particular, innovative metaphors for spiritual development and practical ways of cultivating religious experiences through embodied activities in the world. One result of these changes was a new Christian style, muscular Christianity, which became powerful in the decades around the turn of the twentieth century. Muscular Christians and many others linked problems related to nervous depletion and religious unbelief to the functioning of a crucial human faculty called the will. The will was important because it organized and efficiently conserved the nervous forces in the self. Because of this, and because scientists linked the will and the muscular system, believers began to see physical fitness as an essential way to develop key spiritual and psychological capacities. The result was an astonishing variety of religious fitness regimens and other ways of working out salvation in the neuromuscular self.

Historians have examined different dimensions of the turn to more embodied styles in late-nineteenth-century American culture, but few have linked it to changing physiological and psychological notions. Drawing attention to large-scale cultural changes taking place in the 1890s, John Higham wrote about the dullness of late-nineteenth-century urban culture and the ways that masculinity, youthfulness, and muscle culture were employed as antidotes. Since Higham, there has been a rich literature on these subjects. Studies of changing conceptions of manliness and gender in this period in particular have illuminated (male) American Christian anxieties. Susan Curtis, Janet Fishburn, and Gail Bederman have examined progressive Christians in this period and uncovered the conservative gender assumptions driving them. Their work constituted an important corrective to earlier literature on muscular Christianity that linked calls for a "virile" Christianity not to gender but to issues such as the loss of middle-class status or the breakdown of the Victorian worldview. Bederman also touched on ways that psychologists such as G. Stanley Hall helped fashion gender as an ideological weapon. But there were limitations to Bederman's approach. The driving issue for Bederman was the American Protestant "distaste for feminism." While attention to this issue was important for obvious reasons, it also obscured what I believe was a broader-based sensibility about muscles and spirituality. This literature was deeply physiological: it built notions of self, religiousness, and gender on a physiological foundation. An insightful study of muscular Christianity by Clifford Putney documents how widespread were new ideas about gender, muscularity, and spirituality; but Putney neglects the particular ways that Christians thought about physiology.[1] How did Christians understand their nervous and physiological systems? How did they use physiological and psychological discourses to build new metaphors for spiritual development? These are crucial issues that very few people have examined.

## DISCOURSES ON THE WILL

It is almost impossible to overestimate the importance of the will for believers in this period. Certainly there was no more crucial category for liberal believers, who used this notion to work themselves out of an astonishing number of spiritual difficulties. First of all, they turned to the will to solve neurasthenia. Mental diseases caused by nervous depletion had a number of symptoms, but as Jackson Lears has written, these symptoms were "unified by a common effect: paralysis of the will." Those with inadequate nervous forces generally were fearful, anxious, and indecisive. Neurologists, psychologists, and other advice givers offered similar recommendations, pointing out that the will, as the executive power in the self, was the organ that organized and preserved nervous forces. In an essay reprinted many times and eagerly consumed by American Protestant pastors, William James wrote that, while there were several ways of accessing our nervous energies, the "normal opener of deeper and deeper levels of energy is the will." This conviction was embraced by many. "The difficulty," James thought, however, was "to use it, to make the effort which the word volition implies. But if we do make it[,] . . . it will act dynamogenically on us for a month." It was well known, James could confirm, that "a single successful effort of moral volition, such as saying 'no' to some habitual temptation, or performing some courageous act, will launch a man on a higher level of energy for days and weeks, will give him a new range of power." Using the will was the way to overcome the enervating effects of modern temptations. James illustrated this with a story. "'In the act of uncorking a whiskey bottle which I had brought home to get drunk upon,' said a man to me, 'I suddenly found myself running out into the garden, where I smashed it on the ground. I felt so happy and uplifted after this act, that for two months I wasn't tempted to touch a drop.'" One wonders what happened after the expiration of those energetic two months; but in any case the story contains an important point: that a strong will can, for a time, replenish one's nervous forces. James was one of many psychologists and clinicians recommending a strong will as the antidote to nervousness.[2]

The will was important also because it regulated the economy of nervous forces. The essential dilemma, as Anita and Michael Fellman have made clear, was how to benefit from the dynamism of intense nervous states without losing the integrity and orderliness of the self. Nervous forces could be spent irresponsibly, but they also could be unduly repressed. In either case, nervous forces might wither. The goal was a kind of "self-repressed expression" that involved carefully adjudicating the proper kinds of thoughts and behavior. We saw this in the previous chapter. On the issue of sexual passions, for instance, while undue suppression led to pain, and satiety to nervous weakness, just the right amount generated a legitimate measure of pleasure. One physician illustrated the problem by reflecting on the broken lives of his patients—the "reports of lunatic asylums show that unbridled sexual indulgence is a factor in producing mental disorders, and [that] it is equally certain that undue restraint of a natural and necessary exercise of the sexual instinct is likewise a prominent cause of insanity." A weak will or an overly strong one—both led to disaster. In general, commentators were preoccupied more with the former, with weak wills, and they recommended different regimens of will education and strengthening.[3] Muscular Christianity was a key part of this reform.

If the will had merely solved problems related to indecision and nervous imbalance, this would have been enough to ensure its power in turn-of-the-century America. But there was a final reason the will became central to the self in this period, a final reason that liberal believers in particular clutched at this concept with such intensity. Although many accepted a material model for the brain, even scientists and physicians found themselves searching for something in the self that accounted for human freedom or authorized us as moral agents. Usually they found what they were looking for somewhere in the chains of biological cause and effect, an immaterial force that controlled the material self—the will. When he diagrammed the self in the American *Popular Science Monthly,* the British physiologist W. B. Carpenter (1813–1885) lifted the will above automatic, sensorimotor processes. He asserted that "the operations of the Cerebrum are in themselves as automatic as those of other Nerve centers." But he also insisted that "the Volitional control which we exercise over our thoughts, feelings, and actions operates through the selective attention we determinedly bestow upon certain of the impressions made upon the 'Sensorium' out of the entire aggregate brought thither by the nerves of the internal senses." In other words, the will selects and organizes sensate impressions. For these reasons, the will worked against physiological determinism, lifting human beings above nature and animal instincts. Even a hardheaded materialist like the British physician Henry Maudsley admitted that, while "our appetites and passions prompt or urge their immediate gratification," it was "the nobler function of will, enlightened by reason looking before and after, to curb these lower impulses of our nature." The will was the primary way for human beings to free themselves from the deterministic vectors of biology and nature.[4] Heavily indebted to physicians such as Maudsley and Carpenter, William James and other psychologists saw the self in similar terms.

Of course, thinkers like James went further than the medical authorities they drew on, developing new philosophical insights that employed the will and its forms of knowledge. James is an interesting case because he used the will to overcome so many of the problems troubling his generation: indecision, neurasthenic symptoms, and worries about scientific determinism. Sensing himself caught in a deterministic worldview that made him feel trapped and morally impotent, the young James worked himself back to a middle position by acting as if freedom existed and then contemplating the results. We have already seen the consequences. "I will assume for the present—until next year—that [free will] is no illusion. My first act of free will shall be to believe in free will." In this way, he fashioned belief out of an act of will. When James did this, he affirmed an empirical model of the mind—a mind filled by ideas produced directly by outside stimuli—with the caveat that the mind also had an autonomous "department," the will, that selected among input streams. The crucial issue for us is that, in doing this, James shows how people in this period associated the act of choosing, of focusing attention, with both will and belief. "Effort of attention," James once said, "is . . . the essential phenomenon of 'will.'"

James was unique in linking the same mental states with belief. Belief, he once announced, was "the cessation of theoretic agitation through the advent of an idea which is inwardly stable, and fills the mind solidly to the exclusion of contradictory ideas." Belief involved willfully attending to one idea or one stream of ideas. Belief, attention, and will signified powerful acts of cocreating: cocreating the self, reality, truth, the universe of relations. These concepts wholly altered James's identity and sense of reality. And James was not the only one altered in this way.[5]

In the decades around the turn of the twentieth century, the will and willful action were seen as the foundation stones of consciousness. Several psychologists, including the already mentioned German experimentalist Hugo Munsterberg and the American psychologist James Mark Baldwin, developed these ideas into action theories of consciousness that became widely known. Against conventional views that stimuli from the environment built associative networks in the brain, Munsterberg argued that muscular readiness to *express* inner states was more important than sensations and their mental representations. Munsterberg was looking at the other end of the process. Our actions and our readiness to act, he insisted, were determining factors. In Munsterberg's action theory, as Kuklick has summarized it, "preparedness and unpreparedness for action conditioned the reinforcement and suppression characterizing mental life. We perceived the world just as far as we were prepared to act in it; knowledge depended on the capacity to respond to objects."[6] This reversed the order of experience in the same way that James's theory of emotions had: in both theories, physiological states (and our readiness for them) determined inner, mental events. There were, then, two crucial insights that Munsterberg and other psychologists developed—first, that the will and willful action determined inner states, and second, that the will was located in the muscular self. Taken together, these ideas led to some crucial implications—in particular, that muscular (embodied) actions in the world were the sources of inner events and even spiritual states.

This was a remarkable development. Could inner, spiritual states really be the result of muscular development or physiological activity? Many correctly anticipated popular resistance to this idea, and some, like Hall, a man already worried about public perceptions, moved on the offensive. In an evangelical theological journal, he shrewdly disarmed critics by linking these new psychological insights to other authoritative currents in philosophy and religion. "The more popular sayings of Schopenhauer, that the normal man is two thirds will and only one third intellect, of [the liberal British cleric] F. W. Robertson, that doing is an essential organ of knowing, of Matthew Arnold, that conduct is three fourths of life, or of [Henry] Maudsley, that both history and character are written in the habits of muscles, which constitute about one half of the human body, and are preeminently the organs of the will—these now seem to many not more but less than the truth. We are told that belief is a function, or a part, or even a product of deliberated activity, that thought is repressed action." Had not all responsible authorities concluded that doing, conduct, and muscular activity were the access points to deep parts of the self? Liberal Protestant clerics and muscular Christians borrowed Hall's strategy, settling the question by making the question seem already settled. Henry C. King guided readers through an impressive list of experts—Borden Bowne, John Dewey, William James, Wilhelm Wundt, Thomas Carlyle, and even the authors of Job and Ecclesiastes. All of them knew that outer, muscular actions determined our deepest wishes, inclinations, and beliefs.[7]

Religious Americans and religious liberals in particular were developing their own ideas about the will and its primacy, and though these ideas eventually drew strength from psychological and physiological notions, they appear to have predated them. For nineteenth-century believers unable to produce the prescribed emotions of evangelical conversion, for instance, the will became a crucial alternative starting point. Charting paths out of these evangelical confusions led such liberals down different routes, including those outlined in chapter 1; some sought clearer indications of internal states through physiology, psychology, or their own immediate intuitions. Others merely turned away from feelings and performed their conversions *as acts of will.* Changing discourses on these matters can be monitored in progressive periodicals such as the remarkably popular *Christian Union,* edited for a time by Henry Ward Beecher.[8] Here anxious readers sent letters to the editors, wondering how to cultivate those crucial feelings of faith. Progressive editors like Beecher offered simple answers: Forget about feelings. You get faith by doing things a person of faith should do. "If we wish to feel more for the poor and needy, we must go and do for them, instead of merely asking God to do; and the more we do for them, the more we shall feel for them. If any doubt this, let them try it." If you want to *feel* more, you must *do* more. "For myself," another said, "obedience in detail to the actual commandments of Christ did, once, and for years, change the whole inward world of my habitual thoughts and emotions from confusion to peace." Beecher offered the same kinds of advice, saying that, while "it would be a very unfortunate thing in the community, if men at large should settle down upon the impression that a religious life rose no higher than an ordinary good-natured morality," it also was true that moral actions often came first and religious emotions second. When advising people about how to get faith and keep it, he told them first to act like Christians, to begin Christian living, and then, he surmised, Christ would bestow all the religious "feeling which, with your organization, is necessary and proper." These kinds of interpretive moves reoriented Christian spirituality in the will.[9]

Evangelical misfits like Beecher, Andrew Jackson Davis, and many others began their religious lives by performing this turn from feelings to will. And as the nineteenth century wore on, there were others. Examples from the turn of the twentieth century also are easy to find and are represented well by an autobiographical reflection from George Coe. "Too clear-headed either to interpret my past as that of a sinner outside the gate, or to undergo 'conversion' in any of the numerous revivals, I suffered a period of stress. . . . But when I was already more than half-way through my college course[,] I cut the knot by a rational and ethical act. Assuming that my part in the matter was to continue to commit myself to the Christian way of life, and that internal 'witness' or 'assurance' was not my affair, I resolved that never again would I seek it."[10] He turned away from dramatic feelings and inner states as markers of genuine faith. He would instead act as a Christian; he resolved to *do things*. This experience, he continued, relieved his anxieties and "started a habit of looking for the core of religious experience in the ethical will."

The experience also started a habit of rethinking inherited notions—or, more precisely, helping other people rethink them. In the first half of the twentieth century, Coe was one of the most influential intellectuals reorienting the religious lives of American Christian young people. He was self-assured and could intimidate with probing and provocative questions; but most of the time, people thought he was affable and affectionate, a man who, like King, spent a lot of time helping young people figure out their spiritual difficulties. "A scientific attitude toward all facts and a loving attitude toward all persons"—this was how one of Coe's students remembered him. While a professor at Northwestern, he opened his home to students on Sundays for "conversations," which, though they began with Methodist hymns, quickly moved into less traditional territory. His doctrinal departures were widely noted in the periodical press. (His statement of the proper [that is, liberal] kinds of Christian nurture, *The Religion of a Mature Mind* [1902] was well known to critics as *The Irreligion of an Immature Mind*.) But those Coe cared about most deeply understood that his negations were balanced by affirmative stances on key Christian articles of faith. "Those who knew him at all personally," one friend recalled, "were deeply aware of an intellectual and spiritual receptivity bordering at times upon the mystical[,] which made one sure that in his own often untraditional way he walked with God." Students in particular could "scarcely fail to feel that he was in close touch with Reality," one remembered, adding pointedly: "but he did not overwork traditional terms." Like many religious liberals, he did not "overwork" theological cant about spirit, Christ, and immortality. These were hindrances to clear thinking, or worse, a camouflage for pious hypocrisies. Coe thought authentic Christian witness was doing things, working, acting. One of his favorite verses would have appealed to liberal consciences across the board—"My father worketh hitherto, and I work."[11]

These were ways of being religious marked not by hot evangelical emotions but by faculties of sobriety, intention, and self-control, faculties associated, in a word, with the will. Coe was not the only one promoting this kind of faith. Another liberal Protestant, who wrote a regular advice column on Christian faith and practice, admitted in 1908 that though "feeling that comes spontaneously, that is not manufactured nor strained after, does have its real value, particularly in the sense of reality which it gives," it was not the "real test" of spirituality. The real test was the Christian life—following Christ's example, following his commandments. Feelings would come later. "The only way to right feeling," this Protestant insisted, "is through right conduct and right thinking. We cannot control feeling directly. We train our emotions by obedience and by putting ourselves in the presence of the great objects of faith." In time, he thought, "we may be confident that the feeling will fall finally into line with doing and thinking." These notes were sounded again and again by religious liberals confounded by the emotional rhythms of evangelical religiousness.[12]

It is no exaggeration, then, to say that in this period the will, more than any other concept, solved religious America's urgent spiritual problems. Not only did it help religious liberals replace emotional evangelical exercises with choice and embodied action as key sources of spiritual assurance; it also ensured that their spiritualities, which were often physiologically informed, did not veer toward wholesale materialism. The term helped liberals insist again and again on one crucial concept for liberals, human freedom. And it gave them a vocabulary for free parts of the self that operated outside the bounds of ironclad scientific cause-and-effect, on the one hand, and the omnipotence of the Calvinist God, on the other. "The new psychology is teaching us that the one stronghold of freedom is the power of self-directed attention," one religious liberal wrote in a passage affirming the centrality of will, attention, and "doing the will of God" in

Christian spirituality. "Attention determines motive, motive determines act and acts seal our doom."[13] The proper forms of spirituality required a strong will that produced focused attention and consistent moral action.

## NEUROMUSCULAR BELIEVERS

There were disadvantages, however, to this new emphasis on the will. While there is no doubt that many people drew satisfaction from a newer, will-oriented piety, others saw clearly that such emphases opened up difficulties that had to be reckoned with and eventually resolved. The problem, which intensified already-existing anxieties about modern living, was that if the will had to be cultivated in muscular activities, prospects for human well-being were diminishing—they *had* to be—in a society where machines, not muscles, did most of the work. Was it not true that industrial life was destroying human muscular powers and the moral and religious capacities that these powers produced? While at midcentury some Americans celebrated machines as ways of spreading enlightenment, democracy, and material wealth, by the end of the century many were ambivalent. As Alan Trachtenberg has noted, the machine was the prime cause both "of the abundance of new products changing the character of daily life" and of "newly visible poverty, slums, and an unexpected wretchedness of industrial conditions." Was the machine lifting up our society or tearing it down? Henry George wrote in his famous book, *Social Problems* (1883), that the "greater employment of machinery" resulted in "positive evils" for the working masses, "rendering the workman more dependent; depriving him of skill and of opportunities to acquire it; lessening his control over his own condition and his hope of improving it; cramping his mind, and in many cases distorting and enervating his body." George's critique was more radical than most; but his concerns were shared by many. Religious leaders sustained these anxieties, and in some cases amplified them, in their many antiurban tracts, some of which I have already sampled. Expressing contemporary clerical wisdom, one Catholic modernist wrote that the farmer, not the city dweller, "is the strongest and healthiest member of the social body, he is also the most religious and most moral." One followed from the other. Other liberals pondering problems concerning nervous energies wondered if families should return "to the soil" every third generation. "Vitality appears to be in inverse ratio to the number of years the family has lived away from the soil."[14] YMCA thinkers produced pamphlets on the relationship between urban living, human vitality, and heredity.

Powerfully communicating these anxieties and their scientific ratio-
nales were crossover figures including William James and Stanley Hall.
Both articulated their ambivalence about America's urban-industrial society at different points in their careers, early and late. "A generation or
two ago," Hall complained, "most schoolboys had either farm work, chores,
errands, jobs self-imposed, or required by less tender parents; they *made*
things, either toys or tools." Girls, also, *made things*—"embroidery, bed-
quilting, knitting, sewing, mending," and they could be seen "spinning
and weaving their own or others' clothing." So much of this was gone now.
Cities had brought "so many privileges with so few corresponding duties,"
an atmosphere of amusement and artificiality, with bad air and industrial forms of productivity, all of which weakened willpower and created
"eupeptic minds and stomachs." It seemed that nowadays "machines," Hall
grumbled, "supersede muscles." James too worried about machines, insisting that even in industrial society muscular vigor would remain crucial for
human happiness. "Even if the day ever dawns in which [muscular vigor]
will not be needed for fighting the old heavy battles with Nature, it will
still always be needed to furnish the background of sanity, serenity, and
cheerfulness to life, to give moral elasticity to our disposition, to round off
the wiry edge of our fretfulness, and make us good-humored and easy of
approach." The idea of a fully mechanized society, one in which "machines
will do all our heavy work," James said, made his flesh creep. Thus, even
if modern society took away our economic need for muscularity, we still
needed physical strength for moral and spiritual reasons. "A well-developed
muscular system" was "correlated with calm nerves and strong digestion,"
James wrote, "with joyousness and courage of every sort, with amiabil-
ity and all manner of sound affections and sensibilities." James associated
muscular fitness with spiritual calm, too, as we have seen.[15]

But if modern society was psychologically enervating, what was the
solution? Experts like James and Hall proposed strenuousness of differ-
ing kinds—including warfare and appropriate substitutes like athletics.
James's well-known nostalgia for "primordial and savage" contests and
scenes of "human nature strained to its uttermost and on the rack" illustrates well how pervasive were notions of Darwinian struggle in this era.
In speaking of these matters, James was merely repeating commonplaces.
In one popular article, he related the story of a trip to the idyllic Chautauqua Institution in upstate New York—a healthy-minded "middle-class
paradise, without a sin, without a victim, without a blot, without a tear."
When discharged again into the wicked world, James felt relieved, and
on the train home he saw from his window precisely what Chautauqua

lacked: heroism, strenuousness, "human nature *en extremis.*" He saw construction workers laboring on a new building. Wherever a "scythe, an axe, a pick, or a shovel is wielded, you have [human nature] sweating and aching and with its powers of patient endurance racked to the utmost under the length of hours of the strain"—this was the kind of strain that needed to be "married" to some form of idealism to create a vital culture. Those wielding shovels were, James thought, "our soldiers, . . . our sustainers, . . . the very parents of our life."[16] But other forms of strenuousness were possible—and in fact, among religious liberals who imbibed information from scientific experts, sports and "muscle culture" seemed the best paths to follow. The "hard-won vigor of the pioneer [generation] is lost in a few generations of civilized conditions, unless we develop some artificial substitute for the beast and the savage, the tempest and the plague," the liberal Protestant reformer William DeWitt Hyde said. "That civilized substitute is athletics." Hyde and many others promoted athletics at the time.[17] (See figure 8.)

So widespread was this turn to physical culture that it is difficult to outline its contours precisely. Others, such as the historian Clifford Putney, have tried. Liberal Christian interest in physical culture also was pervasive, with many pastors and lay Christians pointing to ways of "working out their own salvation" in embodied ways. Newman Smyth, before he became a progressive theologian, worked himself out of a philosophical skepticism by—believe it or not—exercising. Studies in mental philosophy furnished him with a haunting skepticism about his own and God's existence. But the college gymnasium helped him vent frustrations, and after a particularly strenuous workout he realized that there was one thing he could no longer doubt: the reality of his sore muscles. "I have never questioned my existence since," he later said. "I solved it by exercise." If Smyth could do it in the gym, others did it on the track, in the pool, or on their bicycles. In the first issue of the cycling journal *The Wheelman,* published during a bicycling revival in the 1880s, all articles took up the issue of clergymen and the bicycle, and all of them celebrated ministers who had stuck with bicycling despite occasional protests from more pedestrian believers. Bicycling could stir the spirit, mollify the mind, and diminish dyspepsia. One clergyman writing anonymously confessed to seeing only "monotony" and ill health until he started cycling, when "as if by magic, away went the spirits that had tormented me so long, and as their cloven feet and writhing tails disappeared in the dark past I was met by the laughing, beautiful faces of the spirits of health and cheerfulness." Others, expressing mental and spiritual conditions in physiological idioms, were convinced that, "if bicycles were more generally used by American preachers, there would

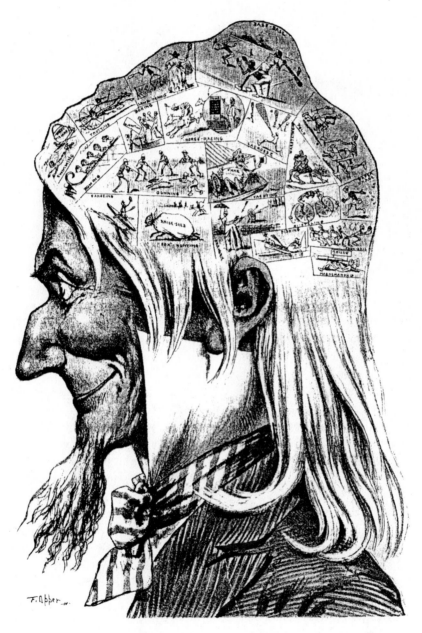

Figure 8.   Though the sports revival was transatlantic, this did not stop British observers from lampooning Americans for silly certainties about muscle culture as a way of building inner capacities. Using an older physiognomy—a skull—to peek into the American psyche, this 1887 *Puck* cartoon points humorously to America's athletic obsessions.

be fewer hollow chests, round shoulders, sensitive stomachs, and torpid livers." The general trend was characterized well by the liberal minister Theodore Munger, who showed that he had assimilated new psychological knowledge thoroughly when he announced that there could "be no health, no thought, no moral feeling, no sound judgment, no vigorous action, except in connection with a sound body." "Any religious experience connected with a weak or diseased body," he said further, "is to be regarded with suspicion." A sizable group of progressive thinkers and "body-as-temple" theologians insisted that the physical body was the "foundation which conditions the intellectual and spiritual superstructure." In this atmosphere it was hard to believe that the meek might inherit the earth. Watch out for "mollycoddles," the Reverend Frank Crane warned. "The road to hell is crowded with [them]"—"slouching, shuffling, blear-eyed, trembling morons."[18]

Muscular Christians thought quite deliberately about how to transform these slouching morons into upright Christians. Josiah Strong, the leader of many muscular Christian initiatives and "the dynamo, the revivalist, the organizer, and . . . the most irrepressible spirit" of the social gospel movement, used Hall's language when thinking about the modern problems of machines, muscles, and spirituality. Anxious that modern life made "less and less demand on muscle," that Americans were becoming nervous and weak and, most alarming of all, that "the physical aspects of the kingdom [of God] are quite ignored," Strong tried to recover the importance of the physiological self in Christian social thought. Strong was in contact with Hall and others interested in scientific psychology, and psychological assumptions about the close connection between the neuromuscular system, thinking, and believing informed his work. (Change in how religious people think and act, Strong confirmed, "is due in part to the progress of science, which has revealed the interdependence of body and mind, and the influence of physical conditions on spiritual life.") Strong was among the first social gospelers to use the concept of the Kingdom of God to talk about physical-spiritual unities, and the concept also worked well as a way to affirm psychological notions about the unified self. The Kingdom, he wrote, was spiritual and physical, "inward and outward," "visible and invisible," and it had to be realized by using both types of human capacities—thinking and doing, mind and body, intellect and will. These were balanced prescriptions, but in fact Strong was calling attention more to one side of things, to muscular doing, to the will. He did this not because embodied actions were more important but because they were more neglected by the churches. In different texts

Strong came out forcefully for a more physiological spirituality. He disliked seeing people who were overweight or unfit; he was alarmed that Christians during every period in history had "despised and abused" their bodies and was surprised that modern Christians were not doing much better; and he insisted that there could be "little usefulness, little intelligence, little moral character, little happiness without the right sort of a body." Physical entities had spiritual effects. Remedying the situation involved Strong in a raft of sports and exercise programs, institutional churches, schools, clubs and leagues, playground associations, immigrant and settlement houses, missionary societies, and that quintessential muscular Christian institution, the YMCA. By 1900 Strong could rejoice that churches were building "facilities for physical culture and recreation—a gymnasium, baths, very likely a swimming pool, and perhaps a bowling alley, which not long since would have been deemed sacrilegious."[19]

In this atmosphere, it seemed increasingly plausible that spiritual vigor depended on physical fitness. Insisting that "the new physiology and the new psychology have thrown a flood of light upon the structure of man's being," and arguing in particular that "body is the basis on which the soul stands when it does its work," one YMCA organizer thought that if you could entice men into the gym, you also could get them thinking about self-culture, self-control, and salvation. "The man who becomes ambitious to keep his body sound is not unlikely later on to become ambitious to adorn and furnish the chambers of his mind," he wrote. "The enthusiasm over running and leaping often precedes a passionate hunger for ideas and for the loftier upbuilding of the soul."[20] Perhaps—but even YMCA organizers could see that some men were using YMCA facilities merely to strengthen their bodies or become healthy. When discourses on salvation elided differences between body and spirit, as these discourses often did, there were some who worried that, in theory or practice, fitness schemes might remain merely bodily pursuits.

YMCA employees made strenuous efforts to prevent this from happening. First of all, they built up a powerful rhetoric concerning the physiological dimensions of faith. Commentators reminded readers not to forget that "a man's mental and spiritual processes are constantly colored by the character of his physiological functioning." A host of sins and temptations resulted from physical ills, abnormalities, and especially neuromuscular fatigue. "There are men who are losing spiritual battles simply because they are physically fatigued." Second, they made an effort to train physical directors who knew and insisted that "the very crown of our work, . . . its highest and ultimate aim" was spiritual. The YMCA advertised physical fitness, one organizer admitted, but it had an "ulterior and higher desire and purpose toward young men, viz.: their spiritual and eternal welfare." In the 1880s many felt that gymnasium instructors should be trained more carefully in how they explained the relations of body and spirit. "Lectures upon physical culture and health should be given to gymnasium members by speakers who will interweave moral and spiritual truths and show the necessity of the development of the whole man."[21] When in 1887 the YMCA put Luther Gulick in charge of the physical department, they found a powerful organizer and exponent of new physiological ideas that unmistakably tethered body and spirit.

## BODY-MIND-SPIRIT

An impatient, driven, and occasionally antagonistic crusader, Luther Gulick (1865–1918) became a key figure in many progressive-era initiatives, including the Playground Association of America, the Camp Fire Girls, the school hygiene movement, and the YMCA. He held prestigious positions as the director of YMCA's physical training at Springfield College in Springfield, Massachusetts, was secretary of the physical department of the YMCA's International Committee, and created the YMCA's famous inverted triangle symbol, which iconographically displayed the principal insight of the new psychology: that body, mind, and spirit were overlapping entities, even different words for the same things. In addition to being an energetic YMCA administrator, Gulick also was probably its greatest thinker and most assiduous popularizer, and he, more than anyone else, shaped the popular discourse on will training and its influence on spirituality. In a number of books on health, hygiene, morality, and religious living, he attached transcendent meanings to physical fitness and promoted in particular the YMCA's physical fitness mission.[22]

Attention to Gulick's work reveals how hard religious liberals had to labor to keep body and spirit together in their new schemes of embodied salvation. Even in the YMCA, and even for believers who parroted biblical verses about the body as a temple for the soul, it was not always clear how physical culture helped in spiritual matters. When Gulick was appointed secretary for the YMCA's physical department, he encountered a good number of officials and colleagues who suspected that the physical department was merely a distraction from other, more important pursuits. Many tolerated the physical department simply because it drew men into the organization. Though Protestant ways of thinking about fitness were rapidly changing, as we have seen, even YMCA workers could be skeptical that the body, athletics, or physical culture might help save souls. Their fears were confirmed when they encountered YMCA physical directors who were ignorant of the YMCA's religious mission or of Christianity in general. Arriving at the YMCA as these issues were being debated, Gulick was surprised to see that many of his physical directors "looked upon the work as merely physical in its nature," or "were not Christians, and the gymnasium was consequently in some instances not merely negative in its influence, but a positive aggressive force tending away from the primary object of the institution." To put it mildly, as Gulick probably did not, the situation was unsatisfactory. "The anomaly of an institution organized primarily for religious work, employing as one of its executive officers, and putting in the place of large influence, a man who was antagonistic both in his life and belief to the fundamental aims of that institution," Gulick grumbled, was an odd contradiction that "had apparently not dawned upon the association world at large." Those who had close contact with young people, such as physical directors and gymnasium instructors, had to remember that "the spiritual work of the association is the most prominent aim. . . . The gymnasium instructor," Gulick insisted, "must be an earnest soul winner."[23]

To physical directors, church members, colleagues, and anyone else willing to listen, he preached tirelessly about the proper relationship between fitness and spirituality. He saw the YMCA mission as consistent in two ways "with all of the latest researches in Psychology, Physiology and also with Theology, first that the body must be cultivated for the sake of the mind; second, that these must be cultivated for the sake of their indirect effect on the soul." He had an apparently unshakable belief, drawn from Germans associated with the gymnastics movement and shared with his friend Stanley Hall, that the starting point for spiritual capacity was located in the muscles. Surveying psychological literature in the *Popular Science Monthly*, he pointed out that "muscular contraction appears to be closely related to the genesis of all forms of psychic activity." "Without the muscular system, material for psychic activity can not be secured. All three of these processes—thinking, feeling, willing—are more or less remotely connected with a rehearsal in the body, both neural and muscular, of the acts by which the original material for the mental process came in." This was Hall's language almost verbatim. It was not merely that thinking, feeling, and willing were *expressed* in the muscular self, but that activity in the muscular self constituted thinking, feeling, and willing. This was the physiological turn I documented earlier.[24] Refined muscular systems correlated in particular with greater powers of attention, will, morality, and emotional control.

The notion that muscle strength indicated deeper mental or spiritual vigor undergirded widespread interest in physical culture and especially body measurement at the turn of the twentieth century. Gulick also was interested in measurement techniques, and he developed and used different systems. (Like other Christians, he thought that a muscular person ipso facto had well-developed inner capacities, especially the will.) In his *Manual for Physical Measurements* (1892), which attempted to measure not just strength, height, weight, heart rate, and lung capacity but also family history, recreational activities, and personal habits, Gulick laid out a comprehensive system of measurement that physical directors and gymnasium instructors could use to get to know and aid young men.[25]

And Gulick pointed to other new devices that, by measuring muscle strength, revealed deeper parts of the self. In *Control of Body and Mind* (1908), one volume of a series of hygiene books he edited, the author, Gulick's sister Frances Jewett, summarized the work of the Italian physiologist Angelo Mosso, who had developed an instrument for measuring muscle strength and endurance called the ergograph (figure 9). The ergograph held the subject's arm, wrist, and hand firmly in place. It also held in place two fingers, allowing the middle finger to pull a weight attached to a string. As the subject raised his finger, a pencil attached to the string recorded how high the subject lifted the weight. As the subject pulled the weight up and let it down repeatedly, he gradually tired and produced a downwardly sloping fatigue curve. This much was unremarkable. The remarkable part was that fatigue curves changed depending on psychological states. If subjects were enthusiastic, they fatigued more slowly; if they were mentally tired (e.g., from intellectual work), their muscles fatigued more quickly. There were several key conclusions here, not lost on Jewett: that muscular fatigue led to mental fatigue and vice versa; that muscular strength led to stronger mental capacities and vice versa; and that Mosso, and presumably other careful observers, could, simply "by looking at the curve," discern "with remarkable truth the state of mind or body of the one who did the pulling." Devices like the ergograph were powerful tools for discerning inner states. In his own books, Gulick referred to such studies to illustrate the dangers of fatigue and how fatigue reduced the whole person, "mentally, morally, physically" to "lower and cruder terms." Different forms of fatigue attacked the will in particular, the executive part of the self, our ability to focus attention, and this in turn made self control and discipline more difficult. Gulick reinforced his YMCA colleagues' beliefs when he agreed that physical illnesses and muscular weakness led to weak wills, which, in turn, led people to submit to all manner of temptations and vices.[26]

Like other muscular Christian organizers, Gulick focused his energies on the perilous religious condition of boys and young men, whose "katabolic,"

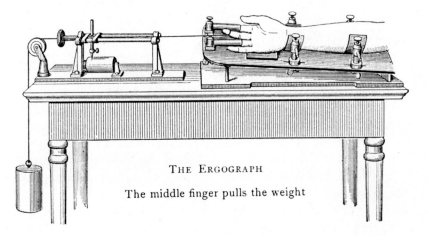

THE ERGOGRAPH

The middle finger pulls the weight

Figure 9. The ergograph measured muscular work and fatigue. From Frances Gulick Jewett, *Control of Mind and Body*, 1908.

or active and energy-expending, tendencies had not been accommodated in feminized programs for moral and religious development. His project was part of a much wider movement to masculinize the churches, a project informed by physiological thinking. He wrote at length about the principal play activities of boys and young men, producing maps and staged charts that showed how play at each age built up the physiological substrata for later psychological, moral, and spiritual acquisitions. The infant and toddler could produce only the most basic sets of muscular actions, but these were the simple building blocks of the self. In the second stage (ages seven to twelve), rudimentary capacities were joined to capacities for social types of play and to corresponding moral reasoning abilities. Young people were introduced to basic ways of reasoning about ethics, individuality, and loyalty. More highly organized forms of play began in the third stage (ages twelve and up), a stage that emphasized teamwork, organization, self-sacrifice, self-control, and obedience. "These qualities appear to me to be a great pulse of beginning altruism, of self-sacrifice, of that capacity upon which Christianity is based," Gulick hypothesized. This adolescent period was a moment of crucial importance, in which instincts for self-sacrifice and intensely other-directed emotion could be developed in play and later focused on religious objects. In general, Gulick felt that games trained the self by cultivating virtues such as courtesy, honesty, and kindness and weaving them into the neuromuscular fabric of the self. Powerful religious living, he argued, is always "founded on deep facts in the psychical life."

One had to establish religion on the deep facts of the self, or it became merely extrinsic and superficial.[27]

Gulick built his understanding of true Christianity on commonly held ideals about gender and male vitality. He shared with other muscular Christians a worry that Protestant churches were too feminine, and he offered his stages of (male) religious development as an alternative to inadequate forms of nurture practiced in most religious contexts. The American church was not nurturing the unique capacities of boys and men. What currently were the dominant characteristics of the church? Gulick had heard too much about "rest, joy, peace, temptations, prayer, trials, resignation, trust, sense of sin, atonement, love to God, hope of heaven"—all things, he said, "involving first introspection and analysis of feelings." "These were feminine, not masculine characteristics," Gulick thought. They were, we should note, also those characteristics that Gulick and other liberals most detested about older forms of evangelicalism. In this way, of course, religious liberals tried to link the feminine with excessive emotion or indulgent mysticism. But the other side of this is that they also sought a measure of these aspects in their own lives, sometimes desperately. I consider this in more detail in the next chapter. In any case, in the role of organizer and katabolic force for other manly men, Gulick insisted on recovering the active and activist elements of faith, the interest in willpower and muscular development, and the strenuous activities of self-sacrifice manifested in heroic efforts to uplift the poor, the sick, and the immigrant. Too often, all these were absent. All these elements might be revived if Christians focused more attention on the unique virtues of boys and men—and if they also fashioned new forms of nurture that cultivated these masculine capacities through specific forms of play and competitive games.

Though Gulick focused his energies on young Christian men, he also was very interested in young women and believed that women too might benefit from physical fitness. Reiterating that "a proper physical education will largely increase the amount of mental and spiritual work we can do"; observing that "women are usually indifferent to the advantages around them in the line of athletic exercises"; and recalling the resulting, sad fact that, among his acquaintances, "I do not know of half a dozen women who are perfectly well," Gulick argued that women who wanted to "do more mental and spiritual work, better mental and spiritual work," would help themselves by adopting a regimen of physical exercise. Exercise conditioned the muscles and the will—and the combination of the two was responsible for self- and emotional control. In some cases, Gulick believed, women needed more of both. But which regimens of fitness might women pursue? What forms of exercise? Unlike men, who needed athletics to develop and test masculine traits such as assertiveness, leadership, and activity, girls and women needed sports that cultivated feminine virtues such as passivity, feeling, and sympathy. Like many others of his generation, Gulick believed that women were essentially different from men, that they were custodians of the home and of moral and religious sentiments. Girls and women still needed to strengthen their wills and keep their bodies fit, but their physiology did not require aggressive or intense exercise. Gulick recommended bicycling or folk dancing. And he was centrally involved in creating separate spaces for the exercise of distinctly female attributes, including the Camp Fire Girls, which was his invention.[28]

## HABITS OF FAITH AND SELF-CONTROL

Linking religious states to physiological ones gave religious liberals seeking certainty on spiritual matters an advantage that was made plain in earlier chapters of this book: mysterious, inner states were brought to the surfaces of the self, to the body, where they could be more easily perceived and reflected upon. Inner states thus externalized also could be more easily manipulated, and for this reason religious figures willing to borrow from physiologists found principles of conduct, duty, habits, and hygiene becoming clearer. Some of this expert advice is summarized in the previous chapter, on nervous energies. But there was an additional literature on the will, muscles, and self-control that became crucial for those trying to reshape American discourses on both spiritual development and how to negotiate a way among good and bad forms of religion.

Liberals recommended muscular action as an important way to shape the spiritual self. The popular author, muscular Christian activist, and college president Henry Churchill King, a pious Congregationalist who did as much as Gulick to apply the conclusions of new psychologists to religious problems, insisted that having a muscular, well-trained body led to an inner calm and spiritual maturity. In his widely read book *Rational Living* (1905), King argued that willful acts, not feelings or other inner conditions, formed the deepest strata in the soul, determining our most fundamental beliefs and dispositions. "Not feelings, not sentiments, moral sensibilities, or aspirations, not principles, not good resolutions, even, but only action, born of the will, truly reveals us." King fully subscribed to the notion that the main way to build this deep, willing strata of the self was to build the muscles; he drew on psychologists promoting the "voluntaristic turn" and agreed with them that the will was the "primary and constitutive function of the mind." Johan Fichte, Harold Hoffding, Friedrich Paulsen, Arthur Schopenhauer—all insisted that the most fundamental, essential feature of consciousness was willful action, in which all other elements of the self participated and found their ultimate expression. "All consciousness is naturally impulsive," King agreed; we were organized for action. This meant that the essence of the self, inner and outer, was shaped in one's outer behaviors—even in one's posture or body style. Though for some this kind of thinking buttressed a (minor) revival of phrenology, King and most others believed it authorized not a specific set of body-spirit correspondences but a new discourse of salvation that turned to habitual actions and character as the most reliable determinants and outward signs of salvation.[29] Using the willing self to produce the correct habits and character became key issues in spiritual development.

How precisely did this work? The Holy Spirit regenerated the self through a series of willed actions, in which human actors cooperated, and these in turn produced routinized neuromuscular patterns (habits). The result was a religious character. "Salvation in its final essence is a change of character," one liberal announced, signaling an important shift away from earlier formulations. "It is less an exemption from the penalty of sin than it is the supplanting of a disposition or bias toward evil and irreligiousness by a permanent disposition or bias toward the good and the religious. This change is wrought by the Holy Ghost operating through the free will of the individual." What is notable here, aside from the fact that liberals (like their more orthodox opponents) had not reconciled the paradoxes of human freedom and holy grace, was that the real *work* of salvation took place on the outer self. Using the will to engage the self in repeated pious and moral *actions* developed the right religious habits, which in turn reconstituted the neuromuscular self, body and mind, as religious. The resulting "religious character" was not merely a set of personality characteristics and routine behaviors; it was an integrated inner/outer religiousness, a "permanent disposition," another liberal wrote, "to freely love, trust, and serve God."[30]

Though observers have mistakenly understood this as a kind of decline from religion to mere morality, in reality liberals were relocating experience in what they considered the deeper and more enduring parts of the self—the working, acting, neuromuscular self.

The patterns of muscular actions that anchored spiritual states were called "habits," and liberal discourses at this time incorporated habits as perhaps *the* crucial ingredient in a stable religious self. Discourses on habit were pervasive in the Protestant establishment in the early twentieth century, a fascinating development that illustrates clearly how American believers were turning to psychological discourses. Surveying these developments, in 1908 the liberal Protestant president of Brown University, W. H. P. Faunce, said that James's famous chapter on habit in his *Principles*, the best-known statement on the subject, had been "preached in a thousand pulpits." Indeed it had. Progressive preachers, reformers, and muscular Christians all drew on physiological studies of habit and on psychologists who, like James, popularized the spiritual implications of these studies. Henry C. King drew specifically on James when he pointed out that in habits "the psychical and physical" was "completely interwoven," and that habits therefore were an "enormous hindrance or help" to our "entire intellectual, moral and spiritual life," a way to "constancy and perseverance in work, . . . self control, . . . self-denial" and "superiority [over bad] moods." There was a way in which willful actors could gradually sediment religious and moral choices in neuromuscular complexes, a process that gradually made these choices automatic and freed the will to attend to other, higher level spiritual attainments. This was how people formed habits. Postures of self-control, self-denial, honesty, and altruism, for example, could become ingrained in the self. Because of this, the discourse on habits was a discourse about an incredibly powerful, and potentially very dangerous, tool, for while the right kinds of habits permanently inscribed religious dispositions in the self, the wrong ways of willing and acting could imprint vice and indolence. "Every small stroke of virtue or of vice leaves its never so little scar," King said, quoting James. Every act, good or bad, was counted "down among the nerve-cells and fibers, . . . registering and storing it up." For neuromuscular Christians, nothing was wiped out.[31]

For these reasons it should not be overlooked that liberals attempting to purge religion of the anxiety-producing emotional rhythms of evangelical Calvinism built into their systems other sources of anxiety. At least one reviewer of King's *Rational Living* objected that older readers, whose habits, muscles, and neuronal channels were already fixed and hardened might find discomfiting the notion that morality and salvation depended on ingrained habits. Proving himself as intense as his Puritan ancestors, King showed no interest in minimizing the discomfort induced by these ideas. "It is a startling fact to face," King preached, "that a man's personal habits are largely fixed before he is twenty; the chief lines of his future growth and acquaintance before he is twenty-five, and his professional habits before he is thirty." This was, King contended, the evidence from physiological psychology. "Our intellectual as well as our moral day of grace is limited. It is of no use to rebel at the facts, it is folly unspeakable to ignore them. . . . With every young person one must, therefore, continually urge: Are you willing to retain just the *personal* habits you have now? You cannot too quickly change them if you wish to make thorough work." And then, as if he had not been explicit enough, King continued: "From your early morning toilet, through the care of your clothing and the order of your room, table manners, breathing, tone of voice, manner of talking, pronunciation, gesture, motion, address, study, to your very way of sleeping at night—all your habits are setting like plaster of Paris. Do you wish them to set as they are?"[32] Even breathing, manners, and tone of voice? These were persnickety prescriptions for religious living.

Embedded in these discourses on will and habit were sharp critiques of other ways of thinking about religious experience. In turning to willpower, habit, and character, these liberals decisively rejected other markers of authentic experience, especially emotion, as I have mentioned. From Hannah Whitall Smith (1832–1911), restless spiritual wanderer and writer of popular devotional books, to the authors of YMCA manuals on religious education, religious liberals agreed that emotions were unreliable foundations for spiritual progress. In a widely read devotional manual that William James praised for its judiciousness on exactly these matters, Smith pointed out that it "is your purpose God looks at, not your feelings about that purpose; and your purpose, or will, is therefore the only thing you need attend to. . . . Let your emotions come or let them go, just as God pleases, and make no account of them either way. . . . They really have nothing to do with the matter. They are not the indicators of your spiritual state, but are merely the indicators of your temperament or of your present physical condition." It was a "psychological fact," Smith wrote, ambidextrously borrowing psychological language to debunk certain religious styles and authorize others, that religious emotions could be "produced by other causes than a purely divine influence, and that they are largely dependent upon temperament and physical conditions. It is most dangerous, therefore, to make them a test of our spiritual union with Christ. It may result in just such a grievous self-deception as our Lord warns against in Luke 6:46–49, 'And why call ye me, Lord, Lord, and do not the things which I say?'" Smith called Christians to live not in their emotions but in their wills—for "the will is the governing power" in human nature, the controlling force "behind our emotions and behind our wishes," the "independent self" that "decides everything and controls everything. . . . Our emotions," by contrast, "belong to us, but they are not ourselves." Smith proceeded with illustrations of the kind that religious liberals often produced, stories about believers who could not understand or control emotional states. A young man could not shake feelings of doubt. A young woman wanted to rebel against Christ.[33] The solution to these dilemmas was to strengthen the will so it might be in control.

Controlling the emotional self was of the utmost importance. "The hysterical everywhere—most of all . . . in the religious life—is fundamentally at fault, though, curiously enough, it is here often not only excused but even urged as a particularly high attainment," groused H. C. King. Placing feeling at the center of Christian life, King thought, substituted a "heathen idea of inspiration," an instance of "being swept away out of our faculties," for "that high and complete surrender of ourselves to God" marked by self-control. There could be no legitimate religious attitude not informed by the will; there could be no genuine revival of religion without the "highest reason and self control." But how did one practice self control? On this matter, King (for one) produced an almost endless series of lectures, advice columns, pamphlets, and sermons explaining that, because "you can not directly determine whether you shall feel or not," because emotion "spontaneously arises" in the presence of external stimuli, it could be controlled only indirectly. The way to overcome an undesirable emotion was to use the will to direct attention and actions to something else. A small boy attracted by the sight of someone else's watermelon could not prevent his mouth from watering; but he could redirect his attention. And he could choose to run away. "And you," King continued, speaking more directly to concerns of the young men he typically addressed, "can not keep your emotions from arising in attention to the exciting object, but you can *think of something else*." Because "every thought, by its presence in the mind, tends to pass into act, and will do so, if it is not hindered by the presence of some other thought," King's counsel here was urgent: Do not dally with unseemly thoughts. This was the same as "playing with sparks over a powder mine" or "putting one's finger on the trigger of a gun and beginning to press it, and yet expecting it not to discharge." One also could control emotions by "acting in the line of those emotions that you think you ought to have." If for example a young man was feeling sad and fearful, he might "take a good, long breath, and stiffen up his backbone, and put on the mien of cheer and courage, and so doing, he is far more apt to become cheerful and courageous." (This was, once again, James's emotion theory applied.)[34]

That willed, muscular actions equilibrated the emotional self was a bit of psychological insight that could be applied in an almost infinite number of situations, religious and secular. Take good posture, for instance. Many thought that psychological facts about the bodily nature of the emotions pointed to the importance of good posture—for good posture allowed the heart, lungs, spine, and entire neuromuscular system to work most effectively. Luther Gulick once pointed out that one who stood erect "looks the world straight in the eye, keeps his chest prominent, his abdomen in and his body under thorough control"; for these reasons, he was likely to experience feelings of confidence, strength, and self-respect. Men who slouched were more susceptible to fits of worry, nervousness, and depression. The mind, Gulick said elsewhere, became "erect and self-confident as the spine and neck and chest become so." To illustrate how correct posture regulated the emotional self, he provided pictures of Teddy Roosevelt in the frontispiece to his *Efficient Life* (1907) (figure 10). He did this to show how "one may maintain a 'strong' carriage during the successive expression of many and divergent emotional states." These wonderful slides illustrate that the goal here was not to resist emotion but to use the neuromuscular self to ensure that inner states were not excessive. By maintaining outer strength and composure, Roosevelt sustained healthy inner emotions and expressed them properly. Roosevelt undoubtedly suggested perfect self-control to H. C. King as well, who was himself a political and religious leader, and who wrote at length on self-control, leadership, and influence. Few things were more important than "the proper and habitual limitation of the emotions," King thought, and this was especially true of destructive passions such as anger, hate, and fear. One should take a deep breath, "stiffen up his backbone, and put on the mien of cheer and courage"—this was the way to cultivate the proper emotions and control undesirable ones. "The leader must show *reserved power*, must make it plain that he has himself in hand, if he is to secure confidence."[35]

Getting the bodily self in order might help the inner self in other ways. To "keep good resolutions," Gulick wrote around New Year's Day in 1910, Americans should think about doing rather than being. This was the familiar emphasis on habit. "Upon a concrete, objective thing to-be-done one can fix attention. A resolution to be more cheerful is not so commendable as a resolution to tell at least one breezy story at the breakfast table every day for a month." And a resolution to be happy was not as effective as a resolution to correct the muscular conditions on which those emotions were fashioned. If one wanted to be

In a merry mood          Laying down the law

Figure 10.   Theodore Roosevelt's posture showed Americans how to use the neuromuscular self to control and express emotions properly. From Luther H. Gulick, *The Efficient Life*, 1907.

sad or discouraged no longer, one should "stand up straight; take deep breaths; discover what tones of voice are most cheerful and make your larynx say 'Good morning!' to somebody in that tone." When "our muscles can be made to express the positive, the constructive, the joyful attitude," when we embody our resolutions in acts in these ways, "we become the thing we act." This was the secret to successful resolutions.[36]

## MUSCULAR MEN, NERVOUS WOMEN

In these and in many other ways new physiological notions changed how American believers understood the inner and outer dimensions of religious experience. Though interest in psychology and physiology was widespread in American culture, YMCA thinkers and other muscular Christians were particularly enthusiastic about using these new sciences to develop innovative, physiological religious styles. When religious believers did this, however, when they defined the religious self in terms of physiological processes, they created for themselves other, unexpected dilemmas. One issue that would not go away, a problem that vexed muscular Christians in almost all of their pamphlets, public pronouncements, and sermons, was gender. How was the physiological self, male and female, related to inner, religious dispositions, needs, and capacities? Did male and female bodies believe differently? Did they produce different kinds of faith? Believers wrestled with these matters and arrived at a number of quite different conclusions.

The first thing to say here is that locating the self, religious or not, in the muscular body probably made more robust those gender notions inherited by turn-of-the-century Americans. All of a sudden the inner self was bonded to the physiological self—and everyone knew that male physiologies were different from female ones. So, in many ways, although liberals showed signs of banishing older warrants for "separate spheres" and female domesticity, they also anchored nineteenth-century gender norms in new, scientific ways. G. Stanley Hall, William James, Luther Gulick, Josiah Strong—all of them usually spoke of gender differences in scientific terms, not religious ones. In any case, the essentialized sexes remained. I would not say, however, as others have, that in general religious Americans in this period used physiological notions as weapons to obliterate "feminization" in the churches. I think the problem was more subtle. Liberal believers wrestled with tensions and ambiguities.

Still, some things were unambiguous: male scientists, moralizers, and believers were the experts, and they did not hesitate to counsel and reform American women. I already have mentioned Gulick's many projects aimed at the proper cultivation of boys, men, and girls. Gulick was not alone in inserting his physiologically inflected forms of faith advice in the periodical literature, and his urgent articles "A Woman's Worst Emotion" and "Emotional Storms in Women," for example, are good illustrations of the trend. In these articles, Gulick applied himself (again) to a classic liberal concern—excessive emotion. And women, of course, presented a particularly difficult problem. Pointing out in the *Ladies Home Journal* of 1908 that the "typical worrying woman is not pretty to look at," that "she stands badly," her "shoulders droop, she is flat-chested," and she wears a wrinkled frown, Gulick informed his readers about the scientific reasons these anxious inner states were manifest in the body. The neuromuscular system was closely linked to the emotions, and worry in particular had been linked to lackluster muscle tone and dyspepsia. Laboratory experiments had proved it. In one such experiment, scientists had made cats swallow chemicals whose paths in the alimentary canal could be monitored by x rays. "It has been demonstrated that as long as Pussy is kept in a worried state of mind—disturbed by trifles, such as teasing, tickled nose, change of position and the like—the stomach does no digestive work." The state of the digestive system, and other systems, were dependent on psychological conditions. In "A Woman's Worst Emotion," Gulick pointed to many physiological consequences of excessive fears and worries. The cure was simple: mental substitutions, diversions, and distraction. Specific instructions included willfully diverting attention to other matters—hobbies, books, gardening, and golf. Or one could take a "moral holiday," advice Gulick borrowed from James. Other instructions, here and in other advice columns, involved familiar discussions about using outer, muscular actions to resolve inner tensions. "We know how an unworried person acts and talks, and we can imitate him." And in the end "one's mind really follows and conforms to one's [outer] attitudes, becoming erect and self-confident as the spine and neck and chest become so." Stand up straight! Smile! In these ways, women in particular might become beautiful—inside and out.[37]

Though most women shared with men these views on gender and supported the muscular and manly initiatives in the churches, there were some who could not believe the obviously distorted images of women that psychologists and other experts were producing. A group of women scientists and social reformers protested loudly. Rhapsodic assertions about female intuition and feeling, and predictions, such as those of Stanley Hall, that one day everyone would worship women as the "object of a new religion and almost of a new worship," struck some as absurd. This kind of worship, the psychologist Kate Gordon responded, was a backhanded compliment to be sure, an "apotheosis" not of womankind, she complained, "but of the vegetable. . . . This attitude toward women did very well in the Middle Ages, but, to tell the truth, the modern woman is made a little bit ill by the incense. She longs for fresh air and common-sense, and is not willing to be a dolt for the sake of being called a deity. In a word, she is ready to resign the charm of her naïveté, and to brave the perils of consciousness and reflection." Should women merely be trained to be wives and mothers? Was it true that intellectual work drained female nervous energies or destroyed reproductive capacities? No science could show this to be the case; no responsible observer could argue that biology meant destiny; and no modern person ought to abridge women's freedom to choose their own futures, educations, and vocations, all equal to men's. Gordon was joined in her call to rethink assumptions about gender by a number of other women scientists, including especially the psychologist Helen Thompson, who demonstrated how confused and unscientific were conventional views concerning sex differences.[38]

The gender stereotypes that Gordon detested were standard fare in psychological directives, which, as I have said, anchored older, essentialized gender notions in newer physiological guises. Because the mind was located deep in the neuromuscular body, it was influenced by differences in physiology. As a consequence, physiological psychologists argued, men and women had different mental capacities: men had more active metabolisms, and this gave them more analytical minds; women had quieter metabolisms, and this led to less analytical power and more emotion and irrationality. Thus men were suited to a life of science and commerce, while women were suited better to social activities and family. When women moved out of their spheres, when they, for instance, studied too much, they siphoned off nervous energies better spent on conviviality and reproduction. It was a commonplace that, if women did too much mental work, they would become nervous, "hysterical," or most seriously, infertile. (The corresponding depletion-to-infertility sequence in men was set in motion by masturbation.) One Protestant summed up psychological wisdom on differences between men and women: "To do things is predominantly masculine. To spiritualize social relations is predominantly feminine. To make Life possible is predominantly masculine. To make Life desirable is predominantly feminine. To seek power is predominantly masculine. To seek beauty is predominantly feminine."[39] These were the ideas informing liberal believers, and many others, on these questions.

But it should be said in closing that the logic of these rigid gender distinctions caught both men and women in uncomfortable ambivalences. The strains involved were obvious for many women who, like Gordon, saw clearly that it denied them their full humanity. And without a doubt, men too were denied possibilities for fullness and fulfillment—especially religious fulfillment, which for these believers represented a complicated balance of inner intensities that were always rationally controlled. It might have seemed medieval to deify women, but there was a deep male desire for the femaleness that these men helped manufacture as their "other." Many liberal believers thought that women easily produced those inner emotions that they needed for balance, happiness, and salvation. In all the talk about control and muscular will, it is easy to forget that the purpose of a strong will was not to annihilate inner emotions but to control and husband them. One had to start with them; and they had to remain robust. Intense emotions, especially in young people, were absolutely essential: they were the inner capital that people needed in order to develop properly. A life of mere toughness, control, and discipline—this led to barren rationality, a sense of alienation, and even religious infidelity. For these reasons it was not uncommon for men to talk about the ways that they welcomed and embraced "feminization"; Gulick for one thought that feminization in certain institutions and dimensions of Christian practice was crucial. Hall did too—and so did many others. It was obvious: women were carriers of the emotions and dispositions that men craved. For all these reasons, the crucial question was not how to build the neuromuscular self and its capacities for control, but how to do so while maintaining a healthy inner intensity. The same careful discriminations had to be made when religious liberals talked about cultivating belief, for while they knew that having a vital faith meant experiencing intense emotions, they worried that these emotions too often spun out of control. So they sought capacities for spontaneity and fervent devotion while insisting that these abilities had to be controlled using willpower and restraint. They yearned for intense inner experiences while developing disciplines for measuring and monitoring them. As they moved tentatively toward these compromise positions, toward finding the ideal balance of inner aptitudes and skills, they turned again and again to science and its new methods for understanding the self and measuring more carefully its possibilities for ecstasy and transcendence.[40]

# 5  "A Multitude of Superstitions and Crudities"

There is little doubt that, in the nineteenth century, American religious liberals used psychological ideas and methods with remarkable adroitness. Those who were confounded by evangelical styles used these new ideas to devise better ways of both mapping the spiritual self and understanding its nervous and spiritual powers. Many used new psychologies to see more clearly the inner self, how it manifested itself in the body, and what the study of bodily processes told believers about spiritual and moral well-being. But it was not until the twentieth century that American religious liberals created what became the most influential way of using psychological notions to reshape religious belief and practice, a discipline they called the psychology of religion. In the twentieth century a number of psychologists of religion used empirical studies of religious experience to critique older, especially evangelical, styles, and fashion new recommendations for how to experience religion authentically. The scientific discourses that these intellectuals created entirely changed American thinking about faith, conversion, and spiritual growth.

Understanding the sources of this development involves understanding a series of personal stories similar to those told by Beecher and Coe, stories of spiritual confusion, personal disappointment, and religious experimentation. The life and work of one pioneer psychologist of religion, Edwin Starbuck (1866–1947), illuminates well the preoccupations and struggles of many first-generation American psychologists of religion, and in this chapter I examine Starbuck's life in detail. Like other psychologists of religion, Starbuck experienced an adolescent conversion that initiated a lifelong interest in the subject. He spent the remainder of his career collecting firsthand accounts of Protestant conversions and arranging and correlating their different dimensions—all because he hoped this work might eliminate local and inessential elements from definitions of (true) religious experience, separate healthy from unhealthy types of religion, and establish a range of legitimate religious thought and action. He was sure that applying scientific methods to the deepest religious experiences—probing and sorting them and studying the "laws" of their growth—would make these deep parts of the self less mysterious. "But to lift [experience] above superstition, to dwell vitally within it, to make it a sure, lasting growing possession of mankind," Starbuck insisted in his 1898 study of religious experience, "it must have a thousand thought-paths leading into its holy of holies." The psychology of religion was Starbuck's "thought-path" to the deep, inner parts of the religious life; and as this science cleared its way to the hot core of religious things, it cut away and demolished obscuring superstitions, old theological notions, and narrow conceptions of faith. "A multitude of superstitions and crudities are doomed to fold their tents," Starbuck rejoiced in a 1902 letter to William James. "People will be living in a new era of religious experience before they know it."[1] Starbuck tirelessly promoted the empirical study of religion not just as a new form of knowledge but also as an essential method for fashioning better and healthier ways of thinking about and practicing religious experience. His life illustrates clearly that scientific studies and methods created new opportunities for religious ways of being in the world.[2]

## FIRSTHAND EXPERIENCES

Starbuck's life was framed by what should by now be a familiar set of ambivalences. Tough minded and credulous, manly and effeminate, willful and emotional, he led a life characterized, he once said, by a warring "between tenderness and toughness, between acceptance and doubt, between inner sensitivity and vigorous intellectuality." His childhood and youth, and especially his failed youthful evangelical conversion, remind us of the nature of some of these ambivalences and some of the struggles common to religious liberals in the nineteenth and early twentieth centuries.[3]

Starbuck was raised a bashful Quaker in Indiana, a farm boy who feared the Holy Spirit when it moved him to speak in religious meetings. Revivalists roaming his hometown and other parts of Indiana had little trouble gathering up even the quietest Quakers in their religious fits, however, and the result for Starbuck was a surprising adolescent conversion that he later regarded with puzzlement, dismay, and occasionally, nostalgia. At first it seemed like a powerful and genuine event; but it was not long before he wondered if social pressures and contagious religious excitements might have produced it. Perhaps the whole episode was contrived and meaningless. Still, the conversion was preceded by strains and anxieties that were real enough. As a youth, Starbuck had struggled with the implications of scientific thinking, spending "long hours of wakeful nights" worried that he was a "creature of terrestrial forces" enmeshed in an iron chain of causality. He doubted free will, the authority of the Bible, and the miracles of Jesus. Starbuck remembered wanting to think, not pray, his way out, but as his doubts deepened he grew desperate. Then he encountered the revivalists. At one of their meetings in 1885, he fell to his knees, improvised a declaration of sinfulness and announced that Christ had saved him. "In the heat of the revival at Centre meetings I went through the forms of this public acceptance, not feeling at the moment the negative implication that my heart had not been on the whole 'given to the Lord,' during the preceding months." Like many religious liberals, he was unable to feel deeply sinful. Evidently his brother shared his liberal sensibilities, for even though he too remained insensible to the "particular 'sins' that needed renouncing," he "fell for the same stunts, then went into seclusion for days afterwards, feeling that he had quite made a fool of himself." Starbuck disguised his own embarrassment by pointing to his brother's, but there is no question that he too was confounded and humiliated by the experience. What had happened to him? Why had he been susceptible to the revival? And why had so many others put aside their reason, given themselves to evangelical emotions, and joined churches? Was it possible that such dramatic experiences were authentic or useful in any way?[4]

These questions stayed with him. In college, at the University of Indiana, Starbuck wondered if religious experiences could be explained in scientific terms, and for a time he embraced the naturalism of several freethinking mentors. He gathered with other heretics and Young Turks in a secret student society, where they discussed poetry and humanism. But there was something false in this identity too. For while Starbuck was eager to forget his momentary lapse into evangelicalism, he found it difficult to dislodge an "ineradicable mysticism" inside him, a feeling that religion might be important, helpful, and sometimes beautiful. He linked this mystical feeling to the Quakerism of his childhood, which had convinced him that, if he watched carefully, he might perceive the Holy Spirit acting in the world. In college and afterward, he searched for the Holy Spirit and found it acting busily among the world's believers in James Freeman Clarke's *Ten Great*

*Religions* and Max Müller's *Lectures on the Science of Religion.* Studying these books and others in comparative religion seemed to help him spiritually. "Not one of the great religions and hardly one of the minor cults," he realized, "has failed to furnish some sort of sustenance to [my] spiritual life." Like other religious liberals, he saw religious experience as the foundation and essence of the world's religions and was critical of the doctrines, theological systems, and rituals that obscured them. Why did the deepest and perhaps most helpful emotions, those found in religious experiences, come packaged in such unseemly and unnatural forms, forms such as ecstatic revival behaviors? Would it be possible somehow to separate these religious experiences from their unseemly contexts and thus recover something of their intensity and spiritual power for modern believers? Starbuck was not the only one interested in such questions. Other early psychologists of religion, such as George Coe and James Leuba, pursued answers to these questions with an intensity that originated in their own puzzling, failed conversions.[5]

When Starbuck enrolled at Harvard Divinity School in 1893, he was still wondering how best to account for evangelical experiences and perhaps recover something of value from them. When he began graduate school, he later recalled, his central guiding principle "was that the study must deal *primarily with the first-hand religious experience of individuals,* not so much with their *theories* about religion as with their actual *experiences.*" Theories about religion, he was sure, were "once removed from the vital springs of conduct and valuation"; historical records and sociological statements about religion were "thrice removed, and consist for all we know of only congealed, discoloured, and distorted semblances of real experience. One must," Starbuck insisted, modifying Emerson, "catch at first hand the feelings of spirituality." But how? How might one catch at first hand these unmediated spiritual impulses? What tool could one use? At some point Starbuck decided to investigate these elusive facts in questionnaires that asked for details about "the feelings of divine presence," "actual feelings of the sense of communion during the ceremony of communion," and above all, what people experienced during conversion episodes. He fashioned questions carefully, hoping, he said, to "awaken" his respondents in certain ways and elicit their immediate reactions. He thought that "what came forth spontaneously would be the most vital and essential elements of the experience," deep inner particulars that were closer to "the operation of life-forces." In many ways, this was a typical errand of late-nineteenth-century liberals: separate the essential inner aspects of religious experience from their less important, outer manifestations. He was the first to use a questionnaire to probe these kinds of religious experiences.[6]

At first, talking to friends and acquaintances about religion seemed like a good beginning; but in time Starbuck regretted trying to study scientifically the inner lives of associates and fellow graduate students. When he distributed questionnaires to contacts in Cambridge and surrounding areas, some thought his surveys were rude and intrusive. (See the very first questionnaire, reproduced in figure 11.) Though Starbuck intended these questionnaires as ways of understanding and fostering the deepest and most essential parts of the religious self, some saw them as cold, scientific instruments likely to eviscerate, not restore, their spiritual capacities. When Starbuck's mentor William James got a copy of the survey, he was full of hesitation. "This is New England," he warned, and "people here will not reply to an inquisitional document of that sort." Starbuck assured James that his plan would work. "I wheedle them; I explain that this is the beginning of a new science in the world—the psychology of religion, and we must have the *facts.*" But at least initially, James appeared to be right. Starbuck received several letters of complaint and recrimination. There were some who did not share Starbuck's enthusiasm for this new science, and many more who were positively worried about "increasing our exact knowledge of the laws of the spiritual life." Was this not just reducing mysterious, spiritual things to natural laws? Even the religious liberal and reformer Thomas Wentworth Higginson complained to James that Starbuck's questionnaire amounted to "moral and spiritual vivisection." He asked James if his approving signature was a forgery. Things got worse when Starbuck presented his findings to C. C. Everett's philosophy of religion class. In this setting, which was normally quite collegial, anxious students assaulted him with objections—and one of them, Edward Borncamp, standing erect and with a face "white with emotion," cried, "It's all a lie!" And all of this took place at liberal Harvard Divinity School.[7] (A more sympathetic classmate and also one of the first women to take courses at Harvard, Anna Diller, later became Starbuck's wife; see figure 12.)

Eventually Starbuck produced two articles on religious experience that he subsequently folded into a book titled *The Psychology of Religion,* published in London in 1898. His was the first full-length book by an American psychologist of religion.[8] Though the book speaks generically about "religion" and "religious experience," it really attempts to measure and account for only one kind of experience—evangelical conversion. Starbuck's personal reasons for focusing on evangelicalism are clear

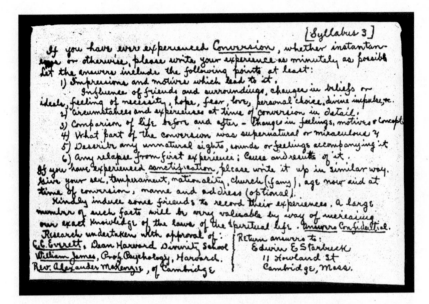

Figure 11. "Moral and spiritual vivisection." Starbuck attempted to dissect America's spiritual life with this, his first conversion survey. From Edwin D. Starbuck, "Religion's Use of Me," 1937. Reprinted with the permission of Ayer Company Publishers.

enough; but he also had intellectual reasons for doing so, for he knew enough about the emerging science of religions to see that American evangelicals, with their uncontrollable fits and holy convulsions, manifested those primitive religious elements that European scholars were studying in aboriginal ceremonies. Starbuck regarded American evangelical conversion as a stand-in category for all ecstatic behaviors, calling it "the most dramatic single storm-centre of religious experience," an event swirling with instincts and primal emotions. Like their European counterparts, American intellectuals such as Starbuck wondered if these and other odd manifestations of the primitive could somehow be harvested for use in the overcivilized modern world.[9]

Needless to say, Starbuck had to leave Cambridge to locate the most primitive religious behaviors. He found evidence of these behaviors on the rough-and-tumble frontier—and mostly in the gesticulating shapes of American Methodists. His 1898 book is full of rowdy Methodist emotions and testimonials, which Starbuck did his best to transform into disembodied statistics. In part 1 of the book, he used different questionnaires.

Figure 12. The Harvard Divinity School Class of 1895. Harvard Divinity School, Photograph Collection, bMS445, Andover-Harvard Theological Library, Harvard Divinity School, Harvard University. Starbuck is the first person in the top row, far left; Anna Diller is standing in the top row, seventh from left; C. C. Everett sits just in front and to the left of Diller; Edward Borncamp, in a calmer moment, relaxes with his hat in the third row, far left.

The first yielded 192 responses (120 women; 72 men) from Protestant Christians across the United States, with Methodists in the majority. He supplemented this questionnaire with more focused surveys on conversion and life-cycle stages. These surveys were distributed in three locations: a Women's Christian Temperance Union meeting in California (in which Methodists again were in the majority); a San Francisco military base, to two regiments of soldiers from Iowa and Tennessee; and a Methodist conference in Santa Barbara, California, to a handful of participants. Starbuck also used data on ages of conversion from the alumni records of Drew Theological Seminary (again, Methodist). In part 1 of the book, Starbuck identified the emotions that initiated and accompanied conversion, linked conversion styles to different temperamental and biological types, and contradicted the views of important neurologists and psychiatrists by suggesting ways that conversion helped young people mature. In part 2 of the book, he identified a second model of religious development, the "gradual-growth" model, which seemed more common among intellectuals. To understand how this second mode of religious experience worked, Starbuck used another, differently worded questionnaire and supplemented this with biographical material about well-known religious liberals such as Leo Tolstoy and Harriet Martineau. Denominations were more evenly represented in this sample, though the majority of respondents were college educated.[10] This fact was not lost on Starbuck or other psychologists of religion. Were educated people less likely to have an evangelical-style conversion?

The striking feature of Starbuck's book is its imposing apparatus of measurement, which Starbuck used essentially to make religious experiences more orderly and comprehensible. There are no fewer than thirty-two figures in the book—remarkable charts on religious development; graphs correlating conversion with age, gender, body growth, emotion, and temperament; and tables measuring the frequency of postconversion anxiety, religious doubt, and the intensity of certain beliefs. Starbuck was mapping inner vectors of doubt and depravity, anxiety and ecstasy, taking inventory of mysterious mental things that had confounded him. He found many ways to use empirical methods to bring "a little coherency and constancy into the midst of that which is constantly flowing"—and many ways therefore to "make it possible to comprehend new regions in the spiritual life of man."[11] Scientific study revealed how spiritual development worked by reducing the astonishing variety of American evangelical experiences, with all of their somatic and emotional variations, to a set of orderly laws and patterns. For Starbuck, this procedure yielded some crucial gains. It had the effect of making the divine force behind religious experiences not a terrifying and unpredictable agent of sudden conversion events, but an architect of an orderly universe who might be admired and understood better by plotting his good works in scientific tables and charts. This was the religious world that Starbuck wanted to live in, a world in which God acted in predictable ways and human beings sensed his immanent presence in nature's laws.

Starbuck's ways of ordering and correlating experiences led to other important spiritual discoveries. While analyzing the laws and general features of evangelical experiences, he stumbled upon the answer to a question that had long troubled him: why some people tried but failed to have dramatic conversions. The answer had to do with temperament. Different personality styles predisposed people to one or anther kind of religious development.

"Where expectation [of conversion] is satisfied," Starbuck explained, "there sensibility is distinctly predominant; but where expectation is disappointed, there intellect is just as distinctly predominant." Those who scored high in sensibility (feeling), and those who were more susceptible to social pressures or were introverted, were more likely to experience dramatic conversions. Psychologists and intellectuals, on the other hand, usually were "intellect predominant." Other surveys, such as those by George Coe, confirmed that better-educated Americans were less susceptible to evangelical forms of religious instruction. This did not mean that young intellectuals did not go through periods of religious conversion, crisis, or adjustment. Such periods were the sine qua non of adolescence. It merely meant that different people had different ways of navigating developmental milestones in this period. Some proceeded gradually. Starbuck did his best to maintain the objective posture required of scientists, but normative glosses leaked in. Conversion moments were important, he said, as long as they were not excessive, and as long as they were quickly controlled using more rational and measured procedures. In this way, at least for Starbuck, psychological studies themselves were an important part of becoming religiously mature.[12]

## MEASURING FAITH

One of the most interesting aspects of Starbuck's work is that it does not pursue the most obvious and effective solution to the evangelical conversion problem. It does not explain conversion away. It does not interpret it as merely the product of social or psychological forces. It does not dismiss conversion as wholly irrelevant or unhealthy. This put Starbuck in a delicate situation, for while he admitted that somatic performances accompanying evangelical conversions often were unseemly, he also knew that the deep emotions they roused were life-sustaining and important. The question, then, became how to recover these deep emotions from phenomena that, at least on the surface, were unappealing. Starbuck had an answer to this question, one that was borrowed and extended by other psychologists, including especially William James.

At first, James appears not to have appreciated Starbuck's attempts to count, correlate, and measure experience. When Starbuck began his empirical work, James, then one of Starbuck's mentors, was chary. The "question-circular method of collecting information had already ... reached the proportions of an incipient nuisance," he remembered telling Starbuck. He expected Starbuck's questions to add nothing significant to the problems of religious experience, eliciting conventional responses couched in familiar

Protestant idioms. But he was mistaken. Respondents testified to a range of interesting awakenings and mystical experiences. Their language seemed ingenuous and natural. On a trip to the American West Coast, James visited Starbuck, then teaching at the newly founded Stanford University, and wrote his wife, Alice, that he was eagerly reading Starbuck's questionnaire data. The data surprised him. "Some of them are *kostlich* [marvelous], and they all give one a splendid feeling of there being such good people in the world. How I *have* wisht, dear Alice, that you might be reading them aloud to me. I know that you would enjoy them as much as I." James's letter is reminiscent of another on the same subject written just after his father's death in 1882, in which he playfully told Alice she had "one new function hereafter"—namely, "you must not leave me till I understand a little more of the value and meaning of religion in Father's sense, in the mental life and destiny of man. . . . I as his son (if for no other reason) must help it to its rights in their eyes. And for that reason I must learn to interpret it aright as I have never done, and you must help me." This moment appears to have arrived when James read Starbuck's conversion narratives. On subsequent occasions James asked Starbuck for more, and he drew extensively from Starbuck's collection in his *Varieties*, as I have already noted.[13] Starbuck's work was a key source for James's book.

Of course, using empirical methods to reform religion was something James had pondered for a number of years. He had been trained in medicine and physiology, and in the late 1870s he collaborated with another young philosopher and psychologist, Stanley Hall, on a series of arguments for an empirical reform of philosophy, a transformation of philosophy along psychological and physiological lines. They made their argument in a couple of articles in the progressive reformist periodical *The Nation*. Their ideas were in line with the ideas of other reforming social scientists. They argued that, without induction and empirical methods, philosophy and religious reflection would remain mired in inconclusive metaphysical speculations. Religion, and Christianity in particular, was in a bad state. Years later, in 1884, James was still wondering "whether there can be any popular religion raised on the ruins of the old Christianity without the presence of . . . a belief in new *physical* facts and possibilities. Abstract considerations about the soul and the reality of a moral order will not do in a year what the glimpse into a world of new phenomenal possibilities enveloping those of the present life, afforded by an extension of our insight into the order of nature, would do in an instant." But actually using the methods of science to answer specifically religious questions, and thus produce a science of religions, does not seem to have occurred to James until the middle of the

1890s. It was at this time that he encountered new facts collected by psychical researchers, scholars of religion such as E.B. Tylor and Max Müller and psychologists of religion like Hall and Starbuck.[14]

It is not surprising, then, that he was intrigued both by Starbuck's raw questionnaire data and by how Starbuck sifted and evaluated these data. But why did reading through Starbuck's accounts of religious experience give James hope and that "splendid feeling"? And why did James incorporate Starbuck's data without adornment and in such detail in the *Varieties*?

The answer had something to do with an ambivalence at the heart of James's work and the work of other psychologists of religion. The more they successfully cast religious phenomena in scientific formulas, the more they complained about being alienated from the deepest and most vital parts of human life. (This was a regular complaint among first-generation social scientists as well, going back to John Stuart Mill.) The psychologist Stanley Hall gave voice to this commonly felt anxiety when he worried that "in our day . . . the hot life of feelings is remote and decadent. Culture represses, and intellect saps its root. The very word passion is becoming obsolete."[15] Hence the appeal of Starbuck's narratives of deep, even primitive religious emotions: These were glimpses into the deepest parts of the self, hot emotions and sensations unmediated by cognition or culture. These emotions were a tonic for enervating, overcivilized lifestyles. And they represented the parts of the self that James, in particular, had trouble accessing.

Though James's yearning for the comforts of faith contributed to his interest in these experiences, this was only part of the reason he wanted to expand his inner life. These parts of the self registered most accurately our perceptions of the (physical and metaphysical) world—and they determined most powerfully our personal qualities, inclinations, and abilities. "The mechanism of the affective life," Starbuck explained, "consists of all the senses in so far as they respond to stimuli that do not admit of discrete handling, the nerve endings in skin, intestines, blood vessels, glands, muscles and joints, the sympathetic nervous system with all its ramifications, and perhaps, also, structures in the central nervous system corresponding to the 'association centers.' The affective life thus involves all the organic reactions in vaso-motor response, circulatory and glandular tone, vascular tension and the like, which experimentation is showing to be the immediate and ever present accompaniment of all sensation." The "feeling life," Starbuck continued, "draws *directly* from experience, and not through the mediation of the cognitive processes; that is, it is itself a source of knowledge." The immediate bodily feeling was constitutive of every mental act; it was the foundation for thinking, believing, reasoning, and forming opinions. Religious wisdom, then, was "direct and immediate," and reports of experience should not be "blurred and distorted by an over-degree of rationality."

Starbuck learned these facts about sensation and perception from James himself, who, when preparing to write his own psychological study of experience, worried that the act of doing so might obscure the part of the self that he was most interested in understanding—the "less articulate and more profound part of our nature." He gave his *Varieties* a descriptive quality in order to present the experiences without discussion or philosophizing. He was merely displaying these experiences, hoping, as Starbuck had, that they might elicit emotional responses or somehow give off traces of intensity. For himself, James told another psychologist of religion, the divine was "limited to abstract concepts which, as ideals, interest and determine me, but do so but faintly, in comparison with what a feeling of God might effect, if I had one. It is largely a question of intensity, but differences of intensity may make one's whole centre of energy shift." Though he could not muster what he called a "living sense of commerce with a God," he knew enough to "envy those who have, for I know that the addition of such a sense would help me immensely."[16] The religious experiences Starbuck collected offered him vicarious satisfactions.

James also appears to have been interested in how Starbuck used statistical methods to understand the value of conversions and related phenomena. In his preface to Starbuck's book, he commented on this. It was "Dr. Starbuck's express aim to disengage the general from the specific and local in his critical discussion, and to reduce the reports to their most universal psychological value," James wrote. "It seems to me that here the statistical method has held its own, and that its percentages and averages have proved to possess genuine significance." James did not explain what he meant, and we are left wondering why he thought the "statistical method" was so significant. We also are left wondering why an intellectual so protective of individualism and metaphysical open-endedness was endorsing a scientific program that reduced the "specific and local" to universal patterns. On one level, certainly, his support of this kind of project seems odd.

But at just this moment (1898–1899), James had another, more urgent difficulty to overcome, one that Starbuck's techniques helped him solve. A year or so after Starbuck published his book, James wrote to a friend that the "well-nigh impossible" task he was pondering for his upcoming Gifford lectures was, first, to defend experience as "the real backbone of the world's religious life—I mean prayer, guidance, and all that sort of thing immediately and privately felt" and, second, "to make the hearer or reader believe, what I myself invincibly do believe, that, although all the special manifestations of religion may have been absurd (I mean its creeds and theories), yet the life of it as a whole is mankind's most important function."[17] James and Starbuck thought about this dilemma at the same time: how could religious experiences in general be promoted without authorizing the many particular and absurd manifestations of them?

Starbuck's statistical generalizations (and accompanying tables) solved James's problem perfectly. They sundered religious experiences from their inessential contexts and showed how they functioned generally to adjust people to new life-cycle stages. Starbuck's statistics lifted the "universal psychological value" out of the idiosyncratic questionnaire data. For different reasons, including James's growing impatience with experimental work, he did not ape Starbuck's methods in his book; but he did borrow the categories Starbuck had so carefully described and help shape, categories such as conversion. And he also shared with Starbuck a sense that displaying these experiences and sorting through their essential characteristics would help modern believers recover what was essential in religious experience and ignore the rest.

## NORMATIVE NOTIONS

There were other ways, too, that psychologists of religion used scientific discourses to uncouple religious experiences from their absurd outer forms. As they did this, as they rooted out religious passions and practices that seemed excessive or unhealthy, they employed a wide-ranging set of psychological notions not just to refine but also to obliterate and cut away.

Because conversion represented the crucial inner core of religion and thus the point "at which a blunder may prove most fatal," it became the subject of a vigorous set of normative discourses. Starbuck borrowed from others, especially Hall and James, in fashioning detailed recommendations. First of all, because conversion was linked to physiological and psychological conditions, simple hygiene and health were essential. Starbuck, for instance, reminded readers that "the avoidance of physical strains which make too great a draft on the nervous system, the observance of the laws of health in the way of wholesome exercise, outdoor games, fresh air, and the like, which stimulate circulation and fill the brain with good rich red blood—these are means which will without doubt be conducive to spiritual health and beauty." There were also specific religious conditions that had to be monitored carefully. Certain doctrines were off-limits: "The fatality of impressing the fact of sin and personal unworthiness, of holding out before the adolescent . . . the horrors of eternal punishment, and of emphasizing unduly the ideal of perfection, instead of stimulating the halting and self-distrustful soul towards wholesome activity—these and numerous other indiscretions which are so frequently indulged in need only be seen to be avoided." It is no surprise that evangelical Calvinism came into focus as the least healthy way of handling conversion. Several psychologists of religion argued that, because conversions came naturally, they did not need to be stimulated artificially with fearful doctrines or judgmental pronouncements. Doing this would waste emotional capital, artificially spike nervous energies, and possibly generate morbid states, anxiety, brooding—sometimes even insanity. Most thought that the sudden, violent conversions characteristic of evangelicalism tended to result not in a "serious sense of God within," but in "increased activity of the passional nature," unstable emotions, and a later incapacity for religion. Thus the "soul is given just enough religious stimulus to act as an inoculation against deeper and more serious interest later." This had been precisely the experience of Starbuck, Coe, and other first-generation psychologists of religion—contrived conversions had led to confusion, malaise, and doubt. There was no question: gradually growing in religion was best.[18]

Such normative notions about spirituality became authoritative in American culture for several reasons, not least of which was that they drew on other "scientific" certainties about gender and race. An important book written by a progressive politician and onetime Methodist preacher named Frederick Davenport shows clearly how discourses about evolution, spirituality, and race reinforced one another. Davenport started out as a minister involved in the Epworth League in Wyoming, a Methodist organization trying to awaken a sense of social responsibility and make "more intelligent Christians." Later his passions for rationality and Christianity deepened, and he turned to solving the more general problem of irrationality in American culture. Davenport agreed that badly managed revivals led to deleterious consequences for body and spirit, and he, too, used physiological and psychological literatures to develop his argument. Davenport used two diagrams to demonstrate the difference between believers who engaged in intemperate enthusiasms and those who turned revival energies into productive channels (see figure 13). The diagram on the left of the figure illustrates the inner workings of "the untrained elements of society," revivalists and revival participants in whom outer forms of stimulation pass uninhibited through the nervous system and out into muscular activities. Resulting impulsive bodily actions appeared as a range of ecstatic behaviors. There were other people, though, illustrated by

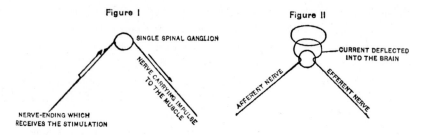

Figure 13.    The neurology of revival and self-control. From Frederick Morgan Davenport, *Primitive Traits in Religious Revivals*, 1905.

the diagram on the right, who had better-developed centers of inhibition and who were able to detain incoming sensations and reflect on them using higher brain functions. The problem then for Davenport, as for other social scientists, was that revivals could stir emotional energies that were not properly controlled or inhibited. Individuals would have to *mature* to a point where they gloried not in "the ecstatic inflow of emotion, the rhapsody, the lapse of inhibition" but in their "rational love, joy, peace, long-suffering, kindness, goodness, faithfulness, meekness—*self-control*." This was a message that all psychologists of religion embraced. Mature religiousness was marked by an ability to control deep emotions, subliminal energies, and other pulses of the irrational.[19]

Of course, some people had more self-control than others. Those most susceptible to the "religious intoxication" proffered at revivals were those who labored with an "exceedingly rudimentary and undeveloped type of mind"—that is, children and childlike races. Davenport turned his attention to the primitive, devoting separate chapters to analyses of ecstatic behaviors among Native Americans and other indigenous peoples, and African Americans. Densely ignorant, vividly imaginative, "thoroughly religious," and "extraordinarily emotional," Negroes in America, Davenport wrote, repeating common assumptions, "found it very difficult to withstand the almost constant tide of revival that sweeps over [their] community." Davenport furnished a number of examples showing how the stimulus of revival led to strong emotions that then issued in a variety of motor discharges. The lack of inhibitory powers in this race was illustrated by the "rhythmic cadence into which they unconsciously drop. . . . Rhythm is the line of least resistance for high emotion. A change in tone level is a rest to the muscles which are producing the vociferous effects. The same phenomenon has appeared among the Hard Shell Baptists, the

Friends and the early Methodists, and has always the same significance." Violent emotion, when stirred inward, issued in incredible muscle contractions that struck people down, immobilizing them. Though believers themselves saw signs of the Holy Ghost in their dramatic muscle automatisms, in reality their behaviors signaled a steep descent into immorality, including especially sexual vice. In a shocking passage, Davenport blamed blacks, now shown scientifically to lack control, for the unconscionable acts of white lynch mobs: "The wide prevalence of the crime of lynching among the whites of the South testifies eloquently to the reign of lust among the blacks." Always the social scientist, Davenport included a chart correlating high incidents of lynching in Kentucky with areas of active revivals. Evidently, revivals had stirred up sexual feelings in blacks and violent urges in ignorant whites; the result was a lynching epidemic. Commentators thought such examples of how not to practice religion helpful. A *Biblical World* review of Davenport's book correctly linked it to the work of Coe, Starbuck, and James, praising it as a book with "great practical value for the teacher and the minister, stimulating thought, and indicating where dangers lie in the work of religious education."[20] There are few better indicators of this liberal generation's fear of irrationality.

One way to dismiss crude religious behaviors was to talk about how categories such as race produced them. This was a strategy used by people like Davenport. Another way to reveal the debased character of certain religious experiences was by linking them to psychopathological states. Several different terms were used in talking about unhealthy mental states and their religious manifestations. One such term was *suggestibility*. Davenport built an entire chapter in his book around it, "Conversion by Suggestion," that explained false conversions confected in revivals by linking them not to deep spiritual forces but to debased, psychopathological ones. Revival converts were impressionable, weak, and out of control. Others used suggestion in similar ways. Worried that authentic religion was "tangled with all forms of abnormal, and even insane, mental vagaries," the liberal Protestant psychologist George Cutten thought psychological insights might help believers "recognize laws of abnormality as we do of normal processes, and we may separate the dross from the metal." Categories such as suggestion helped him do this. Suggestion explained all kinds of excessive practices and credulities—speaking in tongues, witchcraft, stigmatization, and miracles. Suggestible people were those who listened to religious authorities uncritically and believed, those who could not think for themselves, those who were caught up in the ethos of a crowd. Of course, evangelicals were supremely suggestible. And black evangelicals more so. The practices of "Negro" evangelicals were a perfect example of what not to do with your religion. Negroes' suggestibility led not just to spiritual problems, Cutton wrote, but to social ones as well. "The negro saw spirits in everything while in Africa, and if he kept on good terms with spirits his duty was done. He felt no obligation to his fellowmen, and religion had nothing to do with moral conduct." For people like this, it was not inconsistent to be highly religious and highly immoral at the same time, and this was precisely the American Negro's status. When to their immoral character Negroes added "dense ignorance and weak will [combined] with vivid imagination and volatile emotion," they produced a profile of bad religiousness: an excessively emotional religiousness combined with an inadequate sense of duty and self-control.[21]

Starbuck, too, was interested in using psychological categories like suggestion to produce normative judgments about religion, and later in life he directed several research projects that attempted to measure empirically suggestion and other personality traits. Two of his graduate students set out to measure suggestiveness and correlate it with other aspects of religious identity. They surveyed more than five hundred undergraduates at the University of Iowa and subjected a good number of them to sensorimotor tests involving auditory and sensory stimuli, electric shocks, coordination tests, and other tasks designed to examine willpower, reaction time, and suggestibility (see figure 14). When comparing religious liberals and conservatives, they found that conservatives were more suggestible, timid, and extroverted, more likely to have had dramatic conversion experiences, and more likely to be female and church members. Religious liberals, by contrast, scored higher in intellect and self-control. These studies confirmed what religious psychologists had been saying for years: evangelical styles were immature; liberal religious styles were advanced.

But there also was a familiar ambivalence in these studies. These measurements, like those Starbuck did earlier in his life, noted the remarkable power of deep religious feelings and experiences. Perhaps, one of the experimenters wrote, the conservatives had richer or more energetic lives and feelings of "adjustment and peace which enables the individuals to use more effectively the relatively inferior capacities which, according to the tests, they seem to have."[22] A backhanded compliment to be sure—but it is impossible to ignore the traces of nostalgia and longing that haunt this study and others like it. Starbuck and his students did not want to demolish belief but to rescue it from the bad forms that obscured

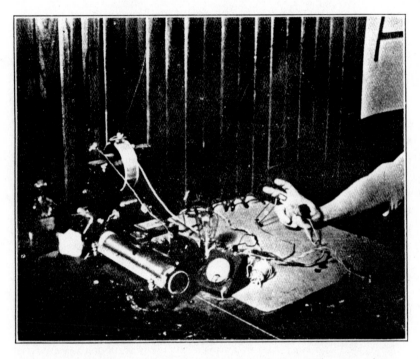

Figure 14.   Testing suggestibility with electric shock. From Robert Daniel Sinclair, "A Comparative Study of Those Who Report the Experience of the Divine Presence and Those Who Do Not," 1930. From the Redpath Chautauqua Collection, University of Iowa Libraries, Iowa City, Iowa.

it. Evangelicalism in particular represented a confounding puzzle: it was a detestable, excessive religiousness that nevertheless contained deep and useful religious emotions.

### RELIGIOUS FEELINGS

Once purified in all these ways, religious experience became a powerful category that psychologists of religion and other liberals promoted with extraordinary enthusiasm and effectiveness. Starbuck was one of the most vigorous proponents of, for example, arguments showing not just that deep religious feelings (when rightly understood) healed and saved but also that they proved the existence of God. Insisting that religion was concerned above all with "the affective life," and expressing the common functionalist view that religious feelings, like other feelings and instincts, adjusted human beings to larger realities encompassing them, Starbuck, in an article published in 1904, argued that feelings "[give] us as valid an account of external facts and relations, truth and reality as the cognitive [life]." He reasoned that because religious feelings were universal, and because most other inner dispositions can be relied upon for true knowledge about the world, religious feelings point to the existence of an objective spiritual reality encompassing us. Feelings were "never purely subjective." Study of the feelings allowed us to probe the edges of a much larger universe of relations.[23] (Starbuck was not alone in wondering about these questions. Many psychologists at the time were concerned with precisely these issues, examining in particular how the physiology of sensation and perception pointed to links between subjective states and outer, objective things.) Starbuck was more inclined than most to transform these kinds of arguments into theistic proofs, however, perhaps because he himself had experienced a number of mysterious religious awakenings. His halfhearted evangelical conversion was merely the beginning; later in life he had several other powerful religious "illuminations," and he never lost that part of his personality he once called his "ineradicable mysticism."

As is well known, James had similar suspicions about the existence of a spiritual dimension, but settled for a tentative assessment of the problem in a section of the *Varieties* on his "over-beliefs." In private, however, he encouraged Starbuck. In August of 1904 he wrote, "I can see but vaguely just what sort of outer relations our inner organism might respond to, which our feelings and intellect interpret by religious thought." When Starbuck's article came out late that year, James told him that his thesis "in this article is both important and original, and ought to be worked out in the clearest possible manner" and "as concretely as possible." It was a difficult argument to make convincingly, James admitted, and "the real crux" of it "is when you come to define objectively the ideals to which the feeling reacts. 'God is a Spirit'— *darauf geht es an*—on the last available definition of the term Spirit. It may be very abstract."[24] The God of scientific believers like Starbuck was abstract indeed; but all other possible gods, including especially those imagined by more conventional American Christians, were accessible only by believing in preposterous doctrines or performing unseemly and irrational worship exercises.

There was a lot at stake in these arguments. Anxious that the Bible's authority had been undermined by both biblical critics and scientific accounts of time and history, American intellectuals turned expectantly to experience as a new, self-certifying foundation for belief. Starbuck showed that religious experience, shorn of its distortions and excesses, injected life-giving elements into the self. Other believing psychologists made similar arguments. "The cold, half-dying belief of the intellect is often warmed into life by getting into touch w/ the vital forces of the feeling background, and once so vivified and identified w/ the deepest currents of one's life, is seldom thereafter subject to doubt or assailable by argument," one psychologist wrote. The only satisfactory foundation for modern faith was this—religious feeling. The same medicine was a tonic for troubled believers. "A touch of mysticism may be quite good enough to lend vitality to one's religion, even when in theological matters one has become skeptical." "Many a man of culture and intellectual power who is well versed in the science and criticism of our day," another psychologist of religion wrote, describing perfectly his own situation (and Starbuck's), though "unable to subscribe to any creed or even to worship with any church, finds springing up within him a stream of inarticulate but genuine religious experience . . . which is the very water of life." This thinker also distributed questionnaires on religious experience, and he too was struck by how subjects with robust religious experiences were contented religiously. Quoting one of his religious (but post-Christian) subjects, this thinker said that the experience itself was "enough to live by." "It is a part of my being, and has for the rest of my being an importance and a value that are supreme, and that suffices me." The task for psychologists of religion was, through "painstaking and systematic study of a large body of facts carefully and critically collected and sifted," to understand these experiences better and help believers incorporate them in their lives.[25] This was of course Starbuck's primary task as well.

To put a sharper point on this, we might say that psychologists of religion produced these experiences for the public. As I already have mentioned, Starbuck saw his vocation as making elusive religious truths more "real" to people, something he did by analyzing how religious experiences worked, writing about them in popular journals, and using his knowledge to help religious and religious education organizations develop faith-producing curricula. He also lectured around the country on psychology and faith. In the *Homiletic Review*, the most popular periodical for American clerics at this time, he wrote immodestly that, of all contemporary religious trends, none had more impact on the "actual religious life of the world to-day" than "the great interest that has sprung up within the last decade in the careful and thoughtful study of religious experience." Such study "has helped to show many things about religion that could hardly have come any other way," bringing "into bold relief the answer to many questions about religion which immediately concern our understanding of what it means, our relation to it, and our personal hold on the things of the spiritual life." The psychology of religion did this in a couple of ways. First, psychologists of religion disseminated and exchanged narratives of religious experience. "The experience of each and every earnest person is original and genuine, and one that others should share, and one that heightens our conception of what are the possibilities of the spiritual life. It is like the exchange of experiences among trusted friends, or the confessions that people make, or the testimonies that they give in prayer-meeting, except on a larger scale." Creating these large-scale discursive "prayer-meetings" dramatically changed the nature of experience and how it was disciplined; experience became a discourse shaped less by pastors and Christian symbols and more by statistical generalizations across cultures formulated by psychologists and educators. Believers have always shared stories about faith, Starbuck wrote, but now the process would lead to an "ability to discriminate among the qualities of spiritual experience." Comparisons of different religious experiences and their outcomes might reveal which experiences were most functional, most useful, and most healthy. With scientific study "we can know enough to feel that we are not wandering entirely in the dark"; we can "be helpful to the hungering of an inquiring soul"; and we can understand and use different methods to move individuals through processes of religious development.[26] One method—the older, evangelical way—did not fit everyone; different temperaments called for different methods.

The transformation in American thinking about religious experience that Starbuck and a few others promoted was far-reaching. Many embraced Starbuck's way of thinking about the two types of conversion—sudden and gradual—and a surprising number agreed that gradual, natural ways of nurturing young people's religious feelings were best. Starbuck's charts and graphs of spiritual growth, and the charts and graphs of other psychologists, found their way into an astonishing number of popular devotional manuals. One pamphlet reproduced a chart on conversion ages and informed pastors that psychologists now agreed that there were certain propitious times to encourage conversion or the "Decision Day" (see figure 15). It was important to guide Sunday-school children between the ages of fourteen and eighteen in particular; this was the time when "the physical nature and the religious nature

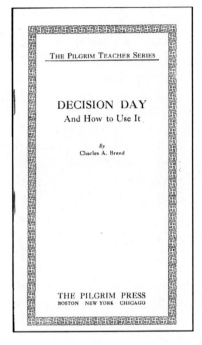

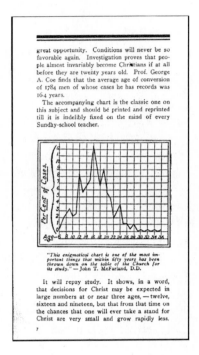

Figure 15.   Pamphlet promoting scientific ways of thinking about religious conversion. From Charles A. Brand, *Decision Day and How to Use It*, 1908.

are in a strange state of turmoil and incompleteness," when the young person had a "longing for something higher and better. . . . Conditions will never be so favorable again." Here, psychological insights added urgency to pastoral labors: there was a small window for conversion opportunities. And of course, psychological insights also reinforced how important conversion experiences were for overall maturity. Still, while youthful conversions were important, those borrowing from Starbuck and other experts agreed that it was never necessary to revert to the "old plan"—to use God's wrath or angry doctrines to motivate Christians. This might produce a herd of converts but no authentic experiences; and pressuring people in this way also would work "upon the emotions in a way that was not wholesome." This was a consistent message in this literature: don't injure believers (and young believers in particular) by foisting upon them contrived or excessive methods. By the early twentieth century, these ideas dominated religious education among mainline American Protestants.[27]

.   .   .

The scientific techniques that religious liberals used helped them find for themselves a middle path between excessive emotion and the spiritually deadening possibilities of their own rational procedures. Starbuck felt an attraction to both extremes, a warring "between tenderness and toughness, between acceptance and doubt, between inner sensitivity and vigorous intellectuality." But Starbuck remained to the end a deeply religious person, interpreting even the working out of these tensions as providential. In fact, late in life he said that the psychology of religion itself had "worked on" him, directing his actions, calling him to its novel affirmations. Apparently his own mystical illuminations assured him of the closeness of God in experience. He felt a resulting "at-home-ness in the universe" that endured for his entire life. This was a sensibility different from the evangelical sensibilities he studied. At the deepest levels, he and other psychologists of religion were unsettled by the evangelical style, which they were able to appreciate only when it was measured and controlled. The transcendent God of American evangelicals and his sudden irruptions in the self were disturbing and confounding. Starbuck thought that the evangelical God was too unpredictable and remote from human needs and aspirations. "Creator gods and absentee deities have never seemed to possess any potency," Starbuck complained once; those notions and other childish ideas about miracles and healings were fanciful and evanescent. But "the feeling of a Presence has had body and substance" in my life, he wrote, moving me to insight, happiness, and a "mighty inwardness." This inwardness, this "sense of an infusing Presence" that Starbuck interpreted within a kind of pantheistic system, was so powerful that it preserved him from conservative believers and materialistic scientists who detested his liberal mediations. There were a number of such critics; Starbuck appears to have disregarded many of them.[28]

The "infusing Presence" that Starbuck and other psychologists of religion felt also powered an incredibly ambitious set of liberal reforms that, within twenty-five years, completely changed how American Protestants and other believers conceived of and practiced religious experience. Psychological interpretations of experience proliferated at an astonishing pace. Trying to understand this vast output, one reviewer complained in 1937 that few "of my readers can have any idea how large is the number of books and papers which have been written to explain religious phenomena from a psychological viewpoint." No one, he said, including himself, could read them all. Many, including especially Starbuck and Coe, also industriously put their new notions into practice. They developed what quickly became dominant religious education associations and fashioned new schemes for religious nurture and Sunday school curricula keyed more to gradual-growth models of faith. Suddenly, lesson plans for Sunday school were specific to age and psychological stage. It is no exaggeration to call this a revolution in how American believers thought about faith. Especially in the first decades of the twentieth century, the effort to put the recommendations of Starbuck, Coe, and others into practice "eclipsed perhaps every other project of the churches," one later observer recalled. "Large numbers of men and women sought specialized training for service in [religious education's] ranks"; new religious specialists helped children believe, adolescents convert, and pastors buttress faith and banish disbelief—all with newly minted scientific methods. A scientifically informed pastoral psychology movement blossomed. All of this represented the apogee of Starbuck's project—a project of probing the universal psychological functions of religious experience and bringing into focus its most useful and healthy forms. Though by the interwar period theologians were critiquing and occasionally abandoning this and other liberal innovations, in the meantime Starbuck could justifiably look back on his life and rejoice that, for a crucial moment at least, he and his colleagues had delivered on promises to usher in a "new era of religious experience."[29]

# 6   Suggestive Explanations

> The story of the conquest of a realm of fable by a campaign of
> enlightenment is always a tale of interest.
>
> JOSEPH JASTROW, *Fact and Fable in Psychology*

For the most part it was consciousness or will-oriented psychologies that helped religious liberals rethink different dimensions of the moral and religious life. In the early decades of the twentieth century, however, as dynamic psychologies and notions of the unconscious became prevalent in American culture, ways of thinking about spiritual matters changed. The unconscious became a powerful source of imaginative reflections about the transcendent parts of human nature. Here was another category, like nervous energies, that believers used to imagine a place for spirit in an otherwise physiological self. Even so, and even though liberals and others embraced the unconscious for these reasons, their yearnings for the divine, and the freedom and creativity the divine provided, had limits. Many worried about the unpredictable, and potentially explosive, forces contained in the unconscious. Some associated it with unseemly evangelical irruptions and ecstatic behaviors. Earlier generations of liberal believers had similar concerns about irrationalism, for, as we have seen, they both insisted on spiritual dimensions of the self and worked hard to contain, measure, and control them. The category they used to contain and measure the unconscious when it appeared on the scene was "suggestion," a concept that secularizing scientists originally employed to explain away all religious intuitions and inner promptings. Though fearless scientific debunkers such as Joseph Jastrow employed this concept as a weapon in their wider campaigns to conquer faith and other childlike inclinations, the history of the category shows that psychological concepts often were used in unexpected ways. Shrewd interpreters that they were, religious liberals employed suggestion not as a weapon against belief but as a new way to stimulate the most credulous parts of the self. They used this category, albeit in careful and measured ways, as another tool to develop spiritual assurance.

## UNCONSCIOUS CREDULITY

The history of the unconscious has been documented extensively in other writings.[1] I recapitulate here only parts of that history that tell us how psychologists and believers were rethinking the spiritual self in this era, especially how their reflections on the unconscious stirred interest in the technologies of self-control that I associate with suggestion.

Ideas about the unconscious have a long history, and though these ideas have been important in different cultures and in select ancient and medieval Christian sources, the unconscious emerged powerfully in the modern West in two principal locations: in the writings of modern post-Kantian philosophers such as Schopenhauer and Schelling, who speculated about impulses, memories, and desires operating outside of conscious control; and in modern therapeutic traditions that employed the category of the unconscious to understand and attempt to treat severe mental illnesses. The key figure in the modern philosophical tradition, a German romantic philosopher whom Americans like Hall and James knew well, was Eduard von Hartmann. (Hall had become acquainted with Hartmann during his student days in Germany.) Drawing on earlier speculation about the unconscious by philosophers such as Schopenhauer, Hartmann put together dramatic examples of the ways unconscious factors influenced memory, the association of ideas, habit formation, and other daily activities. He hypothesized a universal unconscious that fed the unconscious in each individual. Hartmann's ideas appealed broadly to psychologists and other Americans. Late in life, Hall believed Hartmann's "proof of the eccentric . . . marginal nature of consciousness makes him a modern Copernicus. The erection of the Unconscious as a world principle marks the great revolution of views since the Renaissance, which was its prelude, in emancipating the world from the views of the past." Hall's emancipations were complex, as we have seen. For him, the unconscious undoubtedly served the dual role of subverting traditional Christian categories and pointing the way to what Hartmann thought of as a more refined "spiritual monism." Hall pursued a refined monism as well, as we have seen.[2]

The other source of modern notions of the unconscious was a set of therapeutic traditions that priests, exorcisers, and slightly later, psychiatrists used to explain and treat dissociated mental states and other mental pathologies. Though Franz Anton Mesmer, by positing the existence of a pervasive magnetic fluid, successfully redescribed a set of spiritual conditions (for example, possession) in naturalistic terms, his enlightened explanations were soon supplanted by others, especially the mentalist category *hypnosis* (a term used first by James Braid, a nineteenth-century Scottish surgeon). This did not stop an army of itinerant lecturers and expert manipulators of magnetic fluids from fanning out in Europe and America, astounding audiences with magnetically induced trance states, and miraculous healings, mental and otherwise. But hypnosis became the more acceptable explanation of these phenomena. French neurologists working at the Salpêtrière and at the Nancy School used hypnosis to understand better what was involved in altered states of consciousness, trances, sleeplike states, and the appearance in some people of what seemed to be "secondary selves." Pierre Janet was the most important French clinician working in these areas; he had many admirers and correspondents among American physicians and psychologists, including those in the Boston school of psychotherapy—James, Henry Bowditch, Richard Cabot, Morton Prince, James Jackson Putnam, and Boris Sidis (the latter would write an influential dissertation on suggestion under James). As Taves has written, in an 1886 article Janet published the first widely acknowledged experimental evidence for secondary selves. In his *Varieties* fifteen years later, James pointed to Janet's discovery as "the most important step forward that has occurred in psychology since I have been a student of that science." James had different reasons for embracing the unconscious, as we will see.[3]

There was a lot at stake in arguments about the unconscious, and neurologists, clinicians, and others deeply disagreed over whether this obscure part of the self existed. Some of them were sure that it was imaginary, and they set out to explain unremembered actions and other phenomena attributed to a secondary self by showing how intelligent action proceeded physiologically without being conscious. This was the theory of "unconscious cerebration." Thinkers embracing this position, including positivists like Joseph Jastrow and many other American psychologists, rejected the idea that consciousness was divisible.[4] A second group believed that coexistent states of consciousness, hysteria, altered states of consciousness, and other phenomena pointed to different ways that consciousness was more sharply divided into parts. This group believed that dimensions of consciousness could be split off or dissociated. Psychologists in this group argued about whether dissociative states were pathological, as Janet thought, or normal and useful, as the British psychical researcher F. W. Myers argued. In addition, some of those accepting the dissociative model wondered if unconscious mental activity might better account for religious or psychical phenomena—clairvoyance, trance states, and spirit communication. Though thinkers like Myers explained spirit possession and trance states as phenomena produced by shifting energy centers *within* the self, they did not rule out the possibility that external (i.e., supernatural) forces were powering this shift. James and Myers both tended to think of the unconscious not merely as a set-off part of consciousness but also as a metaphysical entity, a reservoir of transcendental power that controlled and enlivened the self, and one that the conscious mind was only dimly aware of. "By placing the pathological, the normal, and the potentially supranormal within a common frame of reference," Taves has summarized adroitly, Myers "created a theoretical space (the subliminal) through which influences beyond the individual, should they exist, might be expected to manifest themselves." Though many psychologists resisted psychical research and worried that talk of dissociated states opened the door to new superstitions, they could do nothing to stop religious reflection on what was admittedly a baffling part of the self.[5]

Some of them did try. Some of them tried to quell the regnant religious clatter about dissociated states and transcendent parts of the self. A group of positivist psychologists and debunkers, of whom more will be said later, used different strategies. Some sought ways of experimentally showing that consciousness was a single, more or less united, entity. One particularly telling episode had to do with the spiritualistic medium Leonora Piper and the discourses that—quite literally—surrounded her. James and other members of the society for psychical research were persuaded that Piper had extraordinary abilities. While she sat in trance states, the spirits that animated her offered astonishingly accurate private information about séance attendees. After investigating Piper and even having her trailed by a detective, key members of the American Society for Psychical Research, including James, found themselves persuaded. But others were convinced neither of Piper's sincerity nor of the fact that consciousness could be invaded by separate, supernatural communications. In 1909, G. Stanley Hall financed six sittings with Piper in her home, where he and a research associate conducted a battery of psychological and physiological tests. Hall set out to disprove the spiritualist claim that channeled voices were in no way connected to physical realities (i.e., bodies). To show that Piper's channeled spirits actually were produced by normal neuromuscular processes, he conducted a series of sensory tests on Piper while she was entranced. Would these spirits feel or comment on these sensations? While conducting routine tests on vision, taste, odor, pressure, and pain, Piper's spirits did not report sensations. Hall persisted. Finally, when applying the maximum twenty-five pounds to Piper's increasingly sore hands, the spirit Hall was trying to find in Piper's body finally responded, asking for relief. This was proof enough for Hall, who reported his results and interpreted them as evidence that the Piper phenomenon was a product of a single neuromuscular consciousness—even if it was a consciousness that was "impulsive," "impressionable," "hysterical," and "neurotic."

But as others would remark in the aftermath, there were different ways of seeing Hall's results. During most of the tests, Piper's spirit seemed to transcend Hall's painful pricks and proddings. Moreover, did the spirit's intervention at the end prove definitively that there were no such things as ghosts? Couldn't a channeled spirit perceive danger and try to protect its host? For all their vigorous testing, as the historian Deborah Coon has noted, "Hall and [his research assistant] Tanner proved little with their tests except that they could do physical damage to Mrs. Piper. Her daughter wrote to protest her mother's sore palms, blistered lips, and numb fingers."[6] Right up to the end of James's life (he died the next year, in 1910), he and Hall battled over the meanings of psychology: Hall insisted that the unconscious merely was the source of our primitive instincts, emotions, and drives; James thought it signified openings to larger, possibly transcendent powers. The unconscious, then, was contested territory.

Hall's efforts to quash the supernatural with twenty-five-pound weights called forth congratulatory cheers from other scientists. But many others were unimpressed. Especially in popular culture, James was having his way, and partly as a result, the subconscious swiftly took shape as a separate, quasi-transcendental part of the self. James did most of the persuading in his *Varieties*. Attempting to produce a "reconciling hypothesis" that restated religious truths in scientific form, James turned to the subconscious as the key mediating category. Religions posited a transcendent "more" in different guises, as gods and angels and forces, but the subconscious, James thought, might be "a way of describing the 'more,' which psychologists may also recognize as real. The *subconscious self* is nowadays a well-accredited psychological entity; and I believe that in it we have exactly the mediating term required. Apart from all religious considerations, there is actually and literally more life in our total soul than we are at any time aware of." Here was a "more" that even scientists recognized. James quoted Myers's article on subliminal consciousness to reinforce the point: Each person had deep, unexpressed psychical layers. There was always a part of the self that was unmanifested, in abeyance, in reserve. In what became a manifesto for religious liberals, James expanded the powers of this self-in-abeyance in "The Energies of Men," identifying "deeper and deeper strata of combustible or explosible material" that could be released by prayer, meditation, and other religious techniques.[7]

Religious liberals often quoted directly from James, borrowed his argumentative strategies, developed sermons using his ideas, and even passed out his lectures to parishioners. Like James, they used the subconscious to contain divine forces just as the mind was being emptied of mystery by new psychologists insisting on the stimulus-response self.[8]

This was precisely what believers needed: a way to locate a supernatural soul in the natural body. The liberal Congregationalist Horace Warner, for one, insisted in 1910 that psychological analyses of the unconscious would eliminate "misunderstandings and unreliable expectations which so often form misleading standards of saving experience" and substitute for older, hazy notions a "clear and luminous . . . pathway of spiritual states." Warner devised elaborate diagrams of ascending spiritual states with instructions on how to practice them. He plotted older Christian salvation stages on top, in waking forms of consciousness, and he identified in subterranean locations the operations of a cooperating Holy Spirit (see figure 16). Warner's elaborate descriptions of conscious Christian states was not unlike analyses of other liberal Christians pursuing detailed descriptions. "What we are essaying to do," he wrote "is to detect and define, as far as the facts now in hand will permit, the scientific succession of demonstrable psychic states in the typical Christian experience." Starbuck, Coe, and others already had taxonomized Christian experience in related ways. Warner listed fairly detailed sequences of emotional states.

But there was always a dilemma in scientifically parsing every moment of faith. Where did the Holy Spirit operate? Was there room for it? Admitting that the Holy Spirit could not be discerned directly in conscious acts, Warner solved the dilemma by inscribing the always operating Holy Spirit in a vast subconscious region, a separate but contiguous part of the self. The Holy Spirit drove the process from underneath, inserting itself (as it had in earlier Christian schemes) especially in crucial breaking points: at dramatic moments of conviction, conversion, and sanctification. The Holy Spirit made cross-border incursions on Warner's diagrams too. The subconscious region was difficult to penetrate intellectually, and Warner's diagrams left this region undeveloped. What he knew of it came from scripture. He also knew that this subconscious region was the source of all conscious activity and the engine that drove salvation. In Warner's maps, the subconscious was the way to reinsert the divine in scientific maps of self.[9]

But if liberals like Warner embraced the subconscious as a way of inscribing the Holy Spirit in the self, they also worried that the subconscious could be unpredictable and potentially explosive. This part of the self seemed to produce extravagant religious notions. Warner's careful

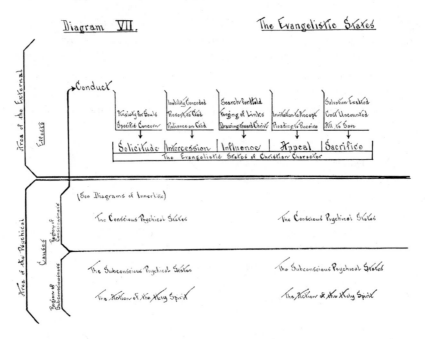

Figure 16. Mapping the external, conscious, and subconscious stages of salvation. From Horace Emory Warner, *The Psychology of the Christian Life*, 1910.

translation of unconscious forces into Christian salvation stages, and his insistence that these stages be confirmed by scripture, betrays a concern with this matter: he was regulating and domesticating the unconscious's irrational pulses. But as spiritual seekers traveled farther out on the religious left, they were less likely to take these cautious steps. Some turned to the unconscious for moments of inspiration, strange intuitions, presentiments, telepathic communications, discussions with departed spirits, ecstatic visions, healings, and trances. These more radical liberals could wax ecstatically about the powers of the subliminal self. These radical visions, of course, produced predictable reactions not just from positivist scientists but also, perhaps more forcefully, from sober progressives and Protestants, believers who wanted to defend belief from unsophisticated handlers on the right and left. "The country has been flooded with hasty interpretations of the subconscious," George Coe worried in 1907. "Apparently, everybody, except the psychologists, is intent, first, upon emphasizing the contrasts between the subconscious operations of the mind and the more familiar ones, and second, upon using the subconscious as a special support of religious, spiritistic, telepathic, or other beliefs." Why did the "popular mind" so hunger for the occult? Why had so many *clergymen* committed themselves to mind reading, telepathy, and other odd beliefs? "I plead for greater caution with regard to our dearest beliefs and hopes," he continued. "To rest them upon such grounds as these is to invite disbelief in the end." The solution to this extreme credulity was to bring the subconscious back into closer relationships with conscious (rational) controls. The credulous subconscious had to be regulated by conscious processes.[10] For many, an entirely free unconscious was an unpredictable and indiscriminate force, something that led to belief in all manner of things. And so discourses of the unconscious opened out into discourses of control and regulation.

## ACCOUNTING FOR THE IRRATIONAL

The discourses of control that the word *suggestion* conjured were wide ranging. Social psychologists used suggestion to control irrational crowds; child psychologists used suggestive techniques to control unruly children; still others thought these techniques might tame primitive peoples and races. One index of how pervasive these discourses were can be found in advertising, an industry that at the turn of the century was turning from rational appeals to techniques of manipulating irrational desires, instincts, and needs. Evidence, calm persuasion, carefully reasoned appeals—none of these seemed to work as well as suggesting something to the unconscious. In 1908, Walter Dill Scott, one of the most influential advertising scholars and the first to import psychological insights into the field, wrote that "the actual effect of modern advertising is not so much to convince as to suggest." Scott used contemporary psychological theory to understand better how conviction, desire, and finally, action were produced by incoming stimuli. He followed the psychological tradition fairly closely, arguing that incoming stimuli were automatically routed through the self and into muscular action—as long as there were no inhibiting ideas. The key to successful advertising was ensuring that this "reflex arc" moved efficiently from advertisement to purchasing behavior. Scott outlined a set of recommendations that used the language of suggestion: Advertisers first had to raise consumer suggestibility by creating a pleasurable advertising environment. Then they had to implant commands or other enticements in the self that were designed to get consumers to buy products. Finally they had to minimize interfering inhibitions and competing images. Controlling the total environment of impressions and sensations was not easy. Scott insisted that we "are constantly subjected to influences of which we had no knowledge"—influences retained by the unconscious and used to form opinions, judgments, and even philosophies of life. In some ways, Scott's work represented the end of the conscious, autonomous consumer. He saw consumers as irrational and confused or at least unaware of the sources of their own desires. His work was similar to the work of other commentators who saw the masses in terms of unconscious impulses, emotions, and automatic reactions.[11]

Advertisers were not the only ones interested in using suggestive discourses to manage irrational forces in the self. The social psychological tradition in particular, which was focused on crowds and irrational group behaviors, was crucial in magnifying these problems in the American imagination. The modern social psychological tradition began with the popular French writer Gustav Le Bon and his classic *The Crowd* (1896), a book cited extensively by American psychologists of religion and religious liberals concerned about the irrational. Le Bon, a well-known French pundit who detested socialism and communism and wanted to find ways to renew French culture, worried about the riots and strikes that had so troubled French history, from the French Revolution to left-wing demonstrations of the late nineteenth century. He also was aware of French clinical psychology, with its interest in hypnotism and dissociated states. His combination of interests fed scholarship that would be useful especially to leaders and society's experts; as Graham Richards has said, "understanding the 'laws' of crowd behaviour would enable national leaders to cultivate patriotic pride and self-confidence." Le Bon believed that in crowds people reverted to a more primitive, irrational, and even hypnotic state, a state easily manipulable by leaders who, in Le Bon's analogy, acted like mass hypnotists. Le Bon hoped that this message would help leaders use the laws of hypnotism and suggestion to control the irrational energies of the crowd and, through ruthless discipline and manipulation, bend them to nationalist interests. His hopes were realized in unexpectedly dramatic ways. His views helped determine French military tactics in World War I, and they shaped decisively the political and psychological strategies of Hitler, Stalin, and Mussolini, each of whom read and thoroughly assimilated Le Bon's ideas.[12] After Le Bon, psychologists tended to equate the unconscious with the masses.

In the United States as well, psychologists worried about the crowd and its uncontrollable impulses. One important group—prominent Jewish American psychologists, whom Andrew Heinze has recently analyzed—associated the unconscious with mass irrationalism, in part because of memories of European pogroms and anti-Semitism. (Non-Jewish religious liberals and American skeptics held similar views, though Heinze neglects this wider context.)[13] One important young Jewish psychologist, a graduate student of William

James's named Boris Sidis, borrowed some of Le Bon's insights and, like him, focused on the dangerous possibilities of crowd behavior. Sidis went to great lengths not only to describe how preachers and politicians implanted suggestions and produced unconscious effects and automatic behaviors but also to show in detail how this process worked. American society was full of such examples, oscillating as it did between financial panics and epidemics of religious insanity. "The clever stump orator, the politician, the preacher, fix the attention of their listeners on themselves, interesting them in the 'subject.' They as a rule distract the attention of the crowd by their stories, frequently giving the suggestion in some indirect and striking way, winding up the long yarn by a climax requiring the immediate execution of the suggested act."[14] The emotional crowd, the large assembly that, by its nature, inhibits individualism and instills conformity; the power of persuasive speeches and didactic commands; and the highly contagious religious emotions—all these things made people suggestible, stripping them of their voluntary mechanisms of control. All interfering impressions and contrary ideas were filtered out; all doubts and appetites for indecision were smothered by the stifling, contagious crowd. Everyone was entranced, hypnotized. Preachers suggested repentance and conversion, and auditors, robbed of their individuality, stepped forward.

Sidis even devised mathematical formulas to measure the economy of suggestive forces, adding long methodological appendices and an accompanying diagram of "mob energy" to show how suggestion's powers might exponentially increase (see figure 17). As suggestions cascaded down upon a passive mob, each individual absorbed the suggestions and increased "the emotion of the mob in volume and intensity. Each new attack is followed by a more violent paroxysm of furious demoniac frenzy. The mob is like an avalanche: the more it rolls the more menacing and dangerous it grows. The suggestion given by the hero, by the ringleader, by the master of the moment, is taken up by the crowd and is reflected and reverberated from man to man, until every soul is dizzied and every person is stunned. In the entranced crowd, in the mob, everyone influences and is influenced in his turn; every one suggests and is suggested to, and the surging billow of suggestion swells and rises until it reaches a formidable height." The total energy of this suggestive cascade could be calculated in the following way. The energy of the master, or hero, set arbitrarily at 50 units, awakens a half-measure (25 units) of energy in each of his 1,000 auditors. Each auditor in turn awakens a half-measure of energy (12.5) in all others. The total level of energy aroused by the master is therefore 25 times 1,000 (25,000). The total energy awakened by

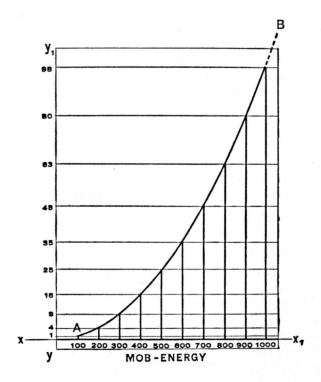

The horizontal line X X₁ represents the number of individuals in the mob from 100 to 1,000; the perpendiculars represent the rates of mob-energy; and the curve A B is the curve of mob-energy.

Figure 17. Plotting "mob-energy." From Boris Sidis, *The Psychology of Suggestion*, 1898.

each individual in the crowd is 12.5 times 1,000 (12,500). And since each individual awakens 12,500 units of suggestive energy, and since there are 1,000 individuals, the total units of energy can rise to 12,525,000, which is the sum of the original energy generated by the master and the aggregate energy produced by auditors. Though these calculations, like other calculations I have analyzed in this book, strike us as odd and perhaps nonsensical, they nicely represent Sidis's main concern. The cumulative forces of the unconscious were careening out of control—awakening, disinhibiting, inciting people to frenzy. Mob energy grew like wildfire. "Like a cannibal it feeds on human beings."[15]

The category of suggestion itself could cannibalize and feed on things around it, especially when it careened among ideas ripening in skeptical minds. Some embraced it as a way to explain everything. Opponents of revival enthusiasms in particular employed the notion ambidextrously, to furnish natural or psychological explanations for supposedly supernatural happenings. Many scoffers riffed on Sidis or Le Bon. "It is evident that no supernatural agency is necessary to explain the peculiar bodily exercises that attended the Great Revival in the western country," the historian Catharine Cleveland wrote in 1916, analyzing the Kentucky revivals of 1800. "The individual, seized either at home or in public, had, previous to the seizure, received some suggestion through the sense of sight or hearing that resulted in bodily reaction." Some hint, image, or word had nestled into the unconscious and was waiting to emerge at the right moment. Suggestion expanded in Cleveland's hands to encompass almost every supernatural marvel. What about believers who, when stricken by the spirit, suddenly expatiated in learned tones on the Bible or exhorted sinners? What about children of six or seven who could "use language beyond their years" and speak convincingly from the Bible? "The cells which had stored up the impressions so received were discharged by the unwonted excitement which had affected the nervous system," Cleveland explained. Everyone in these settings "expressed themselves only in terms perfectly familiar to one acquainted with religious phraseology. The ideas were all suggested by, or taken directly from, the hymns, the Bible, and other books of a religious nature." It was even possible on such principles to account for the "'amazing language' of the scoffer or deist who caught the contagion." Could suggestion make a scoffer preach the Bible? This was a powerful notion indeed![16]

While revived crowds and other mass behaviors became targets for many thinkers, any religious phenomena that dethroned reason could be subjected to debunking discourses. Though some thought testing spiritualism, psychical phenomena, or other religious behaviors either beneath their dignity or beyond the scope of scientific psychology, many of the most prominent American psychologists could not resist attempting to prove such practices fraudulent.[17] Joseph Jastrow, the single most prolific disseminator of psychological knowledge to the public between 1890 and 1940 and an indefatigable opponent of irrationalism and belief in most of its forms, was certain that, according to Heinze, "the entire enterprise of popular psychology . . . depended on persuading Americans to abandon myth and superstition."[18] Suggestion was his main weapon. "Unconscious suggestion has been one of the most potent influences for the production of alleged marvels and pseudo-phenomena," Jastrow complained. "All the series of experiments brought forward at irregular intervals during the past century to establish supernormal sensibilities have depended for their apparent success (apart from trickery) upon unconscious suggestion of the operators, combined with the shrewd assimilation of the desired or expected result on the part of the subjects." Jastrow thought spiritualist performances, telepathic communications, trances, and visions could be explained by analogies to hypnotic and nonhypnotic suggestive processes. Performers could create suggestive environments, implant ideas in people's heads, and pressure and coax them into believing, acting, and thinking in certain ways. Jastrow led powerful campaigns against spiritualism and Christian Science in particular, no doubt because each threatened to collapse what to Jastrow were crucial distinctions between science and religion. Both spiritualism and Christian Science, Jastrow worried, "pertain to the domain over which medicine, physiology, and psychology hold sway." These systems were catching on rapidly; they were a "contagion" that played on people's emotions and fears. They were therefore a "menace to rationality."[19] Such pronouncements suggested the existence of a psychological orthodoxy and a set of pious fears that held it in place. If ideas and spirits were powerful enough to shape matter or subvert what we knew of its laws, what might happen to scientific pursuits? "If spirits can lift tables and hold them suspended in the air in spite of the operation of gravity," another psychologist worried, "then knowledge is at an end, the whole fabric of science deliquesces into a mere logomachy, . . . and man himself becomes the plaything of every eddy that may happen to roil the waters of his ignorance."[20] This kind of loss of control was any scientist's greatest fear.

Healing techniques hawked by Christian Scientists or other metaphysical entrepreneurs also were explained on suggestive principles. "The belief in supernatural energies has cured diseases at all times and among all peoples," Hugo Munsterberg wrote. "Everywhere the patient sought help through the agents [i.e., priests] of higher forces and everywhere these agents themselves utilized their therapeutic success for strengthening the belief in their over-natural power." Reflecting on the credulous past, Munsterberg judged that the "psychologist would say that it was always the same story, the influence of suggestion on the imagination of those who suffer." There were complications to this one-size-fits-all explanation, different cultures with different metaphysical frameworks, but Munsterberg thought that the psychological mechanisms were the same. He chided modern Americans who, like savages in "darkest Africa" or Siberian shamans—"excitable persons with epileptic tendencies"—were tempted to ascribe divine origins to amazing healings.[21] "We must not forget that it is not the solemn value of the religious revelation, nor the ethical and metaphysical bearing of its objects, which brings success, but solely the depth of the emotion," Munsterberg insisted in his immensely popular *Psychology and Life* (1899). Deep emotions, not divine beings, effectively suggested confidence, wholeness, and healing. It did not matter who or what power you evoked. "To murmur the Greek alphabet with the touching intonation and gesture of supplication is just as strengthening for the health as the sublimest prayer; and for the man who believes in the metaphysical cure, it may be quite unimportant whether the love curer at his bedside thinks of the psychical Absolute or of the spring hat she will buy with the fee for her metaphysical healing." Without a doubt, the contempt underlying Munsterberg's comment had to do with a boundary dispute between scientific psychotherapists and other healers. Psychologists wanted to make therapeutic techniques more scientific, to wrest them free of religious controls and add them to the set of reasons that Americans might embrace more fully the new cadre of psychological experts.[22]

## SUGGESTING REFORMS

Others, however, used suggestive discourses to produce quite different outcomes. In churches, lyceums, and open-air lectures, less skeptical commentators resisted extending suggestive explanations indefinitely. They carefully managed the meanings of the term *suggestion* to show that suggestions explained not religious experience in general but only those religious experiences that were obviously excessive.

For religious liberals interested in using suggestion to explain some but not all religious phenomena, the first step was resisting wholly reductive uses of the term. Religious liberals had different strategies for doing this. One was simply to point out the obvious fact that suggestive analyses actually seemed to buttress philosophical (or religious) idealisms. What better evidence was there that ideas determined reality, that "men tend to be inflammable by ideas," as James had once said? Though medical men adverted to words like *autosuggestion* when explaining heightened or extraordinary states of consciousness, their explanations did not support materialist presumptions. Physicians talked of suggestion and autosuggestion "as if these phrases were explanatory, or meant more than the fact that certain men can be influenced, while others cannot be influenced, by certain sorts of *ideas*," James said, assessing the situation critically.[23] Other commentators, and especially New Thought believers, went to great lengths to show the power of ideas as they determined human reality through suggestive processes. Besides all this, what did it really mean to call something *suggestion*? Did the term have greater explanatory power than other words, such as *influence*? Did it break down obscure or mysterious processes into more basic or more clearly defined ones? Many did not think so. "This term is often used in a loose and vague way, even by good writers, to express the method by which one mind influences another, whether the method employed is argument or explanation or an idea offered in some indirect way," complained the Christian physician Samuel McComb. But McComb reminded his readers that suggestion really was a conversation about the dynamics of the subconscious; it was here that suggested ideas did their work. And how this work took place, and why, was still a mystery. "How the subconscious activity works and how it is related to the physiological apparatus of brain and nervous system, we do not know." We knew the external facts—we knew that "certain ideas offered by another can unlock pent-up energies, remove mental and moral inhibitions," and so on, but "as to *how* these things are done, we must say with [the German physiologist] Du Bois-Reymond, 'Ignoramus.'" Calling this mysterious power *suggestion* had not explained or accounted for it.[24]

Most liberal believers assumed that spirit was immanent in nature—and in human nature—and many therefore were not threatened by psychological monisms or identity theories of mind, spirit, and matter. But some felt uncomfortable or unsatisfied by monisms that were also materialisms, and took it upon themselves to insist that separate, divine forces cooperated with or animated material, or psychological, entities. The Swedenborgian and New Thought writer Horatio Dresser thought it absurd to raise "the mental factor (suggestion) to the divine power," or to confuse the mind and the soul. "The decisive agency is not suggestion in any event, but the divine love which uses the human or mental factor as a means." The real powers operating here were not mental but divine. This was a fairly common position. Dresser worked it out in uncommon detail, though, in the context of an argument with Protestant liberals who tried to debunk Swedenborg's divine visions as mere autosuggestions. Dresser believed a more ecumenical view was required not just to save Swedenborg's truths but any form of revelation, for if autosuggestion is invoked for one, why not the others? Moreover, why not use autosuggestion to explain *everything* as illusory? Escaping from this psychological reduction meant holding onto a solid starting point, which to Dresser meant to "start with God and the spiritual world, and regard the human self as the recipient of life or power through the understanding and the will." This starting point resolved many difficulties.

The other difficulty Dresser saw with "suggestionism" was its implication that religious change was intellectual. Didn't real inspiration sweep more powerfully into the self, altering it, changing not just our thoughts but also our emotions and actions? Mental healing through suggestion operated through thoughts, and it often worked; but spiritual healing involved commitment, emotion, submission, love of God, and ultimately, a reorientation to life. While skeptical psychologists might "see no difference between spiritual 'consciousness' and therapeutic 'suggestion,'" the difference, Dresser insisted, was empirical, and "the man who has not experienced the added value which religious belief implies is not expected to make the distinction." This was very Jamesian. Somehow, there was a difference. "To pass beyond the absorbing idea to vivid realization of the presence of God is to enter a superior region."[25]

Others insisted that reductive explanations that used the category suggestion could not account for the complicated processes taking place in the religious consciousness. The religious consciousness involved other inner things—other attitudes, beliefs, and dispositions. "Suggestion is more than attention," the professor of religious education Karl Stolz wrote; "it embraces a faith state. Belief that the idea held in mind is about to express itself or has already been realized is absolutely essential to the success of suggestion." This kind of vital belief was created best in religious contexts, where religious convictions and beliefs enmeshed the suggestion in a supportive network of concepts. To be effective, a suggestion had to be not just focused in attention but intensely and fervently embraced. Though suggested ideas might initially encounter contradictory ideas or other resistance, in order to be effective they "must be uncritically accepted by the person." More particularly, the suggested idea must be embraced warmly, energetically, and emotionally. "The idea of heat," Stolz said, giving an example, "becomes a suggestion only when a sense of rising temperature is induced." Religious faith promoted these more energetic conscious states. When faith embraced a suggestion, wrapping it with a more real, more emotional urgency, it attached to the suggestion a warm sense of certainty that prepared people to act. Faith was a crucial ingredient in powerful suggestions. Faith brought "a strained expectancy which increases the circulation of the blood, the outlay of nervous force," and the convictions of certainty, and it in other ways stimulated us. In short, the religious consciousness provided a powerful set of subjective conditions in which healing or saving suggestions flourished.[26] For all of these reasons, religious liberals could argue that suggestions and autosuggestions made in religious contexts were more potent. God's providential "means" of grace, like preaching and worship, represented the best suggestions, for here the Bible's suggestions reinforced the preacher's suggestions and the worshipper's autosuggestions. These divinely designed settings produced powerful emotional expectations.[27]

Believers used these arguments and others to resist reductive explanations of religious phenomena like prayer. To them, the religious context always was crucial. "The religious teacher tries to persuade men to believe in God and to take a religious attitude towards their conflicts and losses. He then shows that, having this faith, they must release themselves from the worries and fears which are inconsistent with it," one Christian psychologist wrote. The religious teacher does not, this same writer summarized, "tell [people] to believe in God because they may so escape from their worries and fears"—he does not, like the mental culturist, "tell people to apply psychological methods to induce a belief that there was a God who took care of the birds and flowers, because in this way they could get rid of worry." This, to be sure, "would be to try to buy the consolations of religious faith at the price of mental dishonesty." To be powerful and permanent, faith and its benefits had to be anchored in more permanent, more comprehensive sets of divine teachings.[28] Others agreed that the Christian has a suggestive advantage: Christians felt it a duty to persist in faith and suggestion, they had a powerful antidote to discouragement, and they had the companionship of Christ as they persevered. For these reasons, Christian faith states (when "properly poised") were more permanent than those states induced by mere suggestions.[29] Another benefit was that religious contexts also embedded suggestive techniques in a more balanced set of mental and spiritual disciplines—disciplines that incorporated not just the passivity of suggestion but also emotions and especially willed behaviors. Samuel McComb, one of the founders of an Episcopal faith healing movement called the Emmanuel Movement, warned that suggestive techniques practiced improperly could impair one's self-control and capacity for willed behaviors. Suggestion alone could be dangerous, weakening the religious self. Real religious experience, another liberal thought, "involves choice, the personal acceptance of value, the concealed and subliminal maturing of the principles of the good life, and the concrete expression of faith."[30]

## PEOPLE WITHOUT SELF-CONTROL

These arguments remind us that positions on suggestion and how it worked were enmeshed in normative discourses about the proper forms of religion. And in fact, even reductive uses of suggestion often were incorporated in discourses promoting particular religious views. Most revival debunkers, for instance, were less interested in secularism than they were in a faith purged of irrational elements. The liberal Protestant psychologist George Cutten represented the majority view when he said that, while religion was "tangled with all forms of abnormal, and even insane, mental vagaries," the science of psychology would help believers "recognize laws of abnormality as we do of normal processes, and we may separate the dross from the metal." In his writings Cutten performed this remarkable act of reform with analyses of everything from speaking in tongues to witchcraft, stigmatization, and miracles. He employed suggestion as other liberals had, as a way to account for illegitimate forms of religiousness, and he pointed to the familiar set of particularly suggestible groups: women, children, Southern "Negroes," and evangelicals. Cutten's ideological project is quite clear. "The negro saw spirits in everything while in Africa, and if he kept on good terms with spirits his duty was done. He felt no obligation to his fellowmen, and religion had nothing to do with moral conduct." Highly emotional believers had an unreliable moral compass. Cutten's prescriptions for change, carefully placed here and there in his text, can be summarized quite simply: be less emotional; practice self control. Quoting other experts on mobs, he averred that religious contagions "are held in check only if there are a considerable number of individuals scattered through the population who are trained in the habit of control, who are accustomed to subordinate feeling to rational considerations" and who resist the "tide of imitation and emotion."[31] Like Coe and other liberals, Cutten believed willpower and morality, not emotion, was the center of Christian faith.

Cutten was merely one example of an American using suggestion to forge a new normative religious discourse. The majority of psychologists of religion and other believing social scientists produced experimental results that either implicitly or explicitly authorized liberal religious positions. Later in life, Edwin Starbuck and several students devised empirical studies of experience and suggestibility that I introduced in chapter 5. In two such studies, performed by Starbuck's graduate students Thomas H. Howells and Robert D. Sinclair, these students correlated personality traits with religious styles. Howells's study, published in 1930, divided his subjects into conservatives (i.e., those who wanted to preserve "ancient traditions") and radicals (i.e., those "restless minds who wish for freedom and the open road"). He surveyed 542 undergraduates at the University of Iowa, and, based on their responses to a long questionnaire, identified 50 religious conservatives and 50 religious radicals. Howells then conducted a series of tests on individuals in these two groups. The tests were designed to assess motor and sensory abilities, willpower, suggestibility, motivation, and general intelligence. A series of sensorimotor tests involving auditory and sensory stimuli, electric shocks, coordination, muscle fatigue, and reaction time yielded few differences between the groups.[32]

But the second and third battery of tests, on willpower, suggestibility, and general intelligence, revealed significant differences. The tests on willpower and suggestibility were used to discover if there was "something in the volitional make-up of the orthodox person which renders him more susceptible to intense stimulation or to social suggestion, and therefore more likely to conform to the doctrines and practices of an established faith." Howells used five suggestibility tests. In the first, he showed subjects a picture of the British House of Parliament and then asked them to recall the picture's details, using questions that suggested the existence of elements in the picture that were not there. In the second, he assayed the effect of positive versus negative instructions on small coordination tests. In the third, fourth, and fifth tests, he did electrical shock experiments. In test three he told subjects that gradually the charge would increase and "that presently it would begin to be painful." For more suggestible subjects, this suggestion, and the fear and anticipation it elicited, heightened their experiences of pain and anxiety. In test four Howells applied a low-level current to subjects' hands, told them that the current would slowly be increased, and asked them to indicate when they detected a distinct increase in stimulation. In test five Howells showed subjects the rheostat, said they would experience sensations when it reached a certain level, secretly turned off the charge, and turned the rheostat gradually to that level and beyond, looking at the subject "with a serious and expectant mien." When radicals and conservatives were scored on these measures, Howells saw a clear pattern emerge: There seems, he concluded, "complete agreement among all five of the suggestibility tests in indicating the greater suggestibility of the conservative." Moreover, in the face of suggested punishments or criticism, conservatives faltered. "He [the conservative] is more timid, or, in the common expression, has less 'grit' or 'nerve' than the radical." He also was more influenced by the experimenter. In short, he had less willpower and was "more influenced by the immediate situation." The conservatives—that is, the evangelicals—were more suggestible.[33]

The third and last set of tests confirmed that conservatives could not think for themselves. Their general intelligence, measured by scores in tests on memory, judgment, and problem solving, was noticeably lower than the intelligence of the average radical. The facts that "in most of the tests the differences are large enough practically to guarantee that similar tests of a large number of similarly selected sample groups would show differences of the same kind," and that "the different bits of evidence [from all the tests] are mutually supporting," led Howells to the conclusion that conservatives were "relatively inferior in intellectual ability." Howells concluded his study by correlating questionnaire data on such measures as personality, health, church membership, and self-reported religious experiences with his two types, conservative and radical. Though differences were not always pronounced, he found that conservatives were more likely to go to church, be female, have had a conversion experience, and be older, more extroverted, more social, and more pessimistic.[34]

Howells's study is complemented by that of another graduate student, Robert Sinclair, who used data from the same questionnaire but was interested in understanding differences between those who reported having a religious (conversion) experience and those who did not. He divided students into "positive" ("mystics") and "negative" ("non-mystics") groups. His mystics overlapped considerably with Howells's conservatives. Sinclair's information showed that mystics were more suggestible, less intelligent, less coordinated, and had slower reaction times. They were more likely to "see visions" and "hear voices." Though these results seemed to indicate nonmystical superiority, Sinclair left open the possibility that mystics might be differently organized psychologically, and that their openness to mystical experience might lead to richer inner experiences, more energetic responses to life, and feelings of "adjustment and peace which enables the individuals to use more effectively the relatively inferior capacities which, according to the tests, they seem to have." These were backhanded compliments, to be sure.[35] As my previous chapter shows, though these liberals wanted a touch of experience to dissolve hardened forms of rationality, they clearly preferred what they thought of as sober and rational types of religious behaviors. "A chief trouble with religion today is that it is borne down by the weight of an outmoded tradition and shackled with an unconscious pride of caste and authority," Howells wrote in a different, more reflective, study; today's church did not have "a monopoly of either virtue or spirituality," and it was clear that its creeds, enticements, and superstitious religious behaviors appeared inadequate to the task of satisfying and motivating people. Howells had on his mind a typically liberal errand of religious reconstruction, one that began with differentiating the essential from the incidental and recasting those essentials in new forms. "The world needs to be persuaded to anticipate and even plan the occasional destruction of its little Buddhas, but always it should have courage to substitute more effective symbols" in their place. This was modern science as religious iconoclasm.[36]

In Howell's case, psychological tools were used to critique evangelicals in particular; but in fact psychological tools were employed ecumenically, and suggestion in particular was dispatched as a refining fire for a range of beliefs that seemed aberrant or excessive. Such was the case with liberals who argued against the strange revelations of spiritualist mediums, fortune-tellers, and psychic prognosticators. Combining in lecture demonstrations "the technic of a scientist" with the skills of an entertainer and "a speaker *par excellence*," the psychologist Howard Higgins toured Chautauqua circuits in the 1920s, showing how the psychology of suggestion accounted for psychical phenomena (figure 18). For rhetoric and content, Higgins drew on psychologists of deception such as Jastrow. The first part of his program was a séance that "demonstrated spirit forces, spirit vision, writing by an invisible hand, spirit slate writing," and so on. Carefully, Higgins crafted a séance in which doctors, psychiatrists, Catholic priests, and others in even "the most sophisticated audiences . . . are led to believe in the possibility of fortune-telling!" But this was merely a setup. "Dramatic, intensely interesting, educational and entertaining," the surprise ending that followed was one "in which the technics used to establish belief in fortune-telling are exposed." Moreover, in revealing the principles underlying psychic phenomena, Higgins engaged his audience in a "scientifically sound discussion of the psychology of suggestion—in an effort," Higgins hoped, "to protect the public against fraud." Higgins was interested in the psychology of public speaking and persuasion and thus crucially interested in suggestion: "In order to influence people's beliefs it would seem wise to understand how they get their beliefs." Drawing on psychological studies, suggestion theory, advertising, and psychology of religion texts such as Davenport's, Higgins created a powerfully suggestive environment: he invoked prestigious authorities, spoke with confidence, and repeated points hypnotically. Apparently, his lectures persuaded. Religious listeners in particular were convinced. One "not so easily pleased" seminary class from Concordia Seminary in St. Louis "commented again and again on [Higgins's] excellent program," while other Christians thought the show was "a real contribution to Christian thinking" or "a constructive piece of religious and education work."[37] Other popular psychologists lectured on similar topics, and with similar results. One pastor of a Baptist church in Chicago thought another itinerant psychologist's explanation of spiritualism "clean, amusing, mystifying, distinctly unique, and at the same time a telling blow against one of the worst delusions and false religions of the day." This pastor was not against belief in general, of course—just *this* kind of belief. Lecturers like these were bringing their assaults on

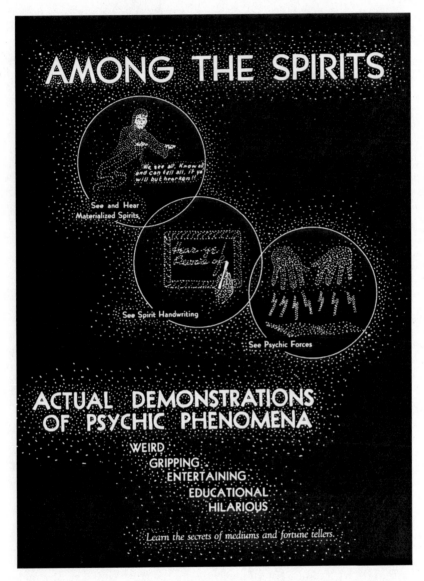

Figure 18.    Advertisement for Howard Higgins's lecture "Among the Spirits," 1920s. From the Redpath Chautauqua Collection, University of Iowa Libraries, Iowa City, Iowa.

spiritualism and other illegitimate systems to towns all over America. The credulous and the misled beware![38]

## PRACTICES OF GOD'S PRESENCE

Though its uses and explanatory powers had limits, as we have seen, suggestion remained a key way to think about how spirituality worked in the modern age. A range of religious liberals used this concept to help themselves overcome sin and achieve spiritual assurance.

One of the most important of these liberals was Henry Wood (1834–1908), a successful businessman who found relief from neurasthenia and dyspepsia in New Thought. Turning his prodigious energies to publishing, Wood wrote a number of influential popular books on mental healing and spiritual growth. Like others bathed in the light of new psychological thinking, Wood knew that mental and bodily states were fully integrated and that inner states strove to be expressed. This meant that managing your inner states was the crucial business of spiritual development: put the right thoughts in, and get the right attitudes and actions out. This kind of thinking undergirded liberal efforts to renew spirituality, to bring a remote God closer, and it functioned similarly in Wood's mind. His "ideal suggestions" were ways of "drawing directly from the Infinite Fountain of life, love and good, through the channel of one's own being"; all real spiritual progress, he insisted, has to be done not merely *"for* one, but *by* and *in"* one's self. "It develops self-reliance and spiritual independence, and strengthens those inner ties which bind every human soul to the parent 'Oversoul.'" Emersonian and new psychological elements combined to produce new spiritual disciplines in Wood and other liberals. Wood's spirituality was an individual act of harmonizing the self with the lawful divine forces that pulsed in and through everyone. He promoted suggestion as a sure way to open the self to these divine forces.[39]

While not deeply reasoned, Wood's spiritual manuals were clear and practical. He laid out in several steps how struggling believers might harmonize with immanent divine forces. To render the mind passive and receptive, Wood recommended retiring at some point during each day, alone and silent, in a restful position. Breathing deeply for a few minutes would relax the body and make the mind more open to "suggestions." Along with this recommendation, Wood provided sets of suggestive phrases in bold, full-page renderings, as well as accompanying meditations on these phrases. Individuals were to read carefully the longer meditations first and then fasten their eyes on the brief suggested phrase for ten to twenty minutes. "Do not merely look upon it, but wholly GIVE YOURSELF UP TO IT, until it fills and overflows the entire consciousness." Then readers were to close "the eyes for twenty to thirty minutes more; behold it with the mind's eye, and let it permeate the whole organism" and, later, to call it to mind during wakeful hours of the night. Believers had to inscribe those suggested phrases in their consciousness. These phrases affirmed that God was immanent in the self, and that human beings were receptive to divine impulses—"GOD IS HERE," "DIVINE LOVE FILLS ME," "I AM NOT BODY." Though confused, depressed, or afflicted believers might find these suggestions efficacious only gradually, they should not despair. The spiritual growth that resulted would not be instantaneous. This was not superstition or magic, Wood wrote. It was a natural and thus spiritually legitimate process of growing. In other books, he made this point more emphatically: "Absorb the ideals repeatedly until they *live* in and with you. They will increasingly become a spontaneous and well-defined feeling. The cure is not magical but a natural growth. Ideals tend toward expression and actualization." Wood used suggestion to rebuild the self from the inside out: "You gradually create a new world for yourself."[40]

Reiterating these suggestions was crucial. Wood recommended carrying them to work or using them in church services or family prayers. The suggestions could be "read slowly in concert, followed by concentration in the silence upon the ideal which forms the climax." Or they could be printed "in large text upon the walls of the room. . . . If made in gold or bright material especially, they may afterward be reproduced in consciousness and stand out to the mind's eye notably at night, in letters of fire. They photograph an idea upon the mind." Drawing on psychological discourses about habit, Wood pointed out that repetition of the suggestion would "wear a deep channel" in the self in which to accommodate "an ever increasing flow of force. . . . Every repetition of an ideal makes its impression deeper. There is more and more of its quality lodged in the subconscious mind. . . . Through reiteration the higher and purer thought develops and strengthens its corresponding brain-cells. Its physical functioning-ground thereby becomes more responsive, fertile and easier to use." Suggestions could be developed into this set of ideal habits, which, in turn, would change the (material) self.[41]

Other writers were more comfortable building systems of suggestion solely from the Bible and its spiritual promises. Though they could praise Wood's popular spiritual system, they improved it with sets of suggestions drawn from God's word. Here, sin and salvation remained crucial

Christian categories, even if suggestion provided new scientific methods of overcoming the one and preparing for the other. "Perfect love casteth out fear," "Be still and know that he is God," "All things are possible to him that believeth," "Thy faith has made thee whole"—one pastor recommended these biblical "suggestions" to believers who doubted, wondered, and worried. He knew from working with parishioners that, if "you will take these suggestions and use them quietly, trustfully, persistently, you can bring about a change in your whole interior life which will register its good results all through your body." His advice was fairly generic: the "inward reconstruction" that might result would banish morbid fears, distrust, and "cynical unbelief."

Most commentators knew that the site at which powerful forces of good and evil battled in the self was the subconscious, and many turned to suggestions to shape this part of the self. Suggestions might help Christians conquer sin, for example. The pastor at Washington Avenue Church in Brooklyn, Robert MacDonald, thanked God that the efficacious remedy for sin finally lay at hand, bestowed providentially by psychologists, a remedy that was "so simple, so strong, so rich that its curative force is difficult to realize and incredible to believe." It was of course the power of suggestion, which MacDonald was certain "will pull down evil and build up good within the soul more speedily and surely than all the remedial punishments of earth." Though the unconscious was thick with "evil instincts, wrong habits, [and] sickening realizations," biblical verses, when implanted properly there, "will spring up and choke out the weeds." The Bible was the "greatest source of powerful suggestions," and believers should whisper these powerful words to themselves at all times of day, remember them at bedtime, and meditate on them daily. This same pastor liked Wood's strategy, with slight modifications: Print out biblical suggestions in large letters, he instructed. "Place it on the wall of your silence chamber, or in some convenient place where you can sit, or lie in most easeful and relaxed position with the eye fixt upon it [sic]." Do not merely read it or gaze at it, but "yield yourself to it completely." A week's daily contemplation of the following biblical verse had cured a believer of morbid fears: "I have no fear. I am strong in the Lord." A week's contemplation of a different verse cured another of lust: "I am God's child. I am pure."[42] The science of suggestion was helping people believe.

Religious liberals toured the country offering advice about the best ways to suggest certainty to the self. The popular preacher and Chautauqua lecturer Elwin L. House (1861–1932), a Congregationalist who dealt "inspiringly and instructively with the fundamental facts of religion as interpreted by reverent modern psychology," insisted to grateful audiences that God's presence might be realized using different systems of suggestion, affirmation, and prayer (see figure 19).[43] House drew eclectically from New Thought, poetry, new psychologists, and the Bible. Like others, he talked about suggestion as the mechanism that explained different kinds of influences on the self. Suggestion was a part of advertising, healing, preaching, prayer, teaching, and child rearing. To use this power to cultivate faith involved quieting the self and concentrating on lodging affirmative statements in the quieted subconscious. Some of the most potent suggestions came when using the means of grace Christ instituted for the church—praying, going to church, preaching. Preaching was the "very highest" form of suggestion, for the preacher delivered God's authoritative word, the Holy Spirit created an atmosphere "charged with inspiration and uplift," and parishioners, for their part, brought sensibilities of faith, which were always necessary for suggestion to work. Prayer and personal Bible study were highly suggestive environments as well. In these situations worship "will thrill us and excite holy emotions, . . . rekindle old memories, awaken fresh sympathies, start new ideas, [and] deepen mighty convictions." House offered specific texts that believers might use.[44]

Believing with psychologists that inner ideas strove to express or actualize themselves, liberals monitored closely the ideas they tried to implant in the subconscious self. "Every mental activity creates a definite anatomical structure in the being who exercises the mental activity," House insisted. Thoughts were actual physical forces. At the very least, they had physical effects. House recommended only positive suggestions, only "affirmations." Like Wood and others, he had auditors repeat that they were a part of God, that God was in them, that they were spirit, and that the spirit was active in them. God would listen, God would save, God would heal. Others reinforced these characteristic emphases, insisting that fearful, unhappy, sinful thoughts led to crippling spiritual states. Autosuggestions about avoiding evil or merely escaping divine punishment conjured all kinds of horrible mental images—"pictures of all that is terrible in unquenchable fire; the everlasting torment of gnawing worms; the bottomless pit and outer darkness." Spirits concentrating on these images reinforced feelings of impotence. Many argued that the consciousness of hell, divine wrath, or the problem of sin, all frozen into the self with evangelical methods, might be replaced by more sanguine suggestions.[45] Contrasting two worship styles, faith and fear, the

# The Psychology of Religion

Body

Mind

Spirit

World
Conscious-
ness

Self
Conscious-
ness

God
Conscious-
ness

REV. ELWIN LINCOLN HOUSE, D. D.
Permanent Address
HOOD RIVER, OREGON

"Spiritual, Sensible, Uplifting, Magnetic."
*Rev. Jason N. Pierce, D. D., Washington, D. C.*

Figure 19.   E. L. House was certain that psychol-
ogy, when used properly, could strengthen Christian
faith. From an advertisement for House's lecture
"The Psychology of Religion," 1920s. From the
Redpath Chautauqua Collection, University of Iowa
Libraries, Iowa City, Iowa.

popular lecturer William Sadler pointed out that the "prayer of faith is
a source of favorable and powerful auto-suggestion to the mind of the
one who prays; while the prayer of doubt and fear may become highly
injurious because of its power of adverse suggestion. . . . Prayer," Sadler
insisted, "may be so prostituted as to become a source of moral weakness
and spiritual defeat." This was Coe's concern, as we saw in earlier chapters.
While these thinkers were quick to exclude evangelicalism from the range
of salvific and sane belief systems, in other ways they were ecumenical.

Liberal Christianity might reign supreme, but anyone from astrologers to hypnotists and quack doctors could reduce fear and increase health. Sadler was a doctor, and he suspected that you could monitor the successes or failures of your belief system by seeing how it registered in the body. Was it producing calm states? Fear and faith both produced characteristic heart rate patterns, postures of the head and body, and nervous or digestive states. Many New Thought practitioners turned to bodily states for signs of inner, spiritual conditions.[46]

While suggestion and autosuggestion tapped subconscious mechanisms, the processes themselves were always controlled consciously. Suggestive therapies always stressed the will. It is useful to point out again, then, that the religious psychologies of mainstream America, and certainly of different liberalisms, even in the postunconscious era, were often *consciousness* psychologies. They were psychologies of control, rationality, and the will. For these reasons, most religious liberals did not approve of hypnosis and other techniques that involved compromising one's self-control. The religious problem in America was precisely that believers were engaging in irrational and "hypnotic" behaviors. Though distressed souls were quite willing to put aside their reason, subduing believers in hypnosis only made them "irrational and unconscious" and too receptive to make clear religious judgments. Hypnosis was an "unnatural" and extreme form of suggestibility that weakened the will. This was disastrous because, in order to cultivate the proper kinds of faith, believers had to both accept suggestive aids and, more important, focus their attention on them.[47] In his outline of the four stages of suggestion, the pastor and (later) dean of the Hartford School of Religious Education, Karl Stolz, began by saying that a "distinct effort of the will" usually was necessary to "lodge the requisite idea in the mind." Always there were ideas and emotions that competed with the suggestion. "Uncritical attitudes, ideas which are emotionally toned, instinctual drives and basic wishes are held in mental focus without conscious effort," Stolz wrote. In order for the suggestion to penetrate the self, it "must be assented to as desirable or overpowering," and the will had to force it to "dominate the personality." Once fixed in the self with willful attention, the believer then had to expect the automatic reactions—new convictions, new ideas, and new actions instantiating the suggestion. Finally, there followed moments of passivity, when the suggested ideal ripened in the unconscious self. In general, though, the process was dependent on a strong will. Others devised techniques for exercising the will. The Reverend Thomas Boyd wrote in 1909 that individuals could practice focusing attention or consciousness on

certain small acts. They could focus on one part of the body and con-
centrate on the idea of heat. Did a warm glow come to that part of the body?
They might stand motionless for five minutes; open and close fingers slowly
and attentively; gaze steadily at an object for a minute without winking
(and gradually lengthen the time); touch someone in pain and say, "I will
the pain to depart"; or "close your eyes and construct the face of a friend,
feature by feature."[48] There were different ways to do it, but most agreed
that strengthening the will helped believers have a healthy and temperate
religious experience.

## HEALING AND BELIEVING

Because liberals borrowed psychological insights about the coextensive
nature of body, mind, and spirit, they saw mental and physical health as
indicators of saving spiritual states. For this reason, commonplace assumptions that liberals exchanged spiritual styles for therapeutic ones must be
qualified in some cases and rebutted in others. Often, interest in therapies
and psychological states was an indication not of religious decline but of
religious seriousness.

"Spiritual healing," Horatio Dresser, for example, once wrote, was "a
regenerative experience accompanying natural processes," a "change of
heart . . . from fear or hate to trust or love." This experience was partly a
change in one's consciousness and partly a supernatural intervention—a
divine-human cooperation that could result in both inner calm and physical health. "The restoration of the physical organism," Dresser thought,
asserting the primacy of the interior, "is incidental to an interior process of
regeneration to which the therapeutic process directly leads." Words like
*healing* were often used to talk about these new therapies, but the "process
was guided by spiritual insight and activity," and this fact made it more
than mere healing or psychotherapy. Metaphysical believers in particular
agreed that the state of the body, in health and sickness, was a reflection of
inner circumstances. Faith produced not just optimism, happiness, and confidence; it also created health and physical vigor. "Faith," another liberal
believer insisted, "is absolutely essential to the normal and ideal working of
every mental power and physical function." Others drew from psychology
and the New Testament to convince Christians that believing and physical
healing had to go together. One commentator worried that Christians had
become "unfamiliar with the doctrine of spiritual health for the body,"
and admonished others to reconsider not just how Jesus's physical healings
were crucial ingredients in his ministry but also the "incompatibility of

God's beauty with disease" and the ways God's power manifested itself in different layers, spiritual and physical, layers that gradually built up the self.[49]

Similar ways of relating healing and salvation were apparent in the Emmanuel Movement, a therapeutic ministry at Boston's Emmanuel Episcopal Church that would be imitated nationwide in the early twentieth century. Though the movement usually is interpreted as a psychological ministry to the sick and neurasthenic, it is more accurate to see it as a movement to restore spiritual power to the church. This was undoubtedly the intention of its founder, Elwood Worcester, who had a doctorate in psychology and had been a student of Wilhelm Wundt. Worcester wanted to revive the church and stave off defections to Christian Science and other new psychological and religious movements. "As a student of religion, I could not help seeing that some of the powers and spiritual uplift of Christ's religion had been lost." The twentieth-century church's low estate had resulted from the abandonment of its ministry of helpful service, as well as from a "loss of faith in the reality and power of the spirit."[50] These were constant refrains in Worcester's writings. As a minister he confessed to feelings of sadness that "in some way something has evaporated out of the gospel of Christ, and the Christian religion." Many ministers, Worcester admitted, "have the sad feeling . . . that it is getting harder and harder for them year by year to do the work of the ministry and to produce the spiritual effect on their people that they long so much to do." Worcester saw two parts to spiritual restoration: healing the church of false and archaic beliefs, and healing individuals suffering from disbelief, nervousness, and other illnesses. Because he was influenced by the body-spirit monism of psychology, Worcester saw the two tasks as intimately related. To heal the church, Worcester prescribed a dose of biblical criticism: he recognized only the "theology of the New Testament as modern critical scholarship has disclosed it" and turned his attention to discarding beliefs that did not pass critical tests. As Worcester saw it, biblical criticism would not only excise the irrational accretions of the church but also isolate important aspects of Christianity that had been ignored or lost. "As a student of the New Testament and of early church history[,] I knew that something valuable had been lost from the Christian religion, and that Christianity had not always been so unsuccessful in its appeal to human nature as it is now." What specifically had been lost? The healing ministry of Jesus Christ himself had been lost, together with "the Gospel of a Savior's love" and "a religion of the Spirit and of Power."[51] Once rediscovered through a critical examination of the Bible, the spirit and the power of faith would purify the church and restore hope.

The second and perhaps more important aspect of Worcester's spiritual renewal concerned the amelioration of spiritual and mental disorders. Here Worcester also used modern tools to excise anything moribund. New psychological techniques would have to help, for older methods were not working. "The kind of spiritual advice and treatment ordinarily dispensed by the Church through its ministers is too unscientific and inexact to be counted on to remove doubts, to calm disturbed minds, to procure sleep, to overthrow degrading habits such as alcoholism or morphinism, to dispel fixed ideas and obsessive fears, and the whole terrible brood of chimeras which render the lives of these persons intolerable." In the body-spirit monism of new psychologies, everything was related: physical cures helped the spirit; resolving doubts led to physical health. Content to leave "organic" (physical) illnesses to physician colleagues, Worcester concentrated on curing the spiritual self, and for this he prescribed a most potent elixir: Christianity. Shorn of its superstitious accretions, Christianity "has ideas and emotions which can release psychic forces strong enough to create a unified state of mind in which inhibitions, weaknesses, [and] disharmonies incline to disappear, with consequent beneficial reaction on the physical organism." A properly toned Christianity cured everything. (There are signs that trumping the doctors with this spiritual panacea sent ripples of discontent through Boston's medical community and set off boundary disputes among doctors and other kinds of healers.) But wasn't Christ both teacher and physician?[52]

Suggestion was a crucial category to Worcester because it helped him accomplish both of his aims. Because it accounted on naturalistic terms for magical, superstitious, or excessive beliefs, it helped Worcester purify the church; because it helped believers understand and perform acts of faith, it helped Worcester transform troubled believers into confident ones.

Worcester embraced suggestion as a way of promoting faith and healing in distressed patients. After triaging patients and sending those with "organic" diseases to medical colleagues, Worcester and other ministers funneled patients into the heart of the Emmanuel Movement, the weekly meetings or "mental health classes." As Taves has written, Worcester "attached religious significance to all three aspects of the weekly meeting—the individual therapy, the service, and the social gathering—and viewed each as having the power to affect healing." Worcester explained his suggestive techniques in countless books and magazine articles. In individualized counseling sessions, he began by making the patient calm by instructing him "how to relax his arms, his legs, his neck, head and body, so that there shall be no nervous tension or muscular effort." He informed his patients that they were relaxed, and that in their relaxed state they should "lazily follow my words." Worcester attached religious significance to the passive state that resulted. Jesus himself had pointed to this state as a prerequisite for spiritual certainty, warning "men against injurious agitation and passion, against anger, fear, and anxious care." Jesus extolled calm and peace. "When our minds are in a state of peace and our hearts open and receptive to all good influence," Worcester said, "I believe that the Spirit of God enters into us and a power not our own takes possession of us." The moral and religious changes that resulted from his treatments, Worcester felt, were too dramatic and long-lasting to be the result of mere relaxation or mechanical psychological principles. Drawing heavily on James and others interested in the subconscious and psychical energies, he was fairly certain that, in suggestive therapies, individuals tapped spiritual energies and used them to help regenerate themselves.[53]

Once patients were relaxed and receptive, they were ready to absorb different suggestions. The Emmanuel Movement as a whole provided a range of ways of suggesting faith and healing. In individual counseling sessions, ministers and others gave curative suggestions in positive and simple statements—pain was diminishing, sleep would certainly return, doubt would change into certainty. These short phrases would be repeated, and individual sessions might last from fifteen minutes to an hour. Individual interviews took place in a partitioned corner of the chancel or in more private settings. The enthusiasm ministers felt when working in these settings, and the power they associated with suggestion, is clear in the account of one minister who wrote that any minister so engaged "will now be thrilled through and through with emotions of reverence and awe. What manner of man ought he to be to touch the delicate and complicated mechanism of the human body; yea, to come in contact with the naked soul! He can now suggest to the subconscious the ideas that it may need to correct or direct or stimulate it." The minister in such situations was "invited into the most secret chambers of the man's being. He is afforded all the advantages that the wisest and best Catholic priest finds in the confessional. In a word, the way is open for him to help remake a man." But these pastoral encounters were merely the beginning. Suggestion was at work in religious services as well, creating not the "lawless and ungovernable mob spirit of strong excitement" characteristic of other forms of religiousness, Worcester noted, but a more rational "mass impression," one with "no excitement, no fanaticism, no sensationalism, but earnest faith tempered by sober thought." In such settings, "when the human spirit is calm and impressionable and open to all good influence, I believe that a higher Spirit, the Spirit of all goodness enters into us, takes possession of us and leads us in better ways." Worcester fashioned suggestive social settings too—music, food, and talk of anything "except sickness."[54]

Nothing succeeded like success. Imitators used similar techniques for healing and believing and discussed these techniques using words like *suggestion, impression,* and *affirmation.* Like Worcester's movement, the healing ministry of Bertram Runnals, rector of an Episcopal church in Corvallis, Oregon, tried to revive the church by borrowing insights from psychology and New Thought. His manual, *Suggestions for Conducting a Church Class in Psycho-Therapy* (1915), began with introductory statements that gathered together the liberal spectrum: there was one by the Episcopal bishop of Spokane, Washington, and another by Annie Payson Call. Call's foreword was essentially a set of relaxation exercises for Runnals's readers, exercises that might help readers prepare body and soul to "receive clear impressions and then to express them in daily life." Every clear impression had to be preceded by suggestive therapies. For his part, Runnals outlined church services that moved believers through the therapeutic sequence: from relaxation and passivity to suggestions for renewed faith and health. His recommended progression went from hymns that produced "an atmosphere of calm and resignation" and opening prayers that might "stimulate a belief in and a desire for the presence of the great Father" to specific Bible readings and study sessions on such topics as self-control, the uses of introspection, and the will. Runnals went so far as to enclose sample promotional materials for the "Emmanuel Class in Personal Religion" and specific directions about how to lead discussions, manage dissent, and arrange the music, decor, and chairs.[55]

Many others in the Protestant mainstream developed practical advice for using suggestion and similar techniques. Addressing himself to the problems of undesirable emotions and spiritual states, one of these Protestants, the Reverend Thomas Boyd, pointed in 1909 to several ways that religious suggestions might be employed. One was merely to command undesirable emotions away. "Affirm with all the positive purpose of your character that hatred has no place or part in your life." If this failed, believers could replace undesirable inner states with their antidotes, substituting thoughts of hate with love, for instance. "Affirm over and over that love dominates you; that you do and will act upon its dictates alone. Hold your attention upon the remedy, and soon its power will fill the mind and heart, and your disturbing disease-producing thought will flee. . . . Every sinful thought," Boyd was sure, "that wars against the soul, poisons the imagination," and "weakens the will" can be "routed[,] and all can be set right by the application of this spiritual chemistry." The resulting admixture functioned like an antiseptic "against the germs of doubt and worry and all disease and pain-producing emotions." Boyd had other tricks for catalyzing this spiritual chemistry. In pastoral situations, he assured patients that powerful faith- and health-producing forces lay close at hand. "The forces I am about to set in motion for your recovery are within yourself," he purred. "There is no magical influence about it. I am going to use my knowledge of the vital forces of life to set them to work harmoniously, to restore you to perfect health. . . . Let your thoughts turn to God in the confidence that he is good, and kind, and loving," and "think of yourself as being one with this perfect life." After thus addressing himself to the spongy underside of the self, the unconscious, Boyd addressed the conscious mind as well, instructing believers to use their conscious minds to focus on the suggestions of health, faithfulness, and courage.[56]

When Boyd gave suggestions, he would also sometimes stand behind patients and "gently strike downward and outward from the top head and forehead, with my hands." In particularly difficult cases he apparently used his hands in different ways. Encountering one young man who stammered, shuffled, shifted his gaze, and had trouble with his temper, digestion, and sleeping—a tough case to be sure—Boyd had him recline, relax, and think of peace and courage and strength. "I stood by his side, making full passes [with my hands] over his head, arms, body, and limbs, for two or three minutes." Standing at his side and "placing my thumb on his forehead at the root of his nose," he coached him with relaxing suggestions and assurances of normal functions of body and mind. Boyd posed himself as a successful operator awed by the mysterious forces that brought healing and spiritual calm. He wondered about the nature of the forces: Were they physical, spiritual, psychological? Were they magnetic fluids? Somehow, "in the presence of this unknown quantity called suggestion, we must stand with confidence in power that works in him thru God." These were the mystical places where healing became believing, and believing, healing.[57]

"Thoughts are forces"—this might serve as the adage of the age. But how precisely were they so? Were thoughts physical waves, streams, or energies? Were they physical things? While speculating about such matters divided those in liberal religious circles, psychological discourses often encouraged believers to think in physiological terms. Even the sober and well-educated dean of Yale Divinity School, Charles Reynolds Brown, affirmed in 1910 that "thoughts are things, and their power for good or ill can be accurately weighed and measured." By linking thoughts to physiological processes, Brown's scientific colleagues at Yale helped him probe the physiological side of our inner life. One professor there suspended a young man on a balanced fulcrum and asked him to "think of some difficult problem in mathematics and to try to solve it mentally." The scale tipped toward the man's head. Then the subject was asked to think about running and playing football. The scale tipped towards his feet. Brown's intention was to prove the power of (religious) ideals; in an ironic move typical of the day, he used science to prove a nonmechanical conception of the self. In any case, Brown could also remind his readers that the Bible had affirmed this long ago: "As a man thinketh in his heart, so he becomes!" Thoughts were real forces.[58]

Others imagined thought forces in more freewheeling ways, unfolding physiological discourses and talk of suggestion into rich systems of healing and believing. Though many of these systems would have seemed eccentric to liberal Protestants like Charles Brown, in fact it was not far from Brown's position to insist, as the spiritualist minister E. W. Sprague did in 1930, that because "mortals are all spirits" everything mental and spiritual took on physical forms. This was a common position among New Thought and metaphysical believers. It meant that through suggestive processes, through thinking in certain ways, a believer could "send his vital forces to any part of the body," setting in motion "magnetic auras and vital fluids of the physical organism," bringing healing, wholeness, and holiness. Sprague developed various suggestive therapies to help people mentally control their physical conditions, and he toured the country for many years, teaching spiritualist truths and proving them with channeled spirit messages and other kinds of empirical tests. Upon retiring at night, Sprague recommended repeating this: "I am feeling better tonight, I will improve in health and strength while I sleep and shall awaken in the morning refreshed and feeling well. Dear spirit friends, help me to be firm and to carry out this determination." He had different phrases for other times of day. Other people had similar ideas. New Thought writers argued that cells, nerves, and organs had different forces and frequencies, insisting that these forces could be cajoled and quickened with different verbal and mental commands. William Walker Atkinson suggested useful commands. "Here stomach! Do this . . ." Heart! Please do that . . .[59]

As powerful as they were, sometimes such suggestions were not enough. Sometimes mental actions did not move physical forces with alacrity. In these cases, these forces could be moved by hand. Sprague, for instance, provided detailed instructions on the spiritual and physical dynamics of therapeutic healing (figure 20). The illustration shows "the spirit hand applying the spiritual forces to the base of the healer's brain while he is treating the patient." The spirit hand recharged the healer's nervous system, as the healer cleared the way for these healing forces by "throwing off the diseased magnetism by snapping it off his finger ends," shunting illness downward through the spine, patting, beating, and massaging painful blockages and opening up the body's energies. As "the last act of his treatment, he should make passes from the head of the patient to his feet, going all around him, gently touching him or coming close to his body to equalize and cause the gentle circulation of the patient's magnetism." Here mental forces were physically handled; but treatments worked best when healers and patients also used the mind to corral or gather the energies. The healer applied treatment by "slapping, patting, rubbing, and willing his healing forces to act upon these [ill] organs, placing his hands upon the diseased organs principally, thinking, and determinedly willing, a cure for his patient." Sprague and other metaphysical believers followed in the footsteps of earlier innovators, especially Andrew Jackson Davis, who used body and mind to collect magnetic forces and cultivate clairvoyance, inspiration, and the highest spiritual states.[60]

For all these liberals, psychological assurances that the mind was somehow coextensive with the physiological self undergirded spiritualities in which healing and believing were metaphors of one another.

. . .

When the great opponent of spiritualism and psychical phenomena Hugo Munsterberg unexpectedly died in the winter of 1916, collapsing halfway through a lecture to Radcliffe undergraduates, it gave his opponents an opportunity to utter the final word on matters spiritual and psychical. For years Munsterberg had studied and debunked mediums and psychics, and he, like Jastrow, used categories such as suggestion to account for these supposedly supernatural phenomena. Just after his death he spoke again, however, this time to a Boston medium, who reported what amounted

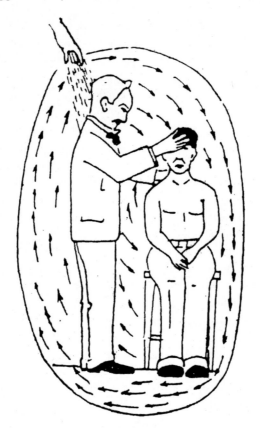

## HOW TO HEAL BY LAYING ON OF HANDS

Figure 20.   Applying spiritual forces to the body. From E. W. Sprague, *The Science of Magnetic, Mental, and Spiritual Healing*, 1930. Reprinted with permission.

to an astonishing reversal. "When I was an inhabitant of the earth I did not then find any proofs that excarnate beings communicate with their earth friends," Munsterberg confessed. "Although I have been in the spirit world but a brief time, I have received absolute proof that excarnate beings can and do communicate with their earth friends." "However valuable the messages I may bring in future time," he continued, "this one to-day is important. Spirit return is a truth. I am Hugo Munsterberg." There was no way for Munsterberg to test, counter, or refute his own incredible statements, which were picked up and printed in a small column in the *New*

*York Times.* As his biographer has written, in this one final moment, "he was appropriated . . . by the public to meet its own needs."[61]

Such examples of a public attempting to undo the careful lifework of a scientist might strike us as perverse, but this is merely an extreme example of how ordinary Americans reworked or resisted scientific discourses—especially when these discourses seemed hegemonic, simplistically reductive, or destructive of deeply held beliefs. And the public had less underhanded ways of turning scientific discourses to their advantage. The brief history of suggestion that I have sketched here is one example of how categories originally fashioned to explain religiousness in secular terms could also be used to reform and, in many cases, promote belief.

# Epilogue

*Intensely Unsettled—Again*

There are several possible endings to this story. One is that, in the end, believers mishandled the sharp edge tools of science and abetted secularization in its different American forms. In fact, this has become a conventional way of thinking about this period and about religious liberals in particular, as I pointed out in my introduction. Though I find this way of thinking about science and liberal religion problematic, there is no question that science unsettled American believers and prompted or helped sustain intellectual journeys out of old-time religions. Some individuals left their childhood faiths behind forever. But as I have tried to show in this book, psychological traditions could aid faith as well as obliterate it. These traditions were used to reform and revive religion—to purify it of nonessentials, to make its spiritual objectives comprehensible and plain. Historians have too often ignored psychological strategies that Americans used to reconstruct older forms of faith or develop new ones. For these reasons, I think the story here is more complicated than clear conflict and decline. I have tried to draw attention to the complex exchanges and ambiguities, and especially the ways that American believers struggled to turn psychology·to their advantage. When we bring all of these developments into focus, the idea that psychology caused religious decline seems dubious or, at best, incomplete.

A second, more illuminating conclusion to my story comes into view as we consider what happened to religion and psychology in the twentieth century. The first striking fact to consider here is the shift in attitudes toward psychology among believers between 1900 and 1950. Before the twentieth century, American believers struggled to mediate between psychology's single vision of the world and religious needs and aspirations. They tried to render psychological symbols and discourses in ways that were either not hostile to faith or clearly supportive of it. There were many dimensions to this project, as we have seen, ranging from liberals borrowing phrenological notions to others using later scientific methods to map and demystify the inner, spiritual impulses that confounded them. In this earlier period and even throughout the first half of the twentieth century, these borrowers sensed that psychology had to be handled carefully, that its meanings had to be monitored and controlled. As the twentieth century wore on, however, American believers appeared less worried about psychology. Their uses of it diversified and became less tinged with anxiety. By the middle of the twentieth century, one perceptive liberal theologian even noted that "too many theologians are content to pay but passing attention to psychology," thinking "that the issues are already settled." Why had the urgent need to harmonize waned? Had the issues been settled? Why were theologians and others suddenly less anxious about using psychological insights?[1]

. . .

The answers have to do with a remarkable set of changes in psychology that began early in the century, changes related to the decline of positivism and the emergence of a broader culture of probablism and uncertainty in science. The role of the revolution in physics in all of this can be overstated, but the dramatic nature of new discoveries in that field did influence psychologists and other intellectuals through indirect and direct channels. The works of Albert Einstein (1879–1955), Max Planck (1858–1947), and Werner Heisenberg (1901–1976) are usually pointed to as crucial, for these men in the early decades of the twentieth century shattered the Newtonian model that had for so many years anchored the positivist worldview. Planck was the first to notice that Newtonian mechanics could not explain certain phenomena, such as the odd behavior of light, which at times appeared to be a continuous electromagnetic wave, as classical mechanics predicted, and at other times seemed to be composed of discontinuous energy packets. Planck named these energy packets "quanta," and quickly other scientists, especially Albert Einstein, called attention to the significance of Planck's quanta by pointing out that they made sense of hitherto inexplicable phenomena, including why electrons ejected from certain metals when they were irradiated by light. Einstein extended the quantum hypothesis to other problems in physics, as did other physicists and mathematicians, and it gradually became clear that *all subatomic objects* had both wave and particle natures. Matter and energy were somehow interchangeable.

The implications of these discoveries entirely reoriented the field. In 1927, the German physicist Werner Heisenberg drew attention to another unsettling implication of quantum science when he showed that the process of observation itself influenced how elementary particles behaved. His "uncertainty principle" stated that, the more we knew about the velocity of a particle, the less we could know about its position. But Heisenberg was not the only one adding complications. The German physicist Max Born (1882–1970) suggested that elementary particles were made up of *nothing but* probabilities: All particles were merely "tendencies to exist" that became (what we call) particles when we added the element of "looking" at them. Was physical reality somehow constituted or at least influenced by our observations of it? Such questions became impossible to avoid even for scientists who detested philosophical speculations. In a well-known 1935 dialogue with Einstein, the Danish physicist Niels Bohr pointed out, in the words of one historian of science, "that recent developments in quantum mechanics demanded a complete renunciation of the classical ideal of causality and a radical revision of attitudes toward the problem of physical reality." "We can no longer consider 'in themselves' those buildingstones of matter which we originally held to be the last objective reality," Heisenberg insisted in another reflection on physics and philosophical problems. "This is so because they defy all forms of objective location in space and time, and since basically it is always our *knowledge* of these particles alone which we can make the object of science. . . . Thus even in science the object of research is no longer nature itself, but man's investigation of nature." Though the meanings of this dramatic reorientation in science were contested, there is no question that things once considered solid had evaporated into unstable energies, paradoxical wave/particle entities, and even human wishes and projections. The world appeared more paradoxical, energetic, and subtle. As a result, positivist scientists made fewer confident proclamations in the 1920s, 1930s, and 1940s. Many wondered about the implications of these new uncertainties and the breakdown of the older, rigidly mechanistic framework.[2]

If the hard sciences in this period experienced a loss of confidence in older certainties, there was no possibility that the human sciences, which so self-consciously modeled themselves on physics, could avoid similar strains. However, for a time in the second, third, and fourth decades of the twentieth century, psychologists ignored uncertainties and proceeded as if an exact human science was possible. By the 1920s, behaviorism was the dominant American psychology and the inheritor of earlier, positivist aspirations to a cause-and-effect account of human nature. Behaviorists could be critical of earlier "new psychologists," who, while attempting to build certain knowledge of the self by studying reflex actions, often found themselves mired in unscientific categories such as mind and conscious-ness. So behaviorists made a final attempt to excise mind altogether: their psychology put in play only measurable behaviors, which were provided in spades by pigeons, monkeys, and especially rats trained to respond in certain ways to stimuli. But though they were well trained, laboratory animals often acted in ways not accountable on behaviorist principles.

Several problems for behaviorists came into focus. First of all, the prin-ciples of conditioning turned out not to be universal. Different species had different preferences and abilities. Some learned easily and others did not. Some appeared to think as they ran through mazes or accomplished cer-tain tasks—and according to some psychologists, such as Edward Tolman (1886–1959), their internal processes and states mattered. Many behav-iorists turned to experiments on motivation, personality, reasoning, and creativity, and some became disillusioned with behaviorism. Though the classic behaviorist theories "were formulated and tested in terms of simple learning, behind the scenes there was always the presumption that these theories could be applied to all behavior," one psychologist remembered. There was also the presumption "that most of the basic laws of learning had already been discovered[,] and all that remained was the minor problem of resolving the few systematic issues that separated the main theorists." But "by the middle of the century it had become clear that the classic theories of learning were limited in scope[,] and that the stature of our scientific knowledge was pre-Galilean rather than post-Newtonian." Other retro-spective judgments were less measured. "Contemporary American scien-tific psychology is the sterilist of the sterile," the psychologist Nehemiah Jordan wrote in 1968, sounding Jamesian accents. "Years of arduous labor and the assiduous enterprise of hundreds of professors and thousands of students have yielded precisely nothing. . . . In the fifty-three years since that 'momentous' occasion [John Watson's 1913 behaviorist manifesto] can *one* positive contribution towards any increased knowledge of man be pointed to? None such can be found."[3]

Others sensed difficulties with behaviorism much earlier and experi-mented with alternatives. Some of the most vigorous assaults on behav-iorism came from the founders of the Gestalt school, many of whom were deeply influenced by developments in physics. Max Wertheimer (1880–1943) was a close friend of Albert Einstein; and Wolfgang Kohler (1887–1967) was profoundly influenced by Planck. The third founder of the Gestalt school was Kurt Kaffka (1886–1941), who, in his classic 1935 statement, the *Principles of Gestalt Psychology*, took up quite directly the problems with psychological positivism. "If there is any polemical spirit in this book," Kaffka wrote, "it is directed not against persons but against a strong cultural force in our present civilization for which I have chosen the name positivism." He defined positivism as efforts to use the concepts and methods of the physical sciences in all other fields of inquiry, and he considered this procedure illegitimate intellectually and harmful morally, as did other Gestaltists. All Gestaltists insisted not just that positivist psychologies disintegrated human values and impoverished us but also that the fundamental tenets of positivist psychologies (especially behaviorism) were patently false. Psychologists had made a "cult" of the fact and fact-finding, and had not considered interpretations, contexts, and how facts assemble into cohesive wholes; they reduced complicated human thoughts and actions to the categories of physics, which were themselves unstable; they collapsed the human self into a set of preposterous maxims concerning behavior; and they developed overspecialized experimental subdisciplines. But the harshest critiques blamed positivism in its various forms for the cultural malaise that gripped Western societies.[4] Science and industrial society were driving unprecedented cultural changes, undercutting older idealist, religious, and humanist traditions without, it seemed, providing suitable replacements.

Dismay was particularly powerful among academics in the birthplace of modern psychology, Germany. Friedrich Paulsen (1846–1908), a philosopher and educator who had studied with Gustav Fechner and who was the leading authority on German education at the turn of the twentieth century, diagnosed what seemed a critical situation.

> Something like disappointment is perceptible because scientific research does not seem to redeem its promise to supply a complete and certain theory of the universe and practical world-wisdom grounded in the very necessity of thought. Former generations had been supplied with such conceptions by religion or theology. Philosophy inherited this place in the eighteenth century. . . . Then a new generation, as distrustful of reason (Hegelian metaphysics) as the former had been of faith, turned to science with expectations that exact research would place us upon sure footing and supply us with a true theory of the world. But that science cannot do. It has become more and more evident that it does not realize such an all-comprehensive world view that will satisfy both feeling and imagination. It only discovers thousands of fragmentary facts, some of them tolerably certain, especially in the natural sciences, which at least supply a basis for practice; some of them doubtful, forever capable of revision, as in the historical sciences. The

result is a feeling of disappointment. Science does not satisfy the hunger for knowledge nor does it supply the demand for personal culture.
It demands the investment of one's full strength and offers but scant
reward. Such disappointment is widespread.

Paulsen was no Gestaltist, but the "disappointment" he acknowledged was
widespread, stemming from the fact not just that behaviorism was wrong
but that its cultural consequences were disastrous. Gestaltists returned
again and again to the same theme. During the last "few hundred years
learning and research have fought any stable mental orientation," Kohler
complained; "can it be mere accident that, in the past, science has tended
to destroy any conviction to which it found mankind clinging, and that
at present it seems eager to destroy what may still be left?"[5]

Disillusionment with older, positivist psychologies proceeded unevenly.
Some intellectuals kept hopes alive for a more complete, scientific account
of the self; others developed new ways of thinking psychologically, and
new psychological schools were born—cognitive, gestalt, humanistic.
These schools proliferated, as did their models of the self. The general
trend in the field, though, was that psychologists, like other scientists,
became more reflexive about their work. This point was made persuasively by James Capshew in 1999. One marker of this reflexive turn,
Capshew noted, was the American Psychological Association's comprehensive review of psychological fields, a massive self-study project initiated in 1952. There were two parts to the study, both of which took many
years to complete: Project A, on the "methodological, theoretical, and
empirical status of psychological science," and Project B, which examined
"occupational, educational, and institutional problems." Project A was
enthusiastically directed by Sigmund Koch (1917–1996), a psychologist
at Duke University who embraced the self-study as a way of calling attention to key psychological concepts that could be used to advance the field
as a whole. Koch solicited, reviewed, and edited almost eighty different
manuscripts for the projected multivolume series. By 1963, six volumes
had appeared. As he directed the project, he came to believe what critics
of the regnant behaviorism had come to believe: that the results of much
experimental work amounted to trivia. He also came to see that hopes for
a single-vision, progressive science required a kind of blind faith that had
become untenable. He planned a seventh volume to the series, a critique
of the field and a contribution (he said) to a "post-positivist psychology,"
a volume that he never completed. Still, Koch spent a good deal of his
later career working on these criticisms and on possibilities for new psychological directions.[6]

Koch's life reveals how unsettling these intellectual changes could be. Koch described these changes in terms usually found in religious or theological contexts—*delusion, spiritual malaise, doubt.* "In my earliest years qua psychologist I was myself victim to the delusion-complex I have sought to describe. But between 1942 (when I started to teach at Duke University) and the early 1950s, the scales fell gradually from my eyes." Before the scales fell, he was an immature undergraduate, vulnerable to the assured proclamations of professors and advisors. "In no time at all, I was a confirmed positivist, with confident answers to the conveniently narrow range of questions that the [field] accredited as 'meaningful.'" As a graduate student at Duke, Koch plunged enthusiastically into experimental work—"naturally, my companion in the venture was to be the rat"—and his early publications marked him as an up-and-coming figure. "I continued in my early post-doctoral years to percolate happily as a comparative analyst of theory and sententious logical positivist lawgiver." He stridently critiqued others who engaged in "informal, sloppy, or indeed 'literary' theorizing." But in private he was having doubts. The problems that troubled him were the same ones others worried about—the universality of scientific, and specifically behaviorist, laws; the influence of beliefs or thoughts (also called "intervening variables") on experimental procedures; and the limitations of observation and measurement. Though he remembered his psychological doubts as being related less to the general "attrition upon positivism that began to become evident . . . in philosophic and other contexts external to psychology" than to "an incipient feeling that the dominating theories of the pre-war era and their post-war successors were disappointingly unproductive of knowledge that was worth having," both factors probably had a role in altering his conceptions. There was, as well, the personal cost of producing such experimental trivialities. In the 1940s and 1950s, Koch felt a dawning spiritual malaise not unlike that felt by other psychologists, European and American, in the early twentieth century. "There was in me a severe malaise of spirit which I warded off by an excess of certitude," he remembered. He had become "anaesthetic" to culture, literature, and the arts, passions cherished before graduate school. "My early passions for literature and the arts . . . were, if not totally obliterated, hermetically sealed off. My *scientific* thinking was not to be vulgarized by such matters!" He began to loathe and avoid work. At some point—and the American Psychological Association's self-study certainly was a part of this—Koch seriously reexamined his work and convictions, a process that "was slow, and not devoid of fear," and one that led to his later belief that the "syndrome" of "positivism" was "the most pervasive feature of Western sensibility from the late nineteenth century through the present." Late in life Koch remained an unsettled psychologist. He was still, he said, without "any messianic idea, 'new' or old, that would unify or reorient psychology, or human knowledge in general, or provide a convenient key to the cosmic ontology, or an ultimate to why such a key cannot be found." But he did know something important: psychology, he said, with more self-deprecating humor than bitterness, "works towards attenuation and denial of the very qualities in its inquirers which could render their inquiry worthwhile."[7]

There were other reasons for this disillusionment with psychology, and the general public was picking up on them. By the 1960s a generation nurtured on behaviorist advice came of age, and, as David Bakan has written, "almost as soon as this generation could sing their own songs" they were chanting sarcastically about soundproof, germ-proof Skinner boxes and other ridiculous mechanical child-rearing devices. These were the baby boomers, and their laidback programs for life experimentation made the laboratory experimentation of psychologists seem artificial and inconsequential. This generation was hard on science in general. Had science's visionary promises been kept? Had science delivered on robotic household servants, flying automobiles, personal helicopters, and cheap sources of energy? Had it improved the quality of life or offered greater national security? Science, for many Americans, was atom bombs, pollution, thalidomide, and napalm. The prototypically rational man was also the one sending them to Vietnam, Robert McNamara. Prophecies of a scientific golden age now appeared ludicrous, as did encouragements, such as those of the anthropologist Alfred Kroeber, to continue believing in scientific progress. "In proportion as a culture disengages itself from reliance on" things like magic and superstition, Kroeber wrote in 1948, "it may be said to have registered an advance." Setbacks came from atavistic attitudes "chiefly among individuals whose social fortune is backward or who are psychotic, mentally deteriorated, or otherwise subnormal." Clearly the ideas of the "most ignorant, warped and insane" in society should be disregarded. "Or," Kroeber asked rhetorically, "are our discards, insane, and hypersuggestibles right and the rest of us wrong?" By midcentury, many were turning against Kroeber and his scientific colleagues, looking for truth in other pursuits—altered states, intuition, meditation, and other activities that "hypersuggestibles" would have excelled in.[8]

Critics proliferated. Joseph Wood Krutch, the powerful writer and sensitive diagnostician of America's modern malaise, thought the massive investment in science was a disastrous miscalculation that left Americans confounded and apprehensive. Our technologies—and psychologies—were killing us. "We have engineered ourselves into a position where, for the first time in history, it has become possible for man to destroy his whole species. May we not at the same time have philosophized ourselves into a position where we are no longer able to manage successfully our mental and spiritual lives?" Were mechanistic models of the self stripping us of dignity and confidence? And, to ask the more important question, were they accurate? Krutch wondered. "Perhaps we have been deluded by the fact that the methods employed for the study of man have been for the most part those originally devised for the study of machines or the study of rats, and are capable, therefore, of detecting and measuring only those characteristics which the three do have in common." These were Kochian accents. But while Krutch himself was troubled and woolly, others, perhaps given less to neurasthenia, came right out and said it: science was pathological. Koch himself had said as much about psychology in his characteristically humorous tracts. But he was outdone by others. In a popular diatribe with the unsubtle title *Science Is a Sacred Cow* (1950), Anthony Standen censured especially scientific studies of human beings, including psychological work that reduced human phenomena to material causes, measured internal states and emotions, and, after it was all over, yielded insignificant results. "Psychologists can't ask the right questions, and they have given up . . . the best way we have of understanding men, but with these limitations they are doing their best," Standen jeered. "It is probable that, hundreds of years from now," he predicted, helping his opponents into history's trash heap, "people will look back at our 'objective' psychologists, with their reflex arcs and their stimuli and responses, in the same way in which we look back at the medieval schoolmen who are alleged to have debated how many angels could dance on the point of a pin." For psychologists observing this situation, these sentiments must have seemed like an astonishing reversal. Many, like Koch, were seeing both their models of mind and their mentalities intensely unsettled.[9]

. . .

In sum then, in the first half of the century, many lost faith in what one commentator has called the "single-vision" psychological positivism of the turn of the century. This loss of faith had to do with both the rise of uncertainty in science and the fragmentation of psychology into different and often opposed schools. These developments did not spell the decline of psychology; quite the contrary—they created the conditions for its proliferation. There is no question that we now live in a culture framed by psychological categories and discourses. But there is a difference between contemporary psychological discourses and the psychology that dominated American culture between 1880 and 1930. That psychology was positivist in a way that ours is not. Today we live in a culture of diverging and multiplying psychological discourses, a culture that is probably both more psychological and more religious at the same time. And it is a culture, therefore, in which psychological and religious hybrids exist more easily and in more combinations.[10]

What are some of those combinations? What are some of the ways that American believers in the second half of the twentieth century used psychological insights to think about or produce faith?

The first thing to mention is the astonishing growth and mainstreaming of psychological discourses in American Christian churches. As I indicated in chapters 5 and 6, the pastoral psychology movement began early in the century and quickly fused Christian categories and modern psychological ones in powerful new discourses of curing and saving souls. The changes were rapid. First, early in the twentieth century, "psychology of religion" courses infiltrated seminaries; then clinically oriented psychology courses developed; then clinical pastoral education became a staple of seminary education. "In 1939," Brooks Holifield has said of this revolution in pastoral practice, "few theological schools had even bothered to teach counseling courses that would introduce students to the newest psychological theories. By the 1950s almost all of them did, over 80 percent were offering additional courses in psychology, and 80 percent could list at least one psychologist on their faculty." Seminaries hastily created and staffed graduate programs in "personality and theology," pastoral counseling, or pastoral theology. Centers, institutes, and chaplaincies, all for pastoral counselors, were created. And seminary faculty founded journals to publish new insights into the many "correlations" between theology and psychology, establishing a new language that let believers move back and forth between psychological insights about mind and religious conceptions of spirit. Here, religious professionals, like earlier religious amateurs, had a concept—"mind"—that allowed them to speak truthfully about the self in scientific and religious terms simultaneously. Of course, some psychologists resisted or even actively opposed pastoral uses of their science; and on the other side, believers sometimes felt agitated by psychological explanations. But most combined psychological insights and affirmative stances on religious faith with alacrity, and religious appropriations of psychology multiplied. In fact, by midcentury, clinical psychologies were everywhere in the American churches. "A good minister cannot now escape personal counseling," the famous liberal Protestant pastor Harry Emerson Fosdick wrote in 1960. "It is in the air."[11]

It is worth saying again that the crucial factor which made these religious-psychological cultures possible was the incredible proliferation of psychological theories and practices, especially new clinical traditions that developed early in the twentieth century. Many clinical traditions could easily be harmonized with religious visions; some quite explicitly buttressed them. Though Freud's clinical views made religion pathological, an infantile neurosis to be outgrown, competing clinical notions already were in play, and many of them, as we have seen, accommodated believers and their perspectives without strain. Elwood Worcester's clinical faith is one such example; an elastic set of therapeutic "suggestive" traditions is another—a religious style that informs believers in many settings today. Other clinical styles also are worth mentioning here. Freud's onetime student Carl Jung produced a psychological system that, while not unequivocally appreciative of religion, and actually hostile to traditional religion, has become a pervasive feature in American religious cultures. Jung is the focus of Christian and New Age retreats, he is preached in American pulpits, used in individual counseling sessions, and invoked incessantly in New Age workshops on dream interpretation, personality traits, past-life regression, and astrology. Jung differed from Freud in his evaluation of the unconscious, which Freud associated with primitive instincts but which Jung thought connected us to symbolic and mythical truths about the universe, truths that American believers could easily associate with God or the transcendent. And of course, Jung is only one theorist among many other "humanistic" psychologists who resolutely turned from positivism and behaviorism. Many others in this trajectory—Abraham Maslow (1908–1970), Victor Frankl (1905–1997), Rollo May (1909–1994), and Carl Rogers (1902–1987), for instance—glimpsed in the self either transcendent states or peak human experiences and taught us how to realize them. Their ideas are ubiquitous in popular self-help books, manuals of religious development, and pastoral settings as well. Their ideas also are crucial for an increasingly large unchurched American population, those who locate religious authority in the self and often self-identify as "spiritual but not religious." By lifting the transcendent out of its older, institutional inhabitations, humanistic psychologists helped create this ubiquitous modern spiritual style.[12]

America's Protestant churches turned to the power of the mind in other, unexpected ways. Were they still around, older metaphysical healers and New Thought practitioners might have felt vindicated, for by the 1950s even mainline Protestants were taking up psychological emphases once regarded as heterodox: positive thinking, mental healing, and the power of the mind to change your fortunes. Best-selling books developed these themes. In a 1958 analysis of best-selling inspirational books published between 1875 and 1955, two sociologists found New Thought emphases everywhere. Their analysis, one reviewer correctly observed, pointed to a recurring emphasis on "the subjective and practical aspects of worship under the banner of a loosely conceived optimism." There was little in the way of dogma, ritual, or eschatology in these best-sellers; all of them, Protestant, Catholic, and Jewish, exchanged older religious notions for a focus on mental health, personality "adjustment," and the benefits of faith as a "power to live by." The best-known popularizer of these ideas was the international celebrity preacher Norman Vincent Peale, a man who moved without strain from Methodism to New Thought and preached a combination of comforting passages from the New Testament, various psychological truths, and familiar "suggestive" techniques developed by New Thoughters like Henry Wood. At every turn his faith was inflected with these popular psychological premises. He and many others also drew on behaviorism—selectively, of course—to speak about "conditioning" positive thoughts, making them automatic, and changing behavior. Books with New Thought emphases continue to span a range from evangelical to metaphysical, and they continue to sell well. A more recent study found these themes in best-sellers in the 1990s—in everything from Gloria Steinem's *Revolution from Within* to Robert Schuller's evangelical *Peace of Mind through Possibility Thinking*. It is no exaggeration to say, as J. Stillson Judah has, that by the 1960s the mind had became America's most powerful religious motif.[13]

One development buttressing this powerful turn to "mind" among religious Americans has been the already mentioned revolution in physics, a rethinking of the basic properties of physical reality that, to believers anyway, suggested ways that mind, not matter, undergirded all things. Excitement about quantum models has moved in several different directions. First, a number of Christian thinkers, especially liberal and "process" theologians and theologically inclined scientists, have argued that the new physics makes possible a reenchantment of the world, a new picture of physical reality as something alive, interconnected, and in some sense at least, conscious. One crucial ingredient in this reenchanted world is *agency*, human and divine, and in thinking about agency many thinkers have depended on quantum metaphors. (It is hard not to imagine how pleased James would have been.) Some have pointed to the work of

Heisenberg and others, calling attention to the observer's role in producing reality and arguing that the messiness of matter and energy, and their interchangeability, suggest ways that consciousness shapes all things. One theologian and ethicist, David Ray Griffin, for instance, has observed that, as "physicists became aware that physical theory gave them only shadows and symbols of reality, rather than reality itself, they became freed from the materialistic worldview and hence open to taking their own conscious experience as real and revelatory." Mapping out the vectors of consciousness in the world has taken thinkers in different directions impossible to summarize here, but one crucial area has been understanding different kinds of mentalist (or psychokinetic) effects in the world, something New Age scientists and consciousness-studies people have been interested in. I will say more on this in a moment. Mind—our mind and, sometimes, an ultimate Mind—shapes so-called material things. Griffin and others also have been interested in the matter-mind collapse implied by the new physics, believing that this new way of thinking suggests an "implicate" order in which all things are "mutually enfolded into each other." Though things appear separate, at deeper levels they are integrated. Some thinkers are expanding this idea into new theological and ecological visions of a living, interconnected universe, a vision some quite deliberately use to battle against "old" dualisms in psychology, science, and theology. New pantheistic or panentheistic theologies have resulted.[14]

The most expansive imaginings of the universe-as-mind-stuff come from New Age believers, who have embraced emphatically the new physics as a source of new metaphors for the divine energies that pulse through all things. *Quantum healing, quantum states, quantum brain*—these have become pervasive refrains among New Age and metaphysical believers. "From the scientific books I've been reading," the New Age celebrity Shirley MacLaine has written, "I've learned that the field of subatomic quantum physics has opened up a whole new world for modern scientists to explore." The quantum world shows us that "everything is linked," that the "universe is a gigantic, multidimensional web of influences, or information, light particles, energy patterns, and electromagnetic 'fields of reality.'" Of course, MacLaine has been mostly interested in what these things tell us about spiritual living. "We are literally made up of God energy, therefore we can create whatever we want in life because we are each co-creating with the energy of God—the energy that makes the universe itself." Drawing on quantum physics, neuroscience, and Vedanta Hinduism, Deepak Chopra, an earnest former endocrinologist and a bestselling New Age writer, has even offered instructions for navigating this quantum world. Referring to Einstein, who "made time and space into fluid things that merge into each other," and who, like other physicists, dissolved matter into quantum energy packets, Chopra went on to divide up the world into three zones: material (matter), quantum (in between), and virtual (pure spirit). Admittedly, traveling in the quantum zone was a spiritually unstable practice; most of us were able to glimpse it in sudden intuitions and fleeting moments of bliss. But mystics and other expert "quantum navigators" had the skill to anchor themselves in this zone and feel its signs—feelings of weightlessness, heightened senses, a sense of energy in the body, and the sense of seeing the "light." Chopra's books, like those of other New Age gurus, such as Wayne Dyer, draw eclectically on devotional practices, including Eastern forms of meditation and yoga, to create the kinds of focused intentions and imaginativeness that might keep aspirants always in this light.[15] It is striking how often Chopra cites research and key figures in physics, psychology, and consciousness studies to create his powerful new religious vision.

Liberal believers have flourished in these indeterminate, energetic worlds, producing different maps of metaphysical vectors and ways of mentally moving them along. William Tiller, a retired Stanford University materials science professor and New Ager, is representative in how he uses science and psychological notions to make metaphysical calculations. In all his books, Tiller's main concern is understanding how people can perceive and control the "vast information territories" of supersensible domains—how, in other words, people can "see" the bits of information and energy that undergird the world. "Practices of inner self management at mental, emotional and physical levels appear to develop additional latent sensory systems in us that allow cognizing of new information by looking inward." His list of self-management techniques is similar to Chopra's: yoga, chi gong, and Eastern meditative practices. But Tiller adds to these his own technical procedures, which he elaborately describes in mathematical formulas and illustrates in charts and tables that probe different dimensions of matter. Unfortunately, the mathematics he uses is mostly incomprehensible to lay readers and probably utterly confounding to specialists, an esoteric translation of nature's energies into a symbolic code that only Tiller and a few like-minded souls can enjoy. There are formulas here for photon fluxes, physical light cones, and Fourier transforms of the sine wave—all marshaled to show that science itself has dematerialized physical matter. The remarkable results show that mind and spirit, when shaped with intention, determine the qualities and appearances of physical things. All of this could be confirmed as well by psychological and neurological studies of meditative states, which, to be sure, produce distinctive ECG and EEG signatures. Mental states produce particular bodily signs. But the effects of intentional mental actions go beyond the body. States of mind have even been shown to influence the properties of water and biological matter, such as DNA, even when held at an arm's length from meditators. Tiller and other New Age thinkers are keenly interested in showing this to be true—that psychological forces reach outside of the self. If all matter really is mental energy, why not? Psychokinetic effects can be traced in different forms—precognition, telepathy, clairvoyance, healing, levitation, and homeopathy. All these phenomena point to the elusive effects of subtle energies and the ways that the mind can move them into the world.[16]

As the Tiller example makes plain, American believers are still borrowing from the human sciences to prove, or at least suggest, the existence and usefulness of different spiritual states. And, it should be said, neurologists, psychologists, and medical doctors are giving them an astonishing amount of material to work with. Especially in the last thirty years, psychologists and others have pointed to a wide range of positive effects of religious belief in clinical studies of stress, substance abuse, mortality, immunity, heart disease, blood pressure, happiness, achievement, and mental illness, among other things.[17] Studies considered under the moniker of "mind-body medicine" in particular have flourished, with mind-body centers and institutes now established at prestigious medical schools in the United States and abroad. The subject matter ranges from psychoimmunology to studies of stress, yoga, and meditation—a signal, if there ever was one, that mental events, those "intervening variables" that positivists shunned, have come back with a vengeance. Studies confirming the positive effects of meditation and prayer have the longest history, beginning with biofeedback studies in the 1960s and expanding recently as clinicians such as the Harvard cardiologist Herbert Benson have popularized the important physiological effects of meditative states. Benson measured the physiological states—heart rate, respiration, blood pressure, and brain wave activity—of different believers while they engaged in repetitive prayers. Catholics said "Hail Mary, full of grace," Hindus repeated mantras, Protestants offered short prayers. Benson even had some subjects substitute simple words for religious phrases, words like *one*. All these activities elicited what he famously called the "relaxation response," a set of physiological states that line up opposite our "fight or flight" readiness responses. (Like earlier psychological studies of religious experience, these studies abetted a distinctly ecumenical appreciation of the health benefits of all the world's religious practices.) Benson, of course, was not the only one. There have been many others interested in mapping the health benefits of religious practices, and this scientific work is cited unceasingly by religious liberals, popular authors, and metaphysicians. Chopra again provides a good example, but he is merely one among many. In his books, he culls from an endless list of studies: work correlating specific EEG signatures and willingness (or ability) to have "spiritual experiences," studies that show the health benefits of meditation, psychological work that links good posture or other outer behaviors with elevated emotions, consciousness studies that argue against materialism, clinical studies of near-death experiences, and so on. These are, again, examples of religious liberals using psychological knowledge to buttress their particular forms of belief.[18]

Though religious liberals often borrow with the most enthusiasm, the range of psychological studies has so broadened that even evangelicals have turned to scientific studies to gain credence for their spiritual states. Even the left-leaning *New York Times* recently reported that brain scans of evangelicals speaking in tongues seemed to support believers' accounts of what was happening. While speaking in tongues, subjects had brain patterns that looked strikingly different from similar scans produced during meditation. During meditation, a highly focused mental activity, the frontal lobes lit up; but when a subject was speaking in tongues, the frontal lobes were quiet. All regions controlling the thinking, willful part of the brain, and the language centers, were quiet, while the regions controlling self-consciousness were active. It was unclear what part of the brain was controlling this process. Was a nonphysical entity driving it? "The amazing thing was how the images supported people's interpretation of what was happening," one of the investigators said. "The way they describe it, and what they believe, is that God is talking through them." There have been studies of other specifically Christian practices as well, including many studies of intercessory prayer, of the neuroscientific foundations of traditional Christian conceptions of faith or spirit, and even arguments for a triune conception of the brain. Some believers are cobbling together elements of a new Christian apologetics using brain imaging or cognitive psychological studies. It should be said that the scientific literature on these subjects, and especially on whether God or religiosity is hardwired into the brain, cuts two ways. There is still no shortage of scientists who insist, performing the New Age reduction in reverse, that spirit actually is matter. Even so, believers cannot be blamed for noticing a sea change from the confident pronouncements of theorists like Freud a hundred years ago, who believed religion was an unhealthy neurosis, to the psychological studies today that link it to health, happiness, and longevity.[19]

It is worth recalling, finally, that these contemporary appropriations of psychological motifs and experimental results are not so different from the strategies used by earlier believers—people who, like Henry Ward Beecher and George Coe, used psychology to reconsider the spiritual self and understand better how it worked. Liberal believers during the time of the first scientific psychology—phrenology—for example, saw that psychology offered a clearer way of peering into the self, a way of seeing confounding inner forces by measuring their traces on the outer self. When the "new psychology" emerged in the last decades of the nineteenth century, it was an improved way of doing the same thing—of seeing in the body the basic elements of the self. Though this psychology and others incorporated possibilities that could cut away at religious conviction, such dangers could be controlled or qualified, at least provisionally, by believing interpreters such as Stanley Hall, William James, and Edwin Starbuck. After the rise of the new psychology, a cascade of religious believers, and especially religious liberals, used psychology in creative and often quite cunning ways—to point to transcendent elements in the self; to understand better how to control emotional and spiritual energies; to increase religious vitality; and to develop faith-producing schemes, suggestions, and affirmations. These traditions represented powerful ways of using psychology to see more clearly both the transcendent elements of the self and the possibilities, which were always elusive, of achieving a greater measure of spiritual assurance.

# Notes

INTRODUCTION

1. The literature on the conflict between science and religion is vast, as is a related literature on the Victorian crisis of faith. A few representative works include Andrew Dickson White, *A History of the Warfare of Science with Theology in Christendom* (New York: D. Appleton, 1896); Walter Houghton, *The Victorian Frame of Mind, 1830–1870* (New Haven, CT: Yale University Press, 1957); and Paul Carter, *The Spiritual Crisis of the Guilded Age* (Dekalb: Northern Illinois University Press, 1971). Revisions to the "warfare" model also have been fairly extensive. See James Moore, *The Post-Darwinian Controversies: A Study of the Protestant Struggle to Come to Terms with Darwin in Great Britain and America, 1870–1900* (Cambridge: Cambridge University Press, 1979); John Hedley Brooke, *Science and Religion: Some Historical Perspectives* (Cambridge: Cambridge University Press, 1991); John Hedley Brooke and Geoffrey Cantor, *Reconstructing Nature: The Engagement of Science and Religion* (Oxford: Oxford University Press, 1998); Jon Roberts, *Darwinism and the Divine in America: Protestant Intellectuals and Organic Evolution, 1859–1900* (Madison: University of Wisconsin Press, 1988); and Paul Croce, *Science and Religion in the Era of William James* (Chapel Hill: University of North Carolina Press, 1995).

2. Newman Smyth, "Orthodox Rationalism," *Princeton Review* 58 (1882): 312.

3. On the marginalization of theology, see, for example, Bruce Kuklick and D.G. Hart, eds., *Religious Advocacy and the Writing of American History* (Grand Rapids, MI: Eerdmans, 1996); George Marsden, *The Soul of the American University: From Protestant Establishment to Established Unbelief* (New York: Oxford University Press, 1994); George Marsden, *The Outrageous Idea of Christian Scholarship* (New York: Oxford University Press, 1997); George Marsden, *The Evangelical Mind and the New School Presbyterian Experience: A Case Study of Thought and Theology in Nineteenth-Century America* (New Haven, CT: Yale University Press, 1970); James Turner, *Without God, without*

*Creed: The Origins of Unbelief in America* (Baltimore: Johns Hopkins University Press, 1985). On the transformation from salvation to self-realization, see E. Brooks Holifield, *A History of Pastoral Care in America: From Salvation to Self-Realization* (Nashville, TN: Abingdon Press, 1983).

4. While it is certain that literature linking liberalism and decline has turned attention away from liberal spirituality, I also think this lack of interest has roots in an earlier historiography. For while intellectual and church historians such as Frank Hugh Foster celebrated liberal decisions to embrace evolution and other progressive intellectual currents, they generally were not interested in liberal experiences of faith or religious practices. Liberals fared well in this literature because they were good thinkers, not interesting believers, preachers, or psychologists. Perhaps the fascination with the intellectual dimensions of liberal life had the double effect of keeping historians focused on both intellectual trends and later (more developed) manifestations of liberalism (instead of "early" or "evangelical" ones). In any case, Daniel Day Williams's book *The Andover Liberals* (1941), Kenneth Cauthen's survey of liberalism (1962), and William Hutchison's *Modernist Impulse* (1976) focus mainly on intellectual and institutional developments in the later period (from the 1880s onward). Frank Hugh Foster, *The Modern Movement in American Theology* (New York: Fleming H. Revell, 1939); Daniel Day Williams, *The Andover Liberals: A Study in American Theology* (New York: King's Crown Press, 1941); Kenneth Cauthen, *The Impact of American Religious Liberalism* (New York: Harper and Row, 1962); William R. Hutchison, *The Modernist Impulse in American Protestantism* (reprint; Durham, NC: Duke University Press, 1992).

5. Jon Butler, "Protestant Success in the New American City, 1870–1920," in *New Directions in American Religious History*, ed. Harry Stout and D. G. Hart (Oxford: Oxford University Press, 1997), 297–98 and 322–24.

6. T. J. Jackson Lears, "From Salvation to Self-Realization: Advertising and the Therapeutic Roots of the Consumer Culture, 1880–1930," in *The Culture of Consumption: Critical Essays in American History, 1880–1980*, ed. Richard Wightman Fox and T. J. Jackson Lears (New York: Pantheon Books, 1983), 3–38, quote on p. 4; and E. Brooks Holifield, *A History of Pastoral Care in America: From Salvation to Self-Realization* (Nashville: Abingdon Press, 1983). Peter Homans, who has for many years written about the history of Freudianism, theology, and Western culture, also saw psychology, and Freudianism in particular, as an overpowering force reshaping culture and secularizing the Western mind. See Peter Homans, *The Ability to Mourn: Disillusionment and the Social Origins of Psychoanalysis* (Chicago: University of Chicago Press, 1989). For Rieff and commentators influenced by his analysis, see Philip Rieff, *The Triumph of the Therapeutic: Uses of Faith after Freud* (Chicago: University of Chicago Press, 1966); Christopher Lasch, *The Minimal Self: Psychic Survival in Troubled Times* (New York: W. W. Norton, 1984); and Robert Bellah et al., *Habits of the Heart: Individualism and Commitment in American Life* (New York: Harper and Row, 1986).

7. Ann Taves, *Fits, Trances, and Visions: Experiencing Religion and Explaining Experience from Wesley to James* (Princeton, NJ: Princeton University Press, 1999).

8. Her work examined the liberalism of Lyman Beecher's children in particular, devising three categories to understand them: "moralists" who "viewed religion almost exclusively in moral terms," "prophets" who pursued "serious" theological studies, and "Christocentric liberals" who adhered to an undogmatic love of Christ. These categories pointed to important differences among early liberals, and to that extent they were useful. But by her own account, Caskey could not always keep Lyman Beecher's children in their (separate) places. Sometimes they occupied all three categories at once. Certainly all of them were Christocentric, and depending on their moods, which Caskey interprets expertly, all of them also described religion in moral terms or explained it in "serious" theological ones.

9. Marie Caskey, *Chariot of Fire: Religion and the Beecher Family* (New Haven, CT: Yale University Press, 1978). See also reviews of Caskey by William R. Hutchison and Paul Carter: William R. Hutchison, review of *Chariot of Fire*, by Marie Caskey, *American Historical Review* 84, no 2 (April 1979): 551–52; Paul A. Carter, review of *Chariot of Fire*, by Marie Caskey, *Journal of Interdisciplinary History* 9, no. 4 (Spring 1979): 766–68. For Cauthen's quotations and his categories, see Cauthen, *Impact of American Religious Liberalism*, 27, 29, and Henry P. Van Dusen, "The Nineteenth Century and Today," in *The Vitality of the Christian Tradition*, ed. George F. Thomas (New York: Harper and Brothers, 1944), 168–69. Hutchison's critique of Cauthen is in William R. Hutchison, *The Modernist Impulse in American Protestantism* (Durham, NC: Duke University Press, 1992), 7–8. See also Leigh Schmidt, *Restless Souls: The Making of American Spirituality* (San Francisco: HarperSanFrancisco, 2005).

10. See Schmidt, *Restless Souls;* and Leigh Schmidt, "The Making of Modern Mysticism," *Journal of the American Academy of Religion* 71, no. 2 (2003): 273–302.

## 1. MINDS INTENSELY UNSETTLED

1. Nelson Sizer, *Forty Years in Phrenology: Embracing Recollections of History, Anecdote, and Experience* (New York: Fowler and Wells Co., 1888), 54–55. It is clear that ministers and lecturers collaborated at local churches, and that pastors used phrenological categories to talk about human nature and salvation. See Sizer, *Forty Years*, esp. 172–74; and John D. Davies, *Phrenology, Fad, and Science: A Nineteenth-Century American Crusade* (New Haven, CT: Archon, 1971), 149–58.

2. For more on itinerant lecturing and preaching in this period, a good starting point is Peter Benes, ed., *Itinerancy in New England and New York* (Boston: Boston University, 1986); earlier studies include Richard Wright's *Hawkers and Walkers in Early America* (Philadelphia: J. B. Lippincott, 1927),

and E. Neville Jackson's *Silhouette* (New York: Scribner's, 1938). Timothy Hall has written an excellent study on a slightly earlier period called *Contested Boundaries: Itinerancy and the Reshaping of the Colonial American Religious World* (Durham, NC: Duke University Press, 1994).

3. Quoted in Nathan Hatch, *The Democratization of American Christianity* (New Haven, CT: Yale University Press, 1989), 10, 170–73. The recent literature on revival in this period is extensive. I have relied mostly on sources that focus on ecstatic experiences, including Ann Taves, *Fits, Trances, and Visions: Experiencing Religion and Explaining Experience from Wesley to James* (Princeton, NJ: Princeton University Press, 1999); Richard Rabinowitz, *The Spiritual Self in Everyday Life: The Transformation of Personal Religious Experience in Nineteenth-Century New England* (Boston: Northeastern University Press, 1989); and Whitney Cross, *The Burned-Over District: Social and Intellectual History of Enthusiastic Religion in Western New York, 1800–1850* (Ithaca, NY: Cornell University Press, 1950).

4. Philip Schaff, *The Principle of Protestantism as Related to the Present State of the Church* (Chambersberg, PA: German Reformed Church, 1845), 25. Similar accounts could be found in the writings of Tocqueville, the English visitors Robert Collyer and Frances Trollope, and many others.

5. Of this "vast army," Baird wrote further that, "although to the inexperienced eye such an army as it moves onward against the enemy may have a confused appearance, the different divisions of infantry being arranged separately[,] . . . to the mind of Him all is systematic order where the uninitiated sees nothing but confusion." Robert Baird, *Religion in America; or, an account of the origin, relation to the state, and present condition of the evangelical churches in the United States* (New York: Harper, 1844), 536–39.

6. Ibid., 578, 583.

7. See Hatch, *Democratization*, 71.

8. Many contemporaries of Sunderland were similarly confused by the cacophony of inspired utterances. When remembering his first vision (1820), Joseph Smith confirmed that his "mind at times was greatly excited, the cry and tumult were so great and incessant. The Presbyterians were most decided against the Baptists and Methodists, and used all the powers of both reason and sophistry to prove their errors, or, at least, to make people think they were in error. . . . In the midst of this war of words and tumult of opinions, I often said to myself, what is to be done?" Joseph Smith, quoted in B. H. Roberts, ed., *History of the Church of Jesus Christ of Latter-Day Saints* (Salt Lake City: Deseret Books, 1964), 1:4–6.

9. Like Beecher, Sunderland experimented with phrenology and mesmerism. See Taves, *Fits*, 130–40. Revivals were not the only reason for intense interest in mind and spirit. Reformed churches (and their liberal offshoots) were sustaining a continuous debate over the mind, sin, and salvation. The best overviews are H. Shelton Smith, *Changing Conceptions of Original Sin* (New York: Scribners, 1955); Daniel W. Howe, *The Unitarian Conscience: Harvard Moral Philosophy, 1805–1861* (Middletown, CT: Wesleyan University Press,

1970); and E. Brooks Holifield, *Theology in America: Christian Thought from the Age of the Puritans to the Civil War* (New Haven, CT: Yale University Press, 2003).

10. Michael McGiffert, ed., *God's Plot: Puritan Spirituality in Thomas Shepard's Cambridge* (Boston: University of Massachusetts, 1994), 145.

11. The assault on orthodoxy was increasingly widespread in American culture, and the literature on this assault and its aftermath is voluminous. For a discussion of how this assault figures in the emergence of liberal religious sensibilities, see, for example, Daniel Walker Howe, "The Decline of Calvinism: An Approach to Its Study," *Comparative Studies in Society and History* 14, no. 3 (June 1972): 306–27; Charles H. Foster, *The Rungless Ladder: Harriet Beecher Stowe and New England Puritanism* (New York: Cooper Square Publishers, 1970); Hatch, *Democratization;* and Taves, *Fits.*

12. His complaint juxtaposes an arid Calvinism with newer formulations relying on intuition and feeling. Moderates and liberals developed theologies of feeling and intuition in the same period. Mary Mann, *Life of Horace Mann* (Boston: Lee and Shepard, 1891), 13.

13. Ibid., 13–14.

14. Henry Ward Beecher, as quoted in "Henry Ward Beecher," *Littell's Living Age* (April 27, 1872): 198. The "gloomy, ascetic piety" quotation is from Orson S. Fowler, *Religion, Natural and Revealed: or, the Natural Theology and Moral Bearings of Phrenology and Physiology: Including the Doctrines Taught and Duties Inculcated Thereby, Compared with Those Enjoined in the Scriptures* (New York: O. S. Fowler, 1840), 65. The same language is ubiquitous in popular progressive evangelical periodicals of the time, such as the *Christian Union* and the *Independent.*

15. Andrew Jackson Davis, *The Great Harmonia* (Boston: B. B. Mussey, 1855), 2:26–27.

16. Two excellent accounts are Kathryn Kish Sklar, *Catharine Beecher: A Study in American Domesticity* (New York: Norton, 1976), and Marie Caskey, *Chariot of Fire: Religion and the Beecher Family* (New Haven, CT: Yale University Press, 1978).

17. Catharine Beecher to Henry Ward Beecher, February 27, 1860, Henry Ward Beecher Papers, Yale University. The same letter shows that these dilemmas were passed to succeeding generations. Catharine asked Henry for spiritual help with their niece, Hatty. "But there is a class of the weak—the discouraged, the lambs of the fold, who are torn and wounded by the thorns of Calvinism and it is for these I plead. Among these you will find sister Harriet's oldest daughter Hattie and I could find you many more." What to do with such "sensitive" souls? The child had said that "Uncle Henry says that 'when I realize the goodness of Christ, his helpfulness, his lenient forgiving, sympathizing spirit, I have faith.' . . . He says again I must 'believe that Christ is willing to save' me. How can I believe it when I do not know that I shall be saved. He never told me he should save me. If he is willing why don't he do it, for I am sure I do not know what to do." Uncle Henry was explaining this in one way,

and "all the Professors" were explaining it in another, with the result that it was "all a dreadful mess!"

18. Harriet Beecher Stowe, *Men of Our Times, or, leading patriots of the day* (Hartford, CT: Hartford Publishing Co., 1868), 532. Beecher talked about his religious difficulties in different ways during the course of his life, and in reconstructing them one has to proceed cautiously. He did not fill his journal with extensive ruminations on these subjects; but he does take up these issues in detail in correspondence with his sister. Her recollections are quoted in the chapter text. See "Henry Ward Beecher," *Littell's Living Age* (April 27, 1872): 198; Clifford E. Clark, *Henry Ward Beecher: Spokesman for a Middle-Class America* (Urbana: University of Illinois Press, 1978), 24–25; and Caskey, *Chariot*, 213–17.

19. Henry Ward Beecher to Harriet Beecher Stowe, undated (perhaps 1848), Henry Ward Beecher Papers, Yale University, his emphasis. The atmosphere at his frontier seminary (Lane) did not help matters, for there he witnessed revivalists and antirevivalists, Calvinists and Arminians, clashing, and had to endure the spectacle of his father's heresy trial. "How I despised and hated this whirling abyss of controversies," he said. This was precisely the time when his mind was "*intensely* unsettled." Quoted in Caskey, *Chariot*, 214–15. (In quotations throughout my book, italics are from the originals.)

20. From Henry Ward Beecher to Harriet Beecher Stowe, undated (perhaps 1848), Henry Ward Beecher Papers, Yale University.

21. On Henry's interest in nature as "a symbol of invisible spiritual truths," see William McLoughlin, *The Meaning of Henry Ward Beecher: An Essay on the Shifting Values of Mid-Victorian America, 1840–1870* (New York: Knopf, 1970), 58. Beecher learned to trust these illuminations, finally believing that "the soul seeks and sees God through nature," and that when nature is seen in this way it "changes its voice, speaking no longer of mere material grandeur and beauty." Nature was "a symbol of invisible spiritual truths, the ritual of a higher life, the highway upon which our thoughts are to travel toward immortality." McLoughlin, *Meaning*, 58–59.

22. Beecher was not alone in keeping notes on character and on "outlines of the lives who have made themselves or have attained any great end by decision of character." Caskey, *Chariot*, 161, 212–23.

23. The argument was not so different from the natural religion arguments of earlier liberals like Francis Bowen, who reasoned from the mind and its structures to God and his qualities. The difference was that Unitarians like Bowen and Henry Ware did not pursue precise body-mind correspondences. Employing an introspective (and metaphysical) philosophy, they argued quite simply that our conscience—that is, our ability to know right from wrong—proved the existence of God, who himself had this capacity and gave it to us. The argument for the existence of God from the mind, they thought, was "even more direct, logical and convincing" than the argument from nature. Howe, *Unitarian*, 94–95. Howe's book also deals with the history of the faculty psychology before phrenologically minded liberals transformed its metaphorical "high" and "low" faculties into specific brain areas. See Howe, *Unitarian*, 40–41, 54–64.

24. There is a longer history to be told about localization of mental functions in the brain and how phrenology fits into this story. Anne Harrington tells this story succinctly in her *Medicine, Mind, and the Double Brain* (Princeton, NJ: Princeton University Press, 1989), 6–10. I have relied on her account and on Daniel Robinson, *An Intellectual History of Psychology* (Madison: University of Wisconsin Press, 1995).

25. Various ways of localizing mental function in the brain were pursued by religious and nonreligious thinkers in the seventeenth and eighteenth centuries. See Robert M. Young, "The Functions of the Brain: Gall to Ferrier (1808–1886)," *Isis* 59, no. 3 (Autumn 1968): 250–68; and H. W. Magoun, "Early Development of Ideas Relating the Mind with the Brain," in *Neurological Basis of Behavior*, ed. G. E. W. Wolstenholme and C. M. O'Connor (London: Churchill, 1958).

26. Clark, *Beecher*, 16–18. Though I am sure that Lyman would have disapproved of Henry's new science, I do not feel, as William McLoughlin does, that the "new science of phrenology . . . provided a foil to the rigid evangelical theology of [Henry's] father and professors." My sense is that Lyman's faith was less rigid and Harry's less pugnacious. Like other liberals, Harry had an irenic personality and moved slowly to new positions. He remained especially aware of displeasing his father and would not talk openly with him about his new ideas. McLoughlin, *Meaning*, 16–18.

27. *American Journal of Phrenology* 24 (1856): 131.

28. Elizabeth Cady Stanton, *Eighty Years and More: Reminiscences, 1815–1897* (New York: European Pub. Co., 1898; reprint, Boston: Northeastern University Press, 1993), 40–44; James Freeman Clarke, *Autobiography, Diary and Correspondence*, ed. Edward E. Hale (New York: Negro Universities Press, 1968), 49. Phrenology saved by providing other comforts as well. "Phrenology saved me from the rock of infidelity; when I saw that the mind was constitutionally adapted to the great principles of Christianity I was enabled to comprehend the fallacy of the base doctrines of the infidel." Phrenology turned people away from skepticism, confusion, and the babble of the sects. See Davies, *Phrenology*, 157–58.

29. George Weaver, *Lectures on Mental Science According to the Philosophy of Phrenology* (New York: S. R. Wells and Co., 1880), 18–23, quote on pp. 21–22; Samuel Gridley Howe, *Address to the Boston Phrenological Society* (Boston: Marsh, Capen, and Lyon, 1836), 18. See also Davies, *Phrenology*, 163. Phrenology was part of a broader curiosity in America about how material forms reflected deeper spiritual realities. This curiosity was manifested in American visual culture and, especially, in speculation about emotion and how emotion influenced the contours of the face and head. For more on how this played out in American Protestantism, see David Morgan, *Protestants and Pictures: Religion, Visual Culture, and the Age of American Mass Production* (New York: Oxford University Press, 1999), 277–79. The nineteenth-century story I am telling here could be contextualized in much larger debates about the somatic signs of authentic religious experience. For these larger debates, see

Leigh Schmidt, *Holy Fairs: Scotland and the Making of American Revivalism* (Grand Rapids, MI: Eerdmans, 2001), xx–xxviii; Leigh Schmidt, *Hearing Things: Religion, Illusion, and the American Enlightenment* (Cambridge: Harvard University Press, 2002); and Taves, *Fits*.

30. For this quotation and a good overview of these problems, see Robinson, *Intellectual History*, 337–41, quote on p. 338. Herbert Spencer was so taken with the science that he designed a "cephalograph" to measure the dimensions of skulls more precisely. Instructions on how to use the cephalograph are in his *Autobiography* (London: Williams and Norgate, 1904), vol. 1, appendix H. See also Angus McLaren, "Phrenology: Medium and Message," *Journal of Modern History* 46, no. 1 (March 1974): 89.

31. Alexander Bain, *The Emotions and the Will* (London: J. W. Parker, 1859), 568, 570.

32. It is hard to know precisely how popular, and how respected among intellectuals, this science was in the second half of the century. Sources disagree. But there is no doubt that it remained powerful in popular cultures; the major phrenological organ, the *American Phrenological Journal*, had a remarkable run, from 1838 to 1911, especially when we compare it with denominational journals from the period. See Davies, *Phrenology*, 164.

33. Charles Colbert, *A Measure of Perfection: Phrenology and the Fine Arts in America* (Chapel Hill: University of North Carolina Press, 1997), 23–25.

34. See Madeleine Stern, *Heads and Headlines: The Phrenological Fowlers* (Norman: University of Oklahoma Press 1971), 108, 236; Davies, *Phrenology*, 119, 123–24. See also Edward Hungerford, "Walt Whitman and His Chart of Bumps," *American Literature* 2, no. 4 (January 1931): 350–84.

35. See Michael Quinn, *Early Mormonism and the Magic World View* (Salt Lake City: Signature Books, 1998); Cross, *Burned-Over*; Davies, *Phrenology*. Positive reviews were common in periodicals popular in the urban (often Congregationalist) Northeast, and especially in the progressive *Christian Union*. Unitarian, Universalist, and other liberal periodicals (*Christian Register, Christian Examiner, The Dial*) and anti-Calvinist-oriented journals also showed interest in the new science. Methodist and Baptist theological journals (*Methodist Review, Baptist Quarterly*) offered mixed views; Presbyterians generally were more critical in their *Princeton Review* and *Presbyterian and Reformed Review*; and Congregationalists were more positive, especially in the *Chicago Advance*, the *Congregationalist*, and the *Boston Recorder*.

36. Beecher's comments on Bain (and other psychologists) are in his *Yale Lectures on Preaching* (New York: J. B. Ford, 1872), 90–92, 96.

37. Quoted in Stern, *Heads*, 81.

38. James Freeman Clarke, quoted in Davies, *Phrenology*, 162–63.

39. Europeans argued that older philosophies of mind fell down in quite specific ways—that, in particular, philosophy had given no account "of the influence of the material organs on the mental powers" or of the "progress of the mind from youth to age"; it had not explained phenomena like "sleep, dreaming, idiocy, and insanity"; it was unable to document and classify accurately

the various faculties and powers of the mind; and it had not been able to shed light on the nature and effects of combinations of mental faculties. In reviewing these charges, Alexander Bain agreed that older ways of thinking about the mind were muddled, and he said that new sciences that linked the mind to the brain and nervous system held out the most promise. Alexander Bain, *On the Study of Character, Including an Estimate of Phrenology* (London: Parker, Son, and Bourn, 1861), 14–17.

40. "Rev. G. S. Weaver," *American Journal of Phrenology* 20, no. 2 (August 1854): 28–29; Weaver, *Lectures*, 20–22.

41. Weaver, *Lectures*, 63.

42. John Hecker, *The Scientific Basis of Education Demonstrated by an Analysis of the Temperaments and of Phrenological Facts* . . . (New York: A. S. Barnes and Company, 1868), 30–31, 47–48, 112–18.

43. Ibid., 30–31, 103.

44. Fowler, *Religion*, xiii, 26, 163.

45. Ibid., 111, 114, 163–65.

46. Rev. T. G. Steward, "Conversion Scientifically Considered," *Philadelphia Christian Recorder*, November 15, 1877.

47. See Alfred Lorraine, "Phrenology," *Ladies Repository* 2, no. 9 (September 1842), 263–64; and Weaver, *Lectures*, 18–23, 60–63, 273.

48. "Phrenological Facts," *American Journal of Phrenology* 7, no. 1 (January 1845): 19.

49. The deacon's story is in Sizer, *Forty Years*, 330; other accounts are in the *American Journal of Phrenology* 4 (1842): 107–9; *AJP* 24, no. 4 (October 1856), 87; *AJP* 11 (1849), 326; and Sizer, *Forty Years*, 31, 93, 244, 306.

50. Sizer, *Forty Years*, 204–5.

51. "Phrenology Exemplified," *Newport Mercury*, December 8, 1838, p. 2.

52. Quoted in Ann Lee Bressler, *The Universalist Movement in America, 1770–1880* (New York: Oxford University Press, 2001), 101.

53. Sizer, *Forty Years*, 130–33, has an interesting episode illustrating this.

54. James L. Corning Sr., "Personal Recollections of Henry Ward Beecher," 1903, 11–12, Henry Ward Beecher Collection, Henry Ward Beecher Papers, Yale University.

55. This dialogue is summarized in Henry Ward Beecher, *Eyes and Ears* (Boston: Ticknor and Fields, 1862), 20–25. Beecher is also quoted from *Yale Lectures*, 93–94.

56. Edward Zeus Franklin Wickes, *Improved Phreno-Chart and Compass of Life* (New York: Mutual Benefit Pub., 1882), 19, 136–38.

57. Ibid., 5, 8–9.

58. Davis's harsh condemnation of orthodoxy is in Taves, *Fits*, 183. His assurances that he and others had tried older systems is from Andrew Jackson Davis, *The Magic Staff: An Autobiography of Andrew Jackson Davis* (Boston: William White, 1871), 490.

59. Davis called the book "unsound and insufficient." Quoted in Robert Delp, "A Spiritualist in Connecticut: Andrew Jackson Davis, the Hartford Years, 1850–

1854," *New England Quarterly* 53, no. 3 (September 1980): 353. For more on Davis's theology and his conflicts with orthodox theologians, see ibid., 350–56.

60. A number of other religious liberals experimented with these systems. For example, the physician and writer Joseph R. Buchanan, drawing on neurophysiological research, phrenological charts, and his own mesmeric experiments, devised extensive systems of correspondences that mapped how the brain and body might be influenced by nonphysical energies. Buchanan hoped that a suitably enlarged scientific method could demonstrate the existence of ambient spiritual forces, and he thought this discovery might lay the groundwork for a new nondogmatic religion. Buchanan agreed with Davis that various techniques could be developed to cultivate one's spiritual impressions and balance the vital forces in the self. These harmonial systems adumbrated the ideas of later New Thought writers like Warren Felt Evans, men and women who also linked outer conditions to inner ones as a way of overcoming the confounding inwardness of Calvinism. Robert C. Fuller, "Joseph R. Buchanan," in *American National Biography*, ed. John A. Garraty and Mark Carnes (New York: Oxford University Press, 1999), 3:840–41. See also R. Laurence Moore, *In Search of White Crows: Spiritualism, Parapsychology, and American Culture* (New York: Oxford University Press, 1977), 10–13; and, for information on Warren Felt Evans and other New Thought figures, Gail Thain Parker, *Mind Cure in New England: From the Civil War to World War I* (Hanover, NH: University Press of New England, 1973).

61. Quoted in Taves, *Fits*, 169–70. For figure 4 and more information, see Andrew Jackson Davis, *Present Age and Inner Life: Ancient and Modern Spirit Mysteries Classified and Explained* (Boston: William White and Co., 1869).

62. Henry Ward Beecher, "The Progress of Thought in the Church," *North American Review* 135, no. 309 (August 1882): 106–7, 116–17.

63. See Taves, *Fits*, 134–35, 202–5. The Hecker references are from *Scientific Basis*, 17.

64. Many on both sides addressed this question. Orthodox Christians linked phrenology to materialism and infidelity, and phrenologists too were sensitive to this problem. See Harold Schwartz, "Samuel Gridley Howe as Phrenologist," *American Historical Review* 57, no. 3 (April 1952): 645; and Davies, *Phrenology*, 149–58.

65. Delp, "Spiritualist in Connecticut," 347, 354.

66. Beecher, *Yale Lectures*, 93–94.

67. On the cultural history of phrenology and its relationship to the new, scientific psychology, see Lucy Hartley, *Physiognomy and the Meaning of Expression in Nineteenth-Century Culture* (Cambridge: Cambridge University Press, 2001), 1–14, 180–88.

## 2. FRAGMENTS OF TRUTH

1. Dorothy Ross, *G. Stanley Hall: The Psychologist as Prophet* (Chicago: University of Chicago Press, 1972), 33; the encounters with Beecher and Sage

are narrated in G. Stanley Hall, *Life and Confessions of a Psychologist* (New York: D. Appleton and Co., 1923), 181–83; Ross, *G. Stanley Hall*, 34; Lorine Pruette, *G. Stanley Hall: A Biography of a Mind* (New York: D. Appleton and Co., 1926; reprint, Freeport, NY: Books for Libraries Press, 1970), 65; and Louis Wilson, *G. Stanley Hall: A Sketch* (New York: G. E. Stechert and Co., 1914), 36.

2. Daniel Robinson, *An Intellectual History of Psychology* (Madison: University of Wisconsin Press, 1995), 341; Edwin Boring, A *History of Experimental Psychology*, 2nd ed. (New York: Appleton-Century-Crofts, 1950), 66–67. Skepticism about precise localizations was replaced by revived interest in localization with Broca's experiments on speech (1861) and Fritsch and Hitzig's experiments on the brain's connection to particular muscle groups (1870). See Boring, *History*, 29. James assesses contemporary scientific debates on localization in William James, *The Principles of Psychology* (New York: Henry Holt and Company, 1893), 1:29–80.

3. Gustav Fechner, quoted in Merle Curti, *Human Nature in American Thought: A History* (Madison: University of Wisconsin Press, 1980), 192; Ralph Barton Perry, *The Thought and Character of William James* (Boston: Little, Brown, and Co., 1935), 2:4; Robinson, *History*, 342–45; Thomas Hardy Leahey, *A History of Psychology: Main Currents in Psychological Thought*, 2nd ed. (Englewood Cliffs, NJ: Prentice-Hall, 1987), 183; Roger Smith, *Inhibition: History and Meaning in the Sciences of the Mind and Brain* (Berkeley: University of California Press, 1992), 120–25.

4. Franklin Fearing, quoted in Smith, *Inhibition*, 19. The history of the reflex action concept is exhaustively treated by Franklin Fearing in *Reflex Action: A Study in the History of Physiological Psychology* (Cambridge, MA: MIT Press, 1970); other treatments of the subject can be found, for example, in Boring, *History*, 35–49, and in William Woodward and Mitchell Ash, eds., *The Problematic Science: Psychology in Nineteenth-Century Thought* (New York: Praeger, 1982).

5. Physiological psychology, Wundt cautioned, "is not a province of physiology; nor does it attempt, as has been mistakenly asserted, to derive or explain the phenomena of the psychical from those of the physical life." *Principles of Physiological Psychology* (London: Swan Sonnenschein and Co., 1904), 2. See also Robinson, *History*, 344–46. Emily Cahan and Sheldon White are excellent on Wundt, Mill, and other psychologists trying to find room for nonphysiological ways of conceiving mind and self. See their "Proposals for a Second Psychology," *American Psychologist* 47, no. 2 (February 1992): 224–35.

6. Perry, *Thought and Character*, 2:586–87; Boring, *History*, 278–80, 332.

7. G. Stanley Hall (hereafter G.S.H.) to his parents, Pentecost 1870, G. Stanley Hall Papers, Clark University, Worcester, MA (hereafter G. S. H. Papers); Pruette, *G. Stanley Hall*, 87.

8. G. S. H., quoted in Ross, *G. Stanley Hall*, 46–48. James is quoted in Linda Simon, *Genuine Reality: A Life of William James* (New York: Harcourt, Brace and Co., 1998), 221.

9. G. S. H. to his parents, Pentecost 1870; G. B. Hall to G. S. H., April 7, 1870; G. S. H. to his parents, April 1870, all in G. S. H. Papers; G. Stanley Hall, *Life and Confessions of a Psychologist* (New York: D. Appleton and Co., 1923), 178.

10. Pruette, *G. Stanley Hall*, 176.

11. Wilson, *G. Stanley Hall*, 52–53.

12. Perry, *Thought and Character*, 2:3; William James to Tom Ward, quoted in Gay Wilson Allen, *William James* (Minneapolis: University of Minnesota Press, 1970), 164. See also Perry, *Thought and Character*, 1:322–23, 2:9–13; Bruce Kuklick, *The Rise of American Philosophy: Cambridge, Massachusetts, 1860–1930* (New Haven, CT: Yale University Press, 1977), 161; Ralph Barton Perry, *The Thought and Character of William James* (briefer version) (Nashville: Vanderbilt University Press, 1996), 107–11. James's friends appear to have been unable to help him during this crisis of faith. Chauncy Wright, for example, one of James's closest companions, was by most measures a "formidably logical and relentless determinist." Oliver Wendell Holmes, on the other hand, something of a mentor, was a "nihilistic skeptic" stoically resigned to materialism despite its unattractive implications. See Allen, *William James*, 125, 165. James started teaching psychology courses in the 1875–1876 school year with a course for graduates, "The Relations between Physiology and Psychology." He taught the undergraduate course the next academic year. Perry, *Thought and Character*, 2:10.

13. Quoted in Kuklick, *American Philosophy*, 161; Perry, *Thought and Character*, 1:323–25; and Paul Jerome Croce, *Science and Religion in the Era of William James* (Chapel Hill: University of North Carolina Press, 1995), 208.

14. Kuklick, *American Philosophy*, 30–31, 239; G. Stanley Hall, "Philosophy in the United States," *Mind* 4 (1879): 97. See also William James, *Manuscript Lectures* (Cambridge, MA: Harvard University Press, 1988), xxxi–xxxiii. The final James quotation is from "Biography, Chronology, and Photography of William James," William James website, www.des.emory.edu/mfp/jphotos.html, accessed March 15, 2008.

15. President Eliot evidently needed little convincing. From the time he became president of Harvard in 1869, Eliot instituted several reforms to model Harvard after the German university. He advanced the elective system, advocated mild freedoms for students (e.g., making morning prayers optional), and in 1870 instituted a graduate division. By 1872, PhDs and SDs were given out by vote of the Academic Council. The Graduate School was organized twenty years later, in 1890. W. J. to Eliot, December 2, 1875, in Perry, *Thought and Character*, 2:10–11. See the *Annual Report of the President of Harvard College, 1875–76*, Harvard University Archives, 4, 6; *Annual Report, 1877–78*, 5–6. These reports also are quoted in Perry, *Thought and Character*, 2:13.

16. The divinity school student worried about materialism was Henry Churchill King, quoted in Donald M. Love, *Henry Churchill King of Oberlin* (New Haven, CT: Yale University Press, 1956), 36.

17. William James, "What the Will Effects," *Scribners* 3 (1888): 240; James, *Manuscript Lectures*, 22, 42; Gerald E. Myers, *William James, His Life*

*and Thought* (New Haven, CT: Yale University Press, 1986), 63. In his public lectures in 1878, he was quick to follow his critique of phrenology by adding that his remarks were "not meant to disparage Phrenology as an art of reading character. . . . I am inclined to think," he continued, in a remarkable phrase that could have been tucked in one of Beecher's lectures, "that prominent eyes are a sign of fluent speech, just as a prominent nose is a sign of decision, and delicate hands of sensibility. But the brain behind the eye need no more be the organ of the first peculiarity than are the nose and the hand of the other two" (22). He repeated these ideas almost verbatim in his 1890 psychology textbook. It is a measure of the ways that physiological thinking dominated American thought and culture that this embattled system of correspondences between body and mind could still be recommended as interesting and useful. Some system of relating inner states to outer ones—any system—was, apparently, better than none at all. The two lectures were "The Senses and the Brain and Their Relation to Thought" (1878) and "The Brain and the Mind" (1878). Both are in James, *Manuscript Lectures*, 3–15 and 16–42.

18. Francis A. Walker, "College Athletics," *Harvard Graduates' Magazine* 2, no. 5 (September 1893): 2–5, 13.

19. James, *Principles*, 1:192–93.

20. A horopter chart is a chart that maps out points in space that the eye can see. Hall is quoted in Perry, *Thought and Character*, 2:14. James's publications on dizziness and hearing included an initial note on dizziness in the *Harvard University Bulletin* 2 (1881): 173, and then "The Sense of Dizziness in Deaf-Mutes," *American Journal of Otology* 4 (October 1882): 239–54. See also Perry, *Thought and Character*, 2:14–15, 23–24; Kuklick, *American Philosophy*, 186–87, 196–97; James, *Manuscript Lectures*, xxxii–xxxv.

21. Perry, *Thought and Character*, 2:24; Perry, *Thought and Character* (briefer version), 198; James, quoted in Morton Hunt, *The Story of Psychology* (New York: Doubleday, 1993), 145. See also James, *Manuscript Lectures*, xxxi.

22. "I heard [Hall] criticize James because he required this candidate for degree to engage in considerable work not along the lines of psychology," one of Hall's companions remembered. F. Eby to D. Ross, in clippings file of correspondence between William James (hereafter W. J.) and G. S. H., G. S. H. Papers. See also Pruette, *G. Stanley Hall*, 109.

23. See Ross, *G. Stanley Hall*, 72–78. Hall's study of Laura Bridgman is reprinted in his *Aspects of German Culture* (Boston: Osgood, 1881). See esp. 257–58. Also see G. Stanley Hall, "The Muscular Perception of Space," *Mind* 3 (1878): 436.

24. Hall, "Muscular Perception," 448–49, 446.

25. Frank M. Albrecht Jr., *The New Psychology in America, 1880–1895* (Baltimore: Johns Hopkins, 1977), 1–6. For a more complete analysis of Hall's influence and the work of his students, see Michael Sokal, "G. Stanley Hall and the Institutional Character of Psychology at Clark, 1889–1920," *Journal of the History of the Behavioral Sciences* 26 (April 1990): 114–24.

26. Pruette, *G. Stanley Hall*, 116–17.

27. Hall was the "only man in his day that could pull down a $1,000.00 a [public] lecture," one student remembered. F. Eby to Dorothy Ross, G. S. H. Papers.

28. G. Stanley Hall, "The Affiliation of Psychology with Philosophy and with the Natural Sciences," *Science* 23, no. 582 (February 23, 1906): 298; G. Stanley Hall, "The New Psychology," *Harpers Monthly* 103, no. 617 (October 1901): 727, 731.

29. G. Stanley Hall, "Rest and Fatigue," *Ainslee's Magazine* (July 1902): 503–8; G. Stanley Hall, "Use of the Muscles," *Worcester (MA) Telegram*, 18 July 1903; G. Stanley Hall, "Psychological Progress" (address delivered at the first dinner of the Liberal Club, Buffalo, NY, November 16, 1883), 30–35, G. S. H. Papers; G. Stanley Hall, "Education of the Heart," *Proceedings of the Southern California Teachers' Association, 16th Annual Session* (Redlands, CA: Redlands Review Press, 1909), 31–38.

30. W. J. to G. S. H., September 3, 1879, G. S. H. Papers; W. J. to G. S. H., October 10, 1879, G. S. H. Papers; W. J. to G. S. H., January 16, 1880, G. S. H. Papers; G. S. H. to W. J., February 15, 1880, William James Papers, Houghton Library, Harvard University; W. J. to G. S. H., March 16, 1880, G. S. H. Papers; Hall, "The Affiliation of Psychology with Philosophy," 299. During the 1880s and 1890s, Hall's experimental output increased steadily. His publications included "Optical Illusions of Motion" (1882), "Reaction-Time and Attention in the Hypnotic State" (1883), "Bilateral Asymmetry of Function" (his only publication in 1884), "Motor Sensations on the Skin" (1885), "Studies of Rhythm" (1886), "A Sketch of the History of Reflex Action" (1890), and others. In 1894 he published eleven articles on different subjects. By the end of his career, Hall had become one of the most productive scientists of his time. Ross, *G. Stanley Hall*, 243–44.

31. Simon, *William James*, 284, 327; James, *Manuscript Lectures*, xxvii; Perry, *Thought and Character*, 2:26–31.

32. William James, "The Dilemma of Determinism," in *Essays on Faith and Morals*, ed. Ralph Barton Perry (New York: Signet, 1962), 147–52, 180, 146.

33. Roswell Angier, "Another Student's Impressions of James at the Turn of the Century," *Psychological Review* 50 (1943): 132–34; Edwin D. Starbuck, "A Student's Impressions of James in the Middle '90s," *Psychological Review* 50 (1943): 131; Simon, *William James*, 245.

34. William James, "Reflex Action and Theism," in *Essays on Faith and Morals*, ed. Ralph Barton Perry (New York: Signet, 1962), 112–14, 142–43. This was not James's most eloquent or reasoned defense of theism, and he did not consider it one of his favorite essays. See Myers, *William James*, 458.

35. Perry, *Thought and Character*, 2:105, 48.

36. Ibid., 1:702; William James, "What the Will Effects," *Scribner's* 3, no. 2 (February 1888): 245, 247.

37. James, *Principles* (briefer version), 273–79.

38. Ibid., 380–81.

39. Ibid., 382–83.

40. William Hallock Johnson, "Free-Will and Physiological Psychology," *Presbyterian and Reformed Review* 13 (July 1902): 429–31; Daniel W. Fisher, "The New Psychology," *Presbyterian and Reformed Review* 2 (1891): 618, 622–23; William J. Tucker, "The Psychology and Physiology of Will," *Universalist Quarterly and General Review* 47, no. 27 (July 1890): 392.

41. Edward H. Griffin, "Psychology as a Natural Science," *Presbyterian and Reformed Review* 12 (July 1901): 560, 566–67; James H. Hyslop, "The New Psychology," *New Princeton Review* 6 (1888): 161–65.

42. See Joseph Crook, "Psychology versus Metaphysics," *Methodist Review* (March 1895): 224–27; F. P. Siegfried, "Catholic Psychology," *American Ecclesiastical Review* 4 (1891): 40–43.

43. George Trumbull Ladd, "Psychology as a So-called 'Natural Science,'" *Philosophical Review* 1 (1892): 28–31, 52. A helpful discussion of the controversy is in Eugene S. Mills, *George Trumbull Ladd: Pioneer American Psychologist* (Cleveland: Case Western Reserve University Press, 1969), 119–30. Interestingly, Ralph Barton Perry hardly mentions Ladd or the controversy.

44. William James, "A Plea for Psychology as a 'Natural Science,'" *Philosophical Review* 1, no. 2 (March 1892): 146–53.

45. Ibid.; William James, "What Is an Emotion?" *Mind* 9 (1884): 204.

46. George Trumbull Ladd, "Influence of Modern Psychology upon Theological Opinion," *Andover Review* 14, no. 84 (December 1890): 571–74; W. B. Clarke, "The Nature and Working of the Christian Consciousness," *Andover Review* 7 (April 1887): 379. In the 1880s and 1890s, there were many articles on Christian consciousness in popular and scholarly journals. See, for example, Clarke, "The Nature and Working of the Christian Consciousness"; G. Harris, "The Function of the Christian Consciousness," *Andover Review* 2 (July–December 1884): 338–52; George Trumbull Ladd, "The Religious Consciousness as Ontological," *Journal of Philosophy, Psychology, and Scientific Methods* 1, no. 1 (January 7, 1904): 8–13; Henry M. Goodwin, "The Christian Consciousness," *New Englander and Yale Review* 44, no. 185 (March 1885): 194–214. See also William R. Hutchison, *The Modernist Impulse in American Protestantism* (Durham, NC: Duke University Press, 1992), 89–91.

47. G. S. Hall, "The New Psychology," *Andover Review* 3, no. 14 (February 1885): 125–127, 247; Newman Smyth, "Orthodox Rationalism," *Princeton Review* 58 (1882): 312. See also Ross, *G. Stanley Hall*, 138–42; and Bruce Kuklick, *Churchmen and Philosophers: From Jonathan Edwards to John Dewey* (New Haven, CT: Yale University Press, 1985), 233–34.

48. G. S. Hall, "The New Psychology," 134; G. S. Hall, "The Relations of Physiology to Psychology," *Christian Register* 69 (October 30, 1890): 699; the passages from Hall's *Jesus, the Christ* are quoted in Hendrika Vande Kemp, "G. Stanley Hall and the Clark School of Religious Psychology," *American Psychologist* 47, no. 2 (February 1992): 293.

49. Pruette, *G. Stanley Hall*, 98.

50. "Psychology for the Pastor," *Methodist Review* 80 (1898): 118–19.

51. C. L. Herrick, "The Physical Basis of Character," *Baptist Quarterly Review* 12 (1890): 191.

## 3. NERVOUS ENERGIES

1. The classic history of the unconscious is Henri Ellenberg, *The Discovery of the Unconscious: The History and Evolution of Dynamic Psychiatry* (New York: Basic Books, 1970). Taves also examines carefully the unconscious and its uses in American culture. See Ann Taves, *Fits, Trances, and Visions: Experiencing Religion and Explaining Experience from Wesley to James* (Princeton, NJ: Princeton University Press, 1999), esp. pt. 3.

2. Edwin Clarke and L. S. Jacyna, *Nineteenth-Century Origins of Neuroscientific Concepts* (Berkeley: University of California Press, 1987), 157–67; Michael Heidelberger, "Naturphilosophie," in *Routledge Encyclopedia of Philosophy* (London: Routledge, 1998); available from www.rep.routledge.com/article/DC092SECT3, accessed February 10, 2007. The Galvani quotation is from Clarke and Jacyna, *Nineteenth-Century Origins*, 167.

3. Robert Fuller, *Mesmerism and the American Cure of Souls* (Philadelphia: University of Pennsylvania Press, 1982), 4–5.

4. Elizabeth Towne, *Practical Methods for Self-Development: Spiritual, Mental, Physical* (Holyoke, MA: Elizabeth Towne Co., 1904), 45; Dougall McDougall King, *Nerves and Personal Power: Some Principles of Psychology as Applied to Modern Health* (New York: F. H. Revell, 1922), 35–36, 43; Towne, *Practical Methods*, 44; Annie Payson Call, *Power through Repose* (Cambridge, MA: University Press, 1891), 9.

5. F. G. Gosling, *Before Freud: Neurasthenia and the American Medical Community, 1870–1910* (Urbana: University of Illinois Press, 1987), 147–49. George Rosen has noted the popularity of this idea in industrializing England, and Dain has documented it in antebellum America. See George Rosen, "Social Stress and Mental Disease from the Eighteenth Century to the Present: Some Origins of Social Psychiatry," *Milbank Memorial Fund Quarterly* 37, no. 1 (January, 1959): 5–32; and Norman Dain, *Concepts of Insanity in the United States, 1789–1865* (New Brunswick, NJ: Rutgers University Press, 1964), 89–91. Also, Jackson Lears has documented a widespread fear about "the decay of sentiment," "the disuse of laughter," "the decadence of enthusiasm," and the "decay of personality" in this period. He quotes the essayist Agnes Repplier, who complained, "The old springs of simple sentiment are dying fast within us. It is heartless to laugh, it is foolish to cry, it is indiscreet to love, it is morbid to hate, and it is intolerant to espouse any cause with enthusiasm." T. J. Jackson Lears, *No Place of Grace: Antimodernism and the Transformation of American Culture, 1880–1920* (Chicago: University of Chicago Press, 1994), 48. This discourse also was linked to a broader discourse on the artificial nature of the city and the ways that the problems of the built environment had to be overcome with more instinctual and natural avocations and forms of "play." See Paul Boyer, *Urban Masses and Moral*

*Order in America, 1820–1920* (Cambridge, MA: Harvard University Press, 1992), 122, 247, 242.

6. Beard is quoted in Fuller, *Mesmerism*, 113. For this paragraph and others, I have also drawn from Donald Meyer, *The Positive Thinkers: Religion as Pop Psychology from Mary Baker Eddy to Oral Roberts* (New York: Pantheon, 1980), 21–27. For information on physiology, degeneration, and the nineteenth-century problem of "culture," see J. E. Chamberlin, "An Anatomy of Cultural Melancholy," *Journal of the History of Ideas* 42, no. 4 (October–December 1981): 691–705.

7. William James, "The Energies of Men," in *Essays on Faith and Morals* (New York: Meridian Books, 1962), 216–37. For James on vital energies, see George Cotkin, *William James, Public Philosopher* (Baltimore: Johns Hopkins Press, 1990), 112–13; Kim Townsend, *Manhood at Harvard: William James and Others* (New York: W. W. Norton, 1996), 169–72; E. Brooks Holifield, *A History of Pastoral Care in America: From Salvation to Self-Realization* (Nashville, TN: Abingdon Press, 1983), 188–92.

8. "Newman Smyth," *Literary World: A Monthly Review of Current Literature* (April 8, 1882): 113.

9. Newman Smyth, quoted in Bruce Kuklick, *Churchmen and Philosophers: From Jonathan Edwards to John Dewey* (New Haven, CT: Yale University Press, 1985), 234; Newman Smyth, "Orthodox Rationalism," *Princeton Review* 1 (1882): 294–312.

10. Clarke and Jacyna, *Nineteenth-Century Origins*, 96–100, 157–59, 211, 287; Barbara Sicherman, *The Quest for Mental Health in America, 1880–1917* (New York: Arno Press, 1967), 127–30. See also Theodore Hough and William Sedgwick, *The Human Mechanism: Its Physiology and Hygiene and the Sanitation of Its Surroundings* (Boston: Ginn and Co., 1906), 286–87.

11. William James, *The Principles of Psychology* (New York: Henry Holt and Company, 1893), 1:124–26; William James, cited in Henry C. King, *Rational Living: Some Practical Inferences from Modern Psychology* (New York: Macmillan, 1918), 150; James, *Talks to Teachers on Psychology: And to Students on Some of Life's Ideals* (New York: W. W. Norton, 1958), 138–40. The psychologist James Baldwin developed the idea that inner excitations always issue in outer reactions into the law of "dynamogenesis," which was "the principle according to which changes in the conditions of sensory stimulation of the nervous system always show themselves in corresponding changes in muscular tension or movement." See entry on "dynamogenesis" in James Mark Baldwin, ed., *Dictionary of Philosophy and Psychology* (New York: Macmillan, 1901–1905), 1:302. I focus on this issue in chapter 4.

12. Beard quoted in Gail Bederman, *Manliness and Civilization: A Cultural History of Gender and Race in the United States, 1880–1917* (Chicago: University of Chicago Press, 1995), 85–88; George Beard, *American Nervousness: Its Causes and Consequences* (New York: G. P. Putnam, 1881; reprint, New York: Arno Press, 1972), vi, 120–21; Beard also quoted in Tom Lutz,

American Nervousness, 1903: An Anecdotal History (Ithaca, NY: Cornell University Press, 1991), 3.

13. Henry Churchill King, The Seeming Unreality of the Spiritual Life (New York: Macmillan, 1911), 25; King, Rational Living, 70, 71, 68.

14. Washington Gladden, "Creative Americans: Henry Churchill King," Oberlin Alumni Magazine (March 1907): 224, 216.

15. George Coe, Spiritual Life: Studies in the Science of Religion (New York: Eaton and Mains, 1900), 73, 80–84, 75, 86–87. See also George Coe, "The Morbid Conscience of Adolescents" (address before the Illinois Society for Child Study, Chicago, June 4, 1898), George Coe Archives, Yale Divinity School, Yale University.

16. James, Talks to Teachers, 146; Oliver Huckel, Mental Medicine: Some Practical Suggestions from a Spiritual Standpoint (New York: Thomas Y. Crowell and Co., 1909), 162; the biblical quotation is Mark 11:22–24; William Sadler, The Physiology of Faith and Fear: Or, the Mind in Health and Disease (Chicago: A.C. McClurg and Co., 1920), 128–29, 100–101. For similar arguments on the subject, see Alfred Schofield, Christian Sanity (New York: A.C. Armstrong and Co., 1908).

17. Philip Wiener, "G.M. Beard and Freud on 'American Nervousness,'" Journal of the History of Ideas 17, no. 2 (April 1956), 269–74; Barbara Sicherman, "The Paradox of Prudence: Mental Health in the Gilded Age," Journal of American History 62, no. 4 (March 1976), 890–912; F.G. Gosling, Before Freud: Neurasthenia and the American Medical Community, 1870–1910 (Urbana: University of Illinois Press, 1987), 111. See also Bederman, Manliness and Civilization, 130; Holifield, Pastoral Care, 189–93, 200–205.

18. Boyer, Urban Masses, 242–48. For more on the American Play Movement and related reforms, see Stephanie Wallach, "Luther Halsey Gulick and the Salvation of the American Adolescent" (PhD diss., Columbia University, New York, 1989), 214–57; and Richard Swanson, "The Acceptance and Influence of Play in American Protestantism," Quest, monograph 11 (December 1968): 59–70.

19. Call, Power through Repose, 80.

20. Josiah Strong, The Times and Young Men (New York: Baker and Taylor, 1901), 151–54; Messages of the Men and Religion Movement, vol. 2, Social Service (New York: Association Press, 1912), 55–56; Allen Hoben, "The Minister and the Boy," Biblical World 39, no. 3 (1912): 184; Richard Cabot, What Men Live By (1914; reprint, Boston: Houghton Mifflin, 1941), 162–63; and Carl E. Seashore, "The Play Impulse and Attitude in Religion," American Journal of Theology 14, no. 4 (October 1910): 505. See also Hamilton W. Mabie, Essays on Work and Culture (Cambridge, MA: University Press, 1898); Horatio Dresser, Human Efficiency: A Psychological Study of Modern Problems (New York: G.P. Putnam, 1912), 147–50; Luther Gulick, Mind and Work (New York: Doubleday, Page, and Co., 1908); and Huckel, Mental Medicine.

21. Strong, Times and Young Men, 154–55.

22. James's practical maxim here was "never to suffer one's self to have an emotion at a concert, without expressing it afterward in some active way,"

and, more generally, to *"keep the faculty of effort alive in you by a little gratuitous exercise every day."* Keeping this faculty alive meant being "systematically ascetic or heroic in little unnecessary points," or doing "something every day or two for no other reason than that you would rather not do it, so that when the hour of dire need draws nigh, it may find you not unnerved and untrained to stand the test." This was standard advice in this strenuous era: be wary of inner emotions that were not expressed in outer acts. James, *Psychology* (briefer version), 148–49. A good number of liberal Protestant moralists took James's advice on this. See, for instance, the YMCA figure Robert Speer and his *A Young Man's Questions* (New York: International Committee of Young Men's Christian Associations, 1903), 121–23.

23. Theodore Munger, *On the Threshold* (Boston: Houghton, Mifflin, and Co., 1887), 203; Vida Scudder, "The Moral Dangers of Musical Devotees," *Andover Review* 7 (January 1887): 52, 50; Edward Howard Griggs, *The Use of the Margin* (New York: B. W. Huebsch, 1912), 52. The period saw the proliferation of antinoise leagues and other related reforms. For more on the symbolism of noise, silence, and sound reformers in this era, see Karin Bijsterveld, "The Diabolical Symphony of the Mechanical Age: Technology and Symbolism of Sound in European and North American Noise Abatement Campaigns, 1900–40," *Social Studies of Science* 31, no. 1 (February 2001): 37–70. The problems of music and culture elicited strong opinions for many reasons, not least of which was the fact that American high culture was replacing (in the view of some) or cooperating (in the view of others) with Protestantism in efforts to propagate morality and order. Arguments over music and other aspects of culture, then, could be as animated and contentious as concerns about religion. Lawrence Levine assays the conversations about culture and its abilities to order disorderly crowds and shape notions of morality and civility in his *Highbrow, Lowbrow: The Emergence of Cultural Hierarchy in America* (Cambridge, MA: Harvard University Press, 1988). For more on the role music played, see Steven Baur, "Music, Morals, and Social Management: Mendelssohn in Post-Civil War America," *American Music* 19, no. 1 (Spring 2001): 64–130. Advice literature on music and other entertainments was vast in this period, much of it included in a broader literature on behavior, manners, and etiquette. This literature is explored in John Kasson, *Rudeness and Civility: Manners in Nineteenth-Century Urban America* (New York: Hill and Wang, 1990). My aim here is to examine clerical or religious advice literature, and literature about spiritual and moral problems in particular.

24. Griggs, *Use of the Margin*, 52–53; Coe, *Spiritual Life*, 214–28. Coe was not alone in worrying about revivals. In lecture notes for talks at Oberlin and in many other publications, H. C. King wrote against revivals. He put many of these cautions together in his *Personal and Ideal Elements in Education* (New York: Macmillan, 1904).

25. George Clarke, "The Novel-Reading Habit," *Arena* 19 (May 1898): 670–79; George T. Ladd, "The Psychology of the Modern Novel," *Andover Review* 12, no. 68 (August 1889): 135; James, *Principles*, 1:126; Griggs, *Use of*

*the Margin*, 51. See also C.C. Everett, *The Psychological Elements of Religious Faith* (New York: Macmillan, 1902), 38–39. For additional discussion see Candy Brown, *Word in the World: Evangelical Writing, Publishing, and Reading in America, 1789–1880* (Chapel Hill: University of North Carolina Press, 2004), 97.

26. Theodore Hough and William Sedgwick, *The Human Mechanism: Its Physiology and Hygiene* (Boston: Ginn and Co., 1906), 376. See also Harvey Green, *Fit for America: Health, Fitness, Sport, and American Society* (New York: Pantheon, 1986), 40–42; and Jonathan Zimmerman, "'When the Doctors Disagree': Scientific Temperance and Scientific Authority, 1891–1906," *Journal of the History of Medicine and Allied Sciences* 48 (1993): 171–97.

27. David Starr Jordan, *The Call of the Twentieth Century: An Address to Young Men* (Boston: Beacon Press, 1903), 58, 63; and Robert Roberts, "Artificial Stimulation," *Association Men* 30, no. 1 (October 1904): 58.

28. Washington Gladden, *Working People and Their Employers* (New York: Funk and Wagnalls, 1885), 148–58, 161, 165. A number of other religious liberals, like William D. Hyde, thought alcohol opened the door to vice and degraded our willpower. See Thomas Edward Frank, "Conserving a Rational World: Theology, Ethics, and the Nineteenth-Century American College Ideal" (PhD diss., Emory University, Atlanta, Georgia, 1981), 242–43.

29. In part this was because depleted men were unable to attract (and fertilize) women. "The more exhausted men become, whether by overwork, unnatural city life, alcohol, recrudescent polygamic inclinations, exclusive devotion to greed and self; whether they become weak, stooping, blear-eyed, bald-headed, bow-legged, thin-shanked, or gross, coarse, barbaric, and bestial, the more they lose the power to lead woman or to arouse her nature, which is essentially passive." From G. Stanley Hall, *Youth: Its Education, Regiment, Hygiene* (1908; reprint, Whitefish, MT: Kessinger Publishing, 2004), 215. See also G. Stanley Hall, "From Generation to Generation: With Some Plain Language about Race Suicide and the Instruction of Children during Adolescence," *American Magazine* 66 (July 1908): 248–54.

30. Josiah Strong, *Our Country: Its Possible Future and Its Present Crisis* (New York: Baker and Taylor, 1891), 120–26; Elwood Worcester, Samuel McComb, and Isador Coriat, *Religion and Medicine: The Moral Control of Nervous Disorders* (New York: Moffat, Yard, and Co., 1908), 128–36. For more on Hall, see Bederman, *Manliness and Civilization*, 109. One chart on the effects of alcohol is in Frances Gulick Jewett, *Control of Mind and Body* (Boston: Ginn and Company, 1908), 230.

31. Gail Bederman, *Manliness and Civilization: A Cultural History of Gender and Race in the United States, 1880–1917* (Chicago: University of Chicago Press, 1995). Jordan is quoted in Edward Larson, *Summer for the Gods: The Scopes Trial and America's Continuing Debate over Science and Religion* (Cambridge, MA: Harvard University Press, 1998), 41; J.H. Denison, "Mental Narcotics and Stimulants," *Andover Review* 9 (April 1888): 408, 397, 406, 397.

32. James, *Principles*, 1:23; Harry Moore, *Keeping in Condition: A Handbook on Training for Older Boys* (New York: Macmillan, 1917), 78–79; and Sylvanus Stall, *What a Young Boy Ought to Know* (Philadelphia: Vir Publishing, 1897). In general, by the late nineteenth century, in discourses on the effects of sexual indulgence (and especially masturbation) the emphasis was switching from physical to mental effects. Earlier it was inflammation, infection, infertility, weakness, dyspepsia, and predisposition to disease; later, and in congruence with new literatures on nervousness especially, the key symptoms were loss of nervous energy, loss of self control, insanity, and nervousness. See Robert H. MacDonald, "The Frightful Consequences of Onanism: Notes on the History of a Delusion" *Journal of the History of Ideas* 28, no. 3 (July 1967): 423–31; and Charles Rosenberg, "Sexuality, Class, and Role in Nineteenth-Century America," *American Quarterly* 25, no. 2 (May 1973): 136–38.

33. Hall's quotations are from Bederman, *Manliness and Civilization*, 102–4, 109; Ross, *G. Stanley Hall*, 384–85.

34. Coe, *Spiritual Life*, 94–96; Lyman Beecher Sperry, *Confidential Talks with Young Men* (New York: Fleming H. Revell, 1892), 12; and Richard Cabot, *Christianity and Sex* (New York: Macmillan, 1937), 34–37.

35. William Hammond, quoted in Anita Clair Fellman and Michael Fellman, *Making Sense of Self: Medical Advice Literature in Late Nineteenth-Century America* (Philadelphia: University of Pennsylvania Press, 1981), 102.

## 4. NEUROMUSCULAR CHRISTIANS

1. John Higham, *Writing American History: Essays on Modern Scholarship* (Bloomington: Indiana University Press, 1970), 73–102; Gail Bederman, "'The Women Have Had Charge of the Church Work Long Enough': The Men and Religion Forward Movement of 1911–1912 and the Masculinization of Middle-Class Protestantism," *American Quarterly* 41, no. 3 (September 1989): 435; Gail Bederman, *Manliness and Civilization: A Cultural History of Gender and Race in the United States, 1880–1917* (Chicago: University of Chicago Press, 1995), 1–44; Susan Curtis, *A Consuming Faith: The Social Gospel and Modern American Culture* (Baltimore: Johns Hopkins, 1991); Janet Forsythe Fishburn, *The Fatherhood of God and the Victorian Family* (Philadelphia: Fortress Press, 1981); Clifford Putney, *Muscular Christianity: Manhood and Sports in Protestant America, 1880–1920* (Cambridge, MA: Harvard University Press, 2001).

2. T. J. Jackson Lears, *No Place of Grace: Antimodernism and the Transformation of American Culture, 1880–1920* (Chicago: University of Chicago Press, 1994), 50; William James, "The Energies of Men," in *Essays on Faith and Morals* (New York: Meridian Books, 1962), 228–29, 222. There were a large number of practical advice manuals on the will as a remedy for nervousness. See, for example, Richard Ebbard, *How to Acquire and Strengthen Will-Power: Modern Psycho-therapy. A Specific Remedy for Neurasthenia and*

*Nervous Diseases* (New York: Fowler and Wells, 1907); and Joseph Collins, *The Treatment of Diseases of the Nervous System: A Manual for Practitioners* (New York: William Wood and Co., 1900).

3. All from Anita Clair Fellman and Michael Fellman, *Making Sense of Self: Medical Advice Literature in Late Nineteenth-Century America* (Philadelphia: University of Pennsylvania Press, 1981), 91–93.

4. Ibid., 115–17.

5. Ralph Barton Perry, *The Thought and Character of William James* (briefer version) (Nashville: Vanderbilt University Press, 1996), 121; Bruce Kuklick, *The Rise of American Philosophy: Cambridge, Massachusetts, 1860–1930* (New Haven, CT: Yale University Press, 1977), 161–64; Richard Gale, "William James and the Willfulness of Belief," *Philosophy and Phenomenological Research* 59, no. 1 (March 1999): 72–73. See also William Woodward, "William James's Psychology of Will: Its Revolutionary Impact on American Psychology," in *Explorations in the History of Psychology in the United States*, ed. Josef Brozek (Lewisburg, PA: Bucknell University Press, 1984), 148–95.

6. Kuklick, *American Philosophy*, 188.

7. Ibid., 187–89; G. Stanley Hall, "The Education of the Will," *Princeton Review* (1882): 306–8; Henry C. King, *Rational Living: Some Practical Inferences from Modern Psychology* (New York: Macmillan, 1918), 158–80.

8. In the early 1870s, the *Christian Union* regularly had one hundred thousand subscribers; by its third anniversary (1873), it "reached the largest circulation," Frank Mott has estimated, "which had ever been attained by a religious periodical." Frank Luther Mott, *A History of American Magazines, 1865–1885* (Cambridge, MA: Harvard University Press, 1938), 66–67, 425–26. The fortunes of the *Christian Union* dramatically changed because of the Beecher trial and other factors in the mid-1870s.

9. F. C. Phinney, "Prayer and Life," *Christian Union* 7, no. 3 (January 15, 1873); W. C. Wilkinson, "Obedience in Detail," *Christian Union* 3, no. 18 (May 3, 1871); Henry Ward Beecher, "The Beginning of Christian Life," *Christian Union* 3, no. 18 (May 3, 1871); and Henry Ward Beecher's article in *The Independent* of May 6, 1858. For more on Beecher's ideas, see his sermon "Morality the Basis of Piety," in *Sermons of Henry Ward Beecher*, 1st series (New York: J. B. Ford, 1873): 389–406. See also George Merriam, *A Living Faith* (Boston: Lockwood, Brooks, and Co., 1876), viii–ix. Taves also talks about ways nineteenth- (and eighteenth-) century liberals turned to the will in their spiritual seeking. See Ann Taves, *Fits, Trances, and Visions: Experiencing Religion and Explaining Experience from Wesley to James* (Princeton, NJ: Princeton University Press, 1999), 46, 123.

10. Coe, "My Own Little Theater," in *Religion in Transition*, ed. Virgilius Ferm (1937; reprint, Freeport, NY: Books for Libraries Press, 1969), 93.

11. Ibid., Arthur L. Swift, "At Union Theological Seminary," *Religious Education* 47, no. 2 (March–April 1952): 95; A. J. W. Myers, "As a Teacher," *Religious Education* 47, no. 2 (March–April 1952): 106; George Michaelides,

"A One Time Secretary Writes," *Religious Education* 47, no. 2 (March–April 1952): 102. This issue of *Religious Education* is a memorial issue on Coe.

12. Henry C. King, "The Professor's Chair," *Congregationalist and Christian World* 90, no. 31 (August 5, 1905): 177. William Hutchison mentions that it was common for modernist Protestants of Coe's generation to be unable to convert in expected ways. See William Hutchison, "Cultural Strain and Protestant Liberalism," *American Historical Review* 76, no. 2 (1971): 410.

13. William DeWitt Hyde, *Outlines of Social Theology* (New York: Macmillan, 1900), 124–33. See also William DeWitt Hyde, *God's Education of Man* (New York: Houghton Mifflin, 1899), 45.

14. Alan Tractenberg, *The Incorporation of America: Culture and Society in the Gilded Age* (New York: Hill and Wang, 1982), 38–42; the liberal Catholic John Lancaster Spalding is quoted in Robert Fuller, *Mesmerism and the American Cure of Souls* (Philadelphia: University of Pennsylvania Press, 1982), 108–9; and Luther Halsey Gulick, *The Efficient Life* (New York: Doubleday, 1907), 182. See also Leo Marx, *The Machine in the Garden: Technology and the Pastoral Ideal in America* (Oxford: Oxford University Press, 2000); and Josiah Strong, *The Times and Young Men* (New York: Baker and Taylor, 1901), 198.

15. Hall, "Education of the Will," 308; William James, "The Gospel of Relaxation," in *Talks to Teachers: And to Students on Some of Life's Ideals* (New York: W. W. Norton, 1958), 136; William James, "Recent Works on Mental Hygiene," *Nation* 19 (July 16, 1874): 43. (The last is collected in William James, *Essays, Comments, and Reviews* [Cambridge, MA: Harvard University Press, 1987], 276–7).

16. William James, *Talks to Teachers: And to Students on Some of Life's Ideals* (New York: W. W. Norton, 1958), 173–76. See also Linda Schott, "Jane Addams and William James on Alternatives to War," *Journal of the History of Ideas* 54, no. 2 (April 1993): 241–54.

17. William DeWitt Hyde, *Are You Human?* (New York: Macmillan, 1916), 3. See also William DeWitt Hyde, "Athletic Virtues," *Homiletic Review* 23, no. 2 (February 1892): 115–16. James and Hall recommended athletics as well. See William James, "Recent Works on Mental Hygiene," *Nation* 19 (July 16, 1874): 43; and James's reviews of three mental hygiene books in James, *Essays, Comments, and Reviews*, 276–77. In his satirical indictment of American society, Thorstein Veblen also points to the connections between religion and athletics. See chapter 12 of *The Theory of the Leisure Class: An Economic Study in the Evolution of Institutions* (New York: Macmillan, 1899).

18. Smyth is quoted in Gary Dorrien, *The Making of American Liberal Theology: Imagining Progressive Religion, 1805–1900* (Louisville, KY: Westminster John Knox Press, 2001), 283; all other quotations are from Putney, *Muscular Christianity*, 50, 59, 45, 57. See also E. Brooks Holifield, *A History of Pastoral Care in America: From Salvation to Self-Realization* (Nashville, TN: Abingdon Press, 1983), 177.

19. The characterization of Strong is from Sydney Ahlstrom, *A Religious History of the American People* (New Haven, CT: Yale University Press,

1972), 798. Strong, *Times and Young Men*, 129, 57; Strong, *Next Great Awakening*, 78; Josiah Strong, *Religious Movements for Social Betterment* (New York: Baker and Taylor, 1900), 14–16, 30–33; Strong, *Next Great Awakening*, 78–9; Strong, *Times and Young Men*, 56–77; Strong, *Next Great Awakening*, 95; Strong, *Times and Young Men*, 7–12; Strong, quoted in Putney, *Muscular Christianity*, 62.

20. Charles E. Jefferson, "The Business of Saving Men," *Association Men* 29, no. 1 (October 1903): 2–4. See also Winfield S. Hall, "The Sin of Physical Neglect," *Association Men* 29, no. 1 (October 1903): 6–7.

21. George J. Fisher, "The Christian Aspects of Personal and Community Hygiene," in *Education and National Character*, ed. H. C. King, Francis Peabody, Lyman Abbott, and Washington Gladden (Chicago: Religious Education Association, 1908), 101–2; W. C. Douglas, "How to Get the Best Spiritual Results from the Physical and Education Departments of Our Work," *Watchman* (July 4, 1889): 442.

22. Stephanie Wallach, "Luther Halsey Gulick and the Salvation of the American Adolescent" (PhD diss., Columbia University, New York, 1989), 1–5, 95–98.

23. Gulick is quoted in Ethel Dorgan, *Luther Halsey Gulick* (1934; reprint, New York: AMS Press, 1972), 26; Luther Gulick, "The Real Work of the Gymnasium Instructor," manuscript, n.d., Luther H. Gulick Papers, Springfield College, Springfield, Massachusetts, 1. See also Wallach, "Luther Gulick," 95–97.

24. Luther Gulick, "The Gymnasium as a Factor in Aggressive Christian Work," n.d., Luther Gulick Papers, Springfield College, Springfield, Massachusetts, 1–2; Luther Gulick, "Psychical Aspects of Muscular Exercise," *Popular Science Monthly* 53, no. 6 (October 1898): 797; Wallach, "Luther Halsey Gulick," 98–102.

25. On the ongoing interest in physiognomy and phrenology, especially in New Thought circles, see R. Marie Griffith, *Born Again Bodies: Flesh and Spirit in American Christianity* (Berkeley: University of California Press, 2004), 110–59. See also Gulick, "Psychical Aspects of Muscular Exercise," 797–98; and Luther Gulick, *Manual for Physical Measurements in Connection with the Association Gymnasium Records* (New York: YMCA, 1892).

26. Frances Gulick Jewett, *Control of Body and Mind* (Boston: Ginn and Co., 1908), 24–29; and Luther Gulick, *Mind and Work* (New York: Doubleday, Page, and Co., 1908) 103, 153.

27. Luther Gulick, "The Psychological, Pedagogical, and Religious Aspects of Group Games," *Pedagogical Seminary* 6, no. 1 (October 1898): 141–42, 144, 139, 149.

28. [Luther Gulick and James Naismith], "Physical Education and Its Relation to the Mental and Spiritual Life of Women," *Physical Education* 1, no. 5 (July 1892): 79, 82. This article is not signed, and I am assuming Gulick and Naismith, the editors of the journal, wrote it. See also Wallach, "Luther Halsey Gulick," 243–45, 250–52.

29. King, *Rational Living*, 145, 146.

30. William George Koons, *The Child's Religious Life: A Study of the Child's Religious Nature and the Best Methods for Its Training and Development* (New York: Eaton and Mains, 1903), 135, 136.

31. Faunce is quoted in Holifield, *History of Pastoral Care in America*, 187; King, *Rational Living*, 61, 87–89. On the rise of a habit discourse, see also Fellman and Fellman, *Making Sense of Self*, 122–25.

32. T. D. A. Cockerell, "Precepts for the Young, and Reflections for the Old," *Dial* 40, no. 472 (February 16, 1906): 151–52; King, *Rational Living*, 62.

33. James, "Gospel of Relaxation," 240; Hannah Whitall Smith, *The Christian's Secret of a Happy Life* (Boston: Willard Tract Repository, 1875; reprint, Westwood, N.J.: Revell, 1952), 66–82.

34. King, *Rational Living*, 181; Henry C. King, *How to Make a Rational Fight for Character* (New York: Association Press, 1902), 18–23.

35. Gulick, *Efficient Life*, 41, 45, 35; Luther Gulick, "A Woman's Worst Emotion," *Ladies Home Journal* 25 (June 1908): 24; King, *Rational Living*, 82–83, 186; King, *Rational Fight*, 20.

36. Luther Gulick, "How to Keep Your Good Resolutions," *Detroit Tribune*, January 16, 1910.

37. Gulick, "A Woman's Worst Emotion," 24; Luther Gulick, "Emotional Storms in Women," *Ladies Home Journal* 5, no. 25 (January 1908): 24.

38. Kate Gordon, "Wherein Should the Education of a Woman Differ from That of a Man," *School Review* 13 (1905): 790. On female support for muscular Christianity, see Bederman, "Women Have Had Charge," 452. For information on Thompson and others women scientists working on gender, see Rosalind Rosenberg, *Beyond Separate Spheres: Intellectual Roots of Modern Feminism* (New Haven: Yale University Press, 1982), 67–83.

39. The quotation is Gulick writing about the Camp Fire Girls in an attachment to a letter he wrote to H. C. King. See Luther Gulick to H. C. King, April 3, 1913, H. C. King Archives, Oberlin College. For more on mental work, nervousness, and infertility in women, see Kim Townsend, *Manhood at Harvard: William James and Others* (New York: W. W. Norton, 1996), 205–6.

40. For Gulick's interest in feminizing the church and religion, see Wallach, "Luther Halsey Gulick," 244. For ways that other liberal men yearned for the female, and especially for feminine emotion, see also Lears, *No Place of Grace*, 241–60. Lears spreads the issue out, as I do in the next chapter, by discussing desire and ambivalence not just for female emotion but also for other things in the same category—Catholicism, Mariolatry, the medieval, and so on. And on the ways male toughness and agnosticism were linked, see James Turner, *Without God, without Creed: The Origins of Unbelief in America* (Baltimore: Johns Hopkins University Press, 1985), 235.

## 5. "A MULTITUDE OF SUPERSTITIONS AND CRUDITIES"

1. Edwin Diller Starbuck, *The Psychology of Religion: An Empirical Study of the Growth of Religious Consciousness* (1898; reprint, London:

Walter Scott, 1914), 10; Edwin Diller Starbuck to William James (hereafter W.J.), August 23, 1902, William James Papers, Houghton Library, Harvard University (hereafter W.J. Papers).

2. For some time, scholars have neglected the scientific and religious pursuits of psychologists of religion. This might be in part because older studies of the late nineteenth century focused on the period's religious emergencies and negations rather than on less visible modes of religious affirmation and reconstruction. For a long time, this era was known as the "critical period" of religious decline in American history. There is still not much work on the pioneer psychologists of religion—Starbuck, George Coe, James Bissett Pratt, G. Stanley Hall—and their ways of rethinking religion. The notable exception has been, of course, the literature on William James, which encompasses an enormous number of dissertations and monographs, including several important studies examining *The Varieties of Religious Experience* and James's other efforts to help fashion a science of religion. Most of these works do not consider in detail broader currents in the psychological study of religion that James was drawing on. Given that James identified himself as a psychologist, engaged a wide range of neurological, physiological, and psychological thinkers in the text, and drew extensively on psychologists like George Coe, James Leuba, Theodore Flournoy, and Edwin Starbuck, it is remarkable that these contexts have been overlooked. (His debt to Starbuck is particularly significant: in his *Varieties*, he uses or refers to Starbuck's scholarship twenty-six times; he draws from Starbuck's questionnaire data thirty-seven times; and he mentions Starbuck by name a total of forty-six times, which is roughly the equivalent of once in every six pages of text.)

One recent work that does succeed in putting psychologists of religion in larger contexts is Ann Taves's book, to which I am much indebted, a book that devotes more than a chapter to how these thinkers explained religious experiences and attempted to reform them (*Fits, Trances, and Visions: Experiencing Religion and Explaining Experience from Wesley to James* [Princeton: Princeton University Press, 1999]). Half a century ago David Bremer noted the "deficiency of historical study in the psychology of religion" and called for new, serious studies of the pioneers in the field—but his call, according to Howard Booth, was ignored. See David Henry Bremer, "George Albert Coe's Contribution to the Psychology of Religion" (PhD diss., Boston University, 1949), 7; and John Howard Booth, "Edwin Diller Starbuck: Pioneer in the Psychology of Religion" (PhD diss., University of Iowa, 1972), 1.

Other than James, the only major figure in the psychology of religion to attract attention has been the founder of American psychology and its driving force, G. Stanley Hall. Unfortunately, the sole scholarly biography of Hall only briefly mentions Hall's "strong religious feelings" and his key role in the psychology of religion. The author, Dorothy Ross, regretted the omission and anticipated disappointment among historians of religion who might have expected "an analysis of the institutional and doctrinal context of American Protestantism to which Hall's mature psychology of religion was directed."

See Dorothy Ross, G. *Stanley Hall: The Psychologist as Prophet* (Chicago: University of Chicago Press, 1972), xvi. See also Taves, *Fits*, 253–307.

3. Edwin Starbuck, "Religion's Use of Me," in *Religion in Transition*, ed. Virgilius Ferm (1937; reprint, Freeport, NY: Books for Libraries Press, 1969), 204–6.

4. Ibid., 214–15.

5. Ibid., 206, 212–22.

6. Ibid., 222–26; Another pioneer in the psychology of religion, a Swiss-born graduate student at Clark University named James Leuba, conducted empirical studies—questionnaires and interviews—of religious experience and published his studies the year before Starbuck (in 1896). But Starbuck initiated his work at Harvard first. See Booth, "Edwin Diller Starbuck," 40–41.

7. Most quotations and the conversion survey are from Starbuck, "Religion's Use of Me," 225–26. The dialogue with James is Starbuck's recollection, printed in Edwin Starbuck, "A Student's Impressions of James in the Middle '90s," *Psychological Review* 50, no. 1 (1943): 129–30.

8. His two articles were "A Study of Conversion," *American Journal of Psychology* (January 1897): 268–308, and "Contributions to the Psychology of Religion," *American Journal of Psychology* 9 (1897–98): 70–124. Starbuck's book was the first in the genre, and his articles were the most ambitious quantitative studies done before 1900. There were, however, other scholars working along the same lines, especially those interested in relating conversion to life-cycle stages. All of them were associated with G. Stanley Hall at Clark University. The very earliest studies were G. Stanley Hall, "The Moral and Religious Training of Children," *Princeton Review* 9 (1882): 26–45; A.H. Daniels, "The New Life: A Study in Regeneration," *American Journal of Psychology* 6 (1895): 61–103; and J.H. Leuba, "The Psychology of Religious Phenomena," *American Journal of Psychology* 7 (1896): 309–85. Leuba's study was the most quantitative.

9. George Coe, "My Own Little Theater," in *Religion in Transition*, ed. Virgilius Ferm (1937; reprint, Freeport, NY: Books for Libraries Press, 1969), 93; Starbuck, "Religion's Use of Me," 223. On liberal conversion failures, see William Hutchison, "Cultural Strain and Protestant Liberalism," *American Historical Review* 76, no. 2 (1971): 410.

10. Starbuck, *Psychology of Religion*, 25–57, 186. There were several prominent social scientists who argued that conversions and other religious states were unhealthy, including the well-known French pundit Gustav Le Bon and the American psychologist Boris Sidis. Starbuck quarrels with Sidis and others in *Psychology of Religion*, 163–79. Sidis thought Starbuck's problem was that he did not know that conversion was a pathological condition!

11. Starbuck, "Religion's Use of Me," 202; Starbuck, *Psychology of Religion*, 6–10.

12. Starbuck, *Psychology of Religion*, 6–10, 72–73; see also George Coe, *The Spiritual Life: Studies in the Science of Religion* (New York: Eaton and Mains, 1900), 120. James Leuba is well known for his efforts to document how education militated against evangelical beliefs. For a summary of his work, see David M. Wulff, "James Henry Leuba: A Reassessment of a Swiss-American

Pioneer," in *Aspects in Contexts: Studies in the History of Psychology of Religion*, ed. Jacob Belzen (Amsterdam: Rodopi, 1994), 25–44. See also Booth, "Edwin Diller Starbuck," 8.

13. See James's preface to Starbuck's *Psychology of Religion*, viii–ix; W. J. to Alice Howe Gibbens James, September 10 and 15, 1898, W. J. Papers; W. J. to Alice Howe Gibbens James, n.d., quoted in Ralph Barton Perry, *The Thought and Character of William James* (Boston: Little, Brown and Co., 1935), 2:323; W. J. to Edwin Diller Starbuck, September 30, 1898, W. J. Papers. Unfortunately, Starbuck's questionnaire data have been lost or destroyed. James thought Starbuck's work was important, and he recommended it to other philosophers and psychologists. See, for example, W. J. to James McKeen Cattell, June 10, 1903, in Frederick J. Down Scott, ed., *William James: Selected Unpublished Correspondence, 1885–1910* (Columbus: Ohio State University), 312–13.

14. James and Hall wrote two separate pieces for one issue of the *Nation* that were printed back to back. See William James, "The Teaching of Philosophy in Our Colleges," *Nation* 23 (September 23, 1876): 178–79; and G. Stanley Hall, "College Instruction in Philosophy," *Nation* 23 (September 23, 1876): 180. Perry, *William James*, 2:327. See also Henry Samuel Levinson, *The Religious Investigations of William James* (Chapel Hill: University of North Carolina Press, 1981), 73–76.

15. Hall is quoted in Gail Bederman, *Manliness and Civilization: A Cultural History of Gender and Race in the United States, 1880–1917* (Chicago: University of Chicago Press, 1995), 95.

16. Edwin Diller Starbuck, "The Feelings and Their Place in Religion," *American Journal of Religious Psychology and Education* 1, no. 5 (1904): 183–85; see also Edwin Diller Starbuck, "Reinforcement to the Pulpit from Modern Psychology: IV. As a Man Thinketh in His Heart," *Homiletic Review* 54 (January 1908): 23; W. J. to James Henry Leuba, April 17, 1904, in William James, *Letters of William James*, ed. Henry James (Boston: Atlantic Monthly Press, 1920), 2:211–12.

17. See James's preface to Starbuck, *Psychology of Religion*, viii–ix; W. J. to Frances R. Morse, April 12, 1900, in James, *Letters of William James*, 2:127. In the preface to Starbuck's book, James recognized that Starbuck's examples were drawn from very particular sources—namely, American evangelicals. And yet James's uncritical suspicion that all experiences followed the pattern remained. See Starbuck, *Psychology of Religion*, x.

18. Starbuck, *Psychology of Religion*, 227–31, 418. See also Starbuck, *Psychology of Religion*, 175–76. The last three quotations are from G. Stanley Hall, *Youth: Its Education, Regimen, and Hygiene* (New York: D. Appleton and Co., 1920), 364–66.

19. Frederick Davenport, quoted in Frank M. Teti, "Profile of a Progressive: The Life of Frederick Morgan Davenport" (PhD diss., Syracuse University, Syracuse, NY, 1966), 42–43; Frederick Morgan Davenport, *Primitive Traits in Religious Revivals: A Study in Mental and Social Evolution* (New York: Macmillan, 1905), 243–44, 323, 21–22, 279.

20. Davenport, *Primitive Traits*, 14, 45–48, 55, 58; Rolvix Harlan, review of *Primitive Traits in Religious Revivals: A Study in Mental and Social Evolution*, by Frederick Morgan Davenport, *Biblical World* 26, no. 3 (September 1905): 237–38. Starbuck shared some of Davenport's ideas on African Americans. See Starbuck, *Psychology of Religion*, 168.

21. George B. Cutten, *The Psychological Phenomena of Christianity* (New York: Charles Scribner's Sons, 1908), 4, 171–73, 165.

22. Robert Daniel Sinclair, "A Comparative Study of Those Who Report the Experience of the Divine Presence and Those Who Do Not," *University of Iowa Studies in Character* 2, no. 3 (1930): 54; see also Thomas H. Howells, "A Comparative Study of Those Who Accept as Against Those who Reject Religious Authority," *University of Iowa Studies in Character* 2, no. 2 (1928), 7, 13.

23. Edwin Starbuck, "The Feelings and Their Place in Religion," *American Journal of Religious Psychology and Education* 1, no. 5 (1904): 169–76; see also Edwin Diller Starbuck, "The Intimate Senses as Sources of Wisdom," *Journal of Religion* 1, no. 2 (March 1921): 129–45.

24. W. J. to Edwin Diller Starbuck, August 24, 1904, published in James, *Letters of William James*, 2:209–10. See also W. J. to Edwin Diller Starbuck, February 12, 1905, W. J. Papers. Others, like the philosopher William Hocking and psychologists of religion such as James B. Pratt, also pointed to experience as evidence that God existed. See Bruce Kuklick, *The Rise of American Philosophy: Cambridge, Massachusetts, 1860–1930* (New Haven: Yale University Press, 1977), 484–86.

25. James Bissett Pratt, *The Religious Consciousness: A Psychological Study* (New York: Macmillan, 1924), 479, 228–29, 474.

26. Edwin Diller Starbuck, "The Scientific Study of Religion," *Homiletic Review* 49, no. 2 (February 1903): 99, 102–5.

27. Charles A. Brand, *Decision Day and How to Use It* (Boston: Pilgrim Press, 1908), 1, 6–7, George Coe Archives, Yale Divinity School, Yale University.

28. Starbuck, "Religion's Use of Me," 204–6, 227–29.

29. Hopkins, "A Critical Survey of the Psychology of Religion," in *Readings in the Psychology of Religion*, ed. Orlo Strunk (New York: Abingdon Press, 1959), 46; H. Shelton Smith, *Faith and Nurture* (New York: C. Scribner's Sons, 1941), 100–104.

## 6. SUGGESTIVE EXPLANATIONS

Epigraph: Joseph Jastrow, *Fact and Fable in Psychology* (Boston: Houghton Mifflin and Co., 1900; reprint, Freeport, NY: Books for Libraries Press, 1971), 234 (page citations are to the 1971 edition).

1. The best and most exhaustive overview is still Henri Ellenberger, *The Discovery of the Unconscious: The History and Evolution of Dynamic Psychiatry* (New York: Basic Books, 1970). For the American side, there are several helpful sources: Robert Fuller, *Americans and the Unconscious* (Oxford: Oxford University Press, 1986); Eugene Taylor, *William James on Consciousness*

*beyond the Margin* (Princeton: Princeton University Press, 1996); Ann Taves, *Fits, Trances, and Visions: Experiencing Religion and Explaining Experience from Wesley to James* (Princeton, NJ: Princeton University Press, 1999).

2. Merle Curti, *Human Nature in American Thought: A History* (Madison: University of Wisconsin Press, 1980), 314–25; Taves, *Fits*, 253–54.

3. All quotations from Taves, *Fits*, 253. I have also used Curti, *Human Nature*, 314–25.

4. Munsterberg represented the group when fretting that the idea of a separated consciousness gave "a foothold for the most complicated mystical theories." Discarnate spirits that also were garrulous worried him. Asserting with impatience that scientists flatly rejected spiritualist mediums, he explained these phenomena not by talking about separate selves but by using the categories hypnotism, illusion, hysteria, hallucination, and nervous disturbance. Hugo Munsterberg, *Psychology and Life* (Boston: Houghton, Mifflin and Co., 1899), 249–55.

5. Taves, *Fits*, 258; Curti, *Human Nature*, 324.

6. The episode is summarized in Deborah Coon, "Testing the Limits of Sense and Science: American Experimental Psychologists Combat Spiritualism, 1880–1920," *American Psychologist* (February 1992): 148–49.

7. William James, *The Varieties of Religious Experience* (New York: Touchstone, 2004), 377–78; James, "Energies of Men," in *Essays on Faith and Morals*, by William James, ed. Ralph Barton Perry (New York: Meridian, 1962), 217, 234.

8. On religious liberals using James, and especially his *Varieties*, see Richard Ostrander, *The Life of Prayer in a World of Science: Protestants, Prayer, and American Culture, 1870–1930* (Oxford: Oxford University Press, 2000), 122; Donald Meyer, *The Positive Thinkers: Religion as Pop Psychology from Mary Baker Eddy to Oral Roberts* (New York: Pantheon, 1980), 315–18; and E. Brooks Holifield, *A History of Pastoral Care in America: From Salvation to Self-Realization* (Nashville, TN: Abingdon Press, 1983), 188–90, 200–201.

9. Horace E. Warner, *The Psychology of the Christian Life: A Contribution to the Scientific Study of Christian Experience and Character* (New York: Fleming H. Revell, 1910), 58–59, 43, 56–59, 87.

10. See George Coe, "The Subconscious," *Methodist Quarterly Review* (October 1907): 765–66. For liberal enthusiasm for a "Subliminal Self" and arguments with debunking opponents, see Andrew Heinze, "Jews and American Popular Psychology: Reconsidering the Protestant Paradigm of Popular Thought," *Journal of American History* 88, no. 3 (December 2001): paras. 42–43 (online at History Cooperative, www.historycooperative.org, accessed February 28, 2008).

11. Scott quotations from Walter Dill Scott, *The Psychology of Advertising: A Simple Exposition of the Principles of Psychology in Their Relation to Successful Advertising* (Boston: Small, Maynard, and Co., 1908), 83, 216; and Richard Wightman Fox and T. J. Jackson Lears, eds., *The Culture of Consumption: Critical Essays in American History, 1880–1980* (New York:

Pantheon Books, 1983), 19–20. Other psychologists of advertising developed detailed taxonomies of suggestions and outlined how to use them. A. J. Snow's 1925 textbook is one example of many. Snow's book displays sample advertisements that illustrate how suggestive techniques could be used. See A. J. Snow, *Psychology in Business Relations* (Chicago: A. W. Shaw Company, 1925). For background information, I also used Robert H. Wozniak's biography of Walter Dill Scott in *Classics in Psychology, 1855–1914: Historical Essays* (Bristol: Thoemmes Press, 1999), 166–69.

12. See Graham Richards, *Putting Psychology in Its Place: An Introduction from a Critical Historical Perspective* (London: Routledge, 1996), 120–22.

13. Heinze's fascinating project is marred by inattention to this wider context. Heinze ignores, for example, ways that religious liberals also recognized the problems of mob violence and demurred to popular Protestant mystical interpretations of the unconscious. See also Heinze, "Jews and American Popular Psychology," para. 5.

14. Boris Sidis, *The Psychology of Suggestion: A Research into the Subconscious Nature of Man and Society* (Boston: D. Appleton and Co., 1898), 297.

15. Sidis has a detailed set of mathematical calculations that accompany this graph. Ibid., 303–5.

16. Catharine Cleveland, *The Great Revival in the West, 1797–1805* (Chicago: University of Chicago Press, 1916; reprint, Gloucester, MA: Peter Smith, 1959), 127, 122–23. Leigh Schmidt discusses these matters and broader enlightenment critiques of American revivals in *Holy Fairs: Scotland and the Making of American Revivalism* (Grand Rapids, MI: Eerdmans, 2001), xviii–xx.

17. They did so because the public was interested in such questions and because these psychologists were interested in carefully differentiating science from pseudoscience and religion. Many operated with a basic antimony: science, rationality, and objectivity versus religion, irrationality, and subjectivity. On boundary disputes between psychologists and religious healers in this era, see Coon, "Testing the Limits"; for broader issues related to how boundaries between science and nonscience are created, see Thomas F. Gieryn, "Boundary Work and the Demarcation of Science from Non-Science: Strains and Interests in Professional Ideologies of Scientists," *American Sociological Review* 48 (1983): 781–95.

18. Andrew Heinze, *Jews and the American Soul: Human Nature in the Twentieth Century* (Princeton: Princeton University Press, 2004), 174. See also 110–13.

19. Jastrow, *Fact and Fable*, 68–70, 27, 32, 39.

20. James Angell, quoted in Coon, "Testing the Limits of Sense and Science," 150.

21. Hugo Munsterberg, *Psychotherapy* (New York: Moffat, Yard, and Company, 1909), 319–20.

22. Hugo Munsterberg, *Psychology and Life* (Boston: Houghton, Mifflin, and Company, 1899), 245–48.

23. James, "Energies of Men," 231.

24. Samuel McComb, *The Power of Self-Suggestion* (New York: Moffat, Yard, and Co., 1909), 4–6.

25. Horatio Dresser, *A Message to the Well: And Other Essays and Letters on the Art of Health* (New York: G. P. Putnam's Sons, 1910), 111–12, 129, 160–62.

26. Karl R. Stolz, *The Psychology of Prayer* (New York: Abingdon Press, 1923), 30–33.

27. Many liberal Christians made this argument. For another example see Elwin Lincoln House, *The Psychology of Orthodoxy* (New York: Fleming H. Revell Co., 1913), 100.

28. Robert H. Thouless, *The Control of the Mind: A Handbook of Applied Psychology for the Ordinary Man* (London: Hodder and Stoughton, 1928), 209–10.

29. See, for example, Lily Dougall, *The Christian Doctrine of Health: A Handbook on the Relation of Bodily to Spiritual and Moral Health* (New York: Macmillan, 1923), 73–75; and Warner, *Psychology of the Christian Life*, 246–48. Warner spoke of a "properly-poised" Christian experience (248).

30. Samuel McComb is quoted in Clerical and Medical Committee of Inquiry into Spiritual, Faith, and Mental Healing, *Spiritual Healing: Report of a Clerical and Medical Committee of Inquiry into Spiritual, Faith, and Mental Healing* (New York: Macmillan, 1914), 43. Karl Stolz, *The Church and Psychotherapy* (New York: Abingdon Press, 1943), 142. See also Dougall, *Christian Doctrine*, 136–37; Thouless, *Control of the Mind*, 35; and William Sadler, *The Physiology of Faith and Fear: Or, the Mind in Health and Disease* (Chicago: A. C. McClurg and Co., 1920), 491.

31. George B. Cutten, *The Psychological Phenomena of Christianity* (New York: Charles Scribner's Sons, 1908), 4, 171–73, 165.

32. Thomas H. Howells, "A Comparative Study of Those Who Accept as against Those who Reject Religious Authority," *University of Iowa Studies in Character* 2, no. 2 (1928), 7, 13.

33. Ibid., 31, 33–39.

34. Ibid., 47, 57.

35. Sinclair, "A Comparative Study," 54.

36. Thomas H. Howells, *Hunger for Wholeness: Man's Universal Motive* (Denver: World Press, 1940), 256, 276.

37. "Among the Spirits: Actual Demonstrations of Psychic Phenomena," lecture promotional materials from Records of the Redpath Lyceum Bureau, Special Collections Department, University of Iowa Libraries. All quotations in the paragraph are from these promotional materials, except Higgins's statement: "In order to influence people's beliefs . . ." This statement is from Howard Higgins, *Influencing Behavior through Speech* (Boston: Expression Company, 1930), 9.

38. "George Leo Wilkins: Incomparable Prestidigitator, In His Unique Lecture *explaining* the Psychical Phenomena of Spiritualism," n.d., Records of the Redpath Lyceum Bureau, Special Collections Department, University of Iowa Libraries, Iowa City.

39. Henry Wood, *Ideal Suggestion through Mental Photography: A Restorative System for Home and Private Use* (Boston: Lee and Shepard, 1902), 103. For background information on Wood, I am indebted to Leigh Schmidt, *Restless Souls: The Making of American Spirituality* (San Francisco: HarperSanFrancisco, 2005), 150–52.

40. Wood, *Ideal Suggestions*, 108–9, 113; and Henry Wood, *The New Old Healing* (Boston: Norwood Press, 1908), 19.

41. Wood, *New Old Healing*, 19–21, 40–41.

42. Charles Reynolds Brown, *Faith and Health* (New York: Thomas Y. Crowell and Co., 1910), 136; Robert MacDonald, *Mind, Religion, and Health: With an Appreciation of the Emmanuel Movement* (New York: Funk and Wagnalls Co., 1908), 106, 107, 136–39.

43. From his lecture promotional materials, "The Psychology of Religion," Records of the Redpath Lyceum Bureau, Special Collections Department, University of Iowa Libraries, Iowa City, n.d.

44. House, *The Psychology of Orthodoxy*, 114–15, 140–50, 100, 115.

45. Ibid., 110, 231, 220; Arthur A. Lindsay, *The New Psychology Complete: Mind the Builder and Scientific Man Building* (1907; reprint, New York: Lindsay Publishing, 1922), 83. For another example, see MacDonald, *Mind, Religion, and Health*, 106–7, 131.

46. Sadler, *Physiology of Faith and Fear*, 491.

47. Ibid.; MacDonald, *Mind, Religion, and Health*, 111. These were common positions. The unconscious was powerful, but other capacities were powerful too. See also Elwood Worcester, *Making Life Better: An Application of Religion and Psychology to Human Problems* (New York: Charles Scribner's Sons, 1936), 106.

48. Stolz, *Church and Psychotherapy*, 141–42; Thomas Parker Boyd, *The How and Why of the Emmanuel Movement: A Hand-book on Psycho-Therapeutics* (San Francisco: Whitaker and Ray Co., 1909), 115–18.

49. Dresser, *Message to the Well*, 156–63; Sadler, *Physiology of Faith and Fear*, 93; Dougall, *Christian Doctrine*, 150.

50. Elwood Worcester and Samuel McComb, *The Christian Religion as a Healing Power: A Defense and Exposition of the Emmanuel Movement* (New York: Moffat, Yard, and Co., 1909), 26; Worcester also quoted in John G. Greene, "The Emmanuel Movement," *New England Quarterly* 7, no. 3 (September 1934): 498.

51. Taves, *Fits*, 314; Worcester quoted in Greene, "The Emmanuel Movement," 512; Elwood Worcester, *Life's Adventure, the Story of a Varied Career* (New York: Charles Scribner's Sons, 1932), 276.

52. Worcester and McComb, *Christian Religion as a Healing Power*, 44, 50; Worcester, *Making Life Better*, 84. *The Christian Religion as a Healing Power* has an appendix with rules regulating interactions between ministers and clergy.

53. Taves, *Fits*, 321–23; Elwood Worcester, Samuel McComb, and Isador Coriat, *Religion and Medicine: The Moral Control of Nervous Disorders* (New York: Moffat, Yard, and Co., 1908), 66–67.

54. "The Remarkable Growth of the Emmanuel Movement," *Current Literature* 14, no. 6 (December 1908): 659; Worcester is quoted in Taves, *Fits*, 323.

55. C. Bertram Runnalls, *Suggestions for Conducting a Church Class in Psycho-Therapy* (Milwaukee: Young Churchman Co., 1915), 19–25, 68.

56. Thomas Parker Boyd, *The How and Why of the Emmanuel Movement: A Hand-book on Psycho-Therapeutics* (San Francisco: Whitaker and Ray Co., 1909), 32–33, 66–67, 70.

57. Ibid., 71, 75–78, 122, 124–26.

58. Brown, *Faith and Health*, 109–11; Proverbs 23:1.

59. E. W. Sprague, *The Science of Magnetic, Mental, and Spiritual Healing, with Instructions How to Heal by Laying on of Hands* (Grand Rapids, MI: E. W. Sprague, 1930), 102, 150; William Walker Atkinson, *Suggestion and Auto-Suggestion* (Chicago: Progress Co., 1909), 158–60.

60. Sprague, *Science of Magnetic Healing*, 65–66, 70–71. Many others used suggestions, hypnotism, and therapeutic touching to restore people's energies.

61. "Word from Hugo Muensterberg [sic]: Boston Woman Quotes Alleged Message from Dead Professor," *New York Times*, December 28, 1916, p. 2; Matthew Hale Jr., *Human Science and the Social Order: Hugo Munsterberg and the Origins of Applied Psychology* (Philadelphia: Temple University Press, 1980), 183.

EPILOGUE

1. Seward Hiltner, "The Psychological Understanding of Religion," in *Readings in the Psychology of Religion*, ed. Orlo Strunk Jr. (New York: Abingdon Press, 1959), 86–87. It is true in fact that at least one harmonizing tradition, the psychology of religion, did decline precipitously in the 1930s and 1940s. This decline mystified many observers, including especially Edwin Starbuck, but it may have had something to do with the phenomena I am describing: psychology diversified and religious people perceived it as less threatening.

2. John Hedley Brooke, *Science and Religion: Some Historical Perspectives* (Cambridge: Cambridge University Press, 1996), 327; Heisenberg is quoted in Bert James Loewenberg, "Toward a New Birth of Freedom," *American Quarterly* 16, no. 3 (Autumn 1964): 499. I also am indebted to Catherine Albanese, *A Republic of Mind and Spirit: A Cultural History of American Metaphysical Religion* (New Haven, CT: Yale University Press, 2007), 397–99; Brooke, *Science and Religion*, 326–36; and, for general information on probablism and uncertainty in science, Paul Jerome Croce, *Science and Religion in the Era of William James* (Chapel Hill: University of North Carolina Press, 1995).

3. All quotations are from Morton Hunt, *The Story of Psychology* (New York: Doubleday, 1993), 278–79. See also 262–63 and 276–77.

4. Kaffka is quoted in Martin Leichtman, "Gestalt Theory and the Revolt against Positivism," in *Psychology in Social Context*, ed. Allan Buss (New York: Irvington Publishers, 1979), 47.

5. Paulsen and Kohler are quoted in ibid., 58, 62.

6. James Capshew, *Psychologists on the March: Science, Practice, and Professional Identity in America, 1929–1969* (Cambridge: Cambridge University Press, 1999), 231.

7. Sigmund Koch, *Psychology in Human Context: Essays in Dissidence and Reconstruction* (Chicago: University of Chicago Press, 1999), 7, 30, 35, 8, 37, 38, 2–3, 41.

8. David Bakan, "American Culture and Psychology," in *Psychology: Theoretical-Historical Perspectives*, ed. Robert W. Rieber and Kurt D. Salzinger (Washington, DC: American Psychological Association, 1998), 223; Kroeber is quoted in Theodore Roszak, *Where the Wasteland Ends: Politics and Transcendence in Postindustrial Society* (New York: Anchor Books, 1973), 213. Roszak is quoting material Kroeber added to the revised (1948) version of his text. I am indebted to Bakan's article for content in this paragraph and also for the laboratory/life juxtaposition I use here (see Bakan, "American Culture," 223).

9. Joseph Wood Krutch, *The Measure of Man: On Freedom, Human Values, Survival, and the Modern Temper* (New York: Bobbs-Merrill, 1954), 28, 33; Anthony Standen, *Science Is a Sacred Cow* (New York: E. P. Dutton, 1950), 139, 122.

10. The language of "single-vision" science I draw from Roszak, *Where the Wasteland Ends.*

11. E. Brooks Holifield, *A History of Pastoral Care in America: From Salvation to Self-Realization* (Nashville, TN: Abingdon Press, 1983), 270–71, 274, 355. See also Francis Strickland, "Pastoral Psychology—A Retrospect," *Pastoral Psychology* 4, no. 7 (October 1953): 9–12.

12. Robert C. Fuller, *Spiritual but Not Religious: Understanding Unchurched America* (Oxford: Oxford University Press, 2001), 137–39; Eugene Taylor, *Shadow Culture: Psychology and Spirituality in America* (Washington, DC: Counterpoint, 1999), 212–15.

13. Bernard Weisberger, review of *Popular Religion: Inspirational Books in America*, by Louis Schneider and Sanford Dornbusch, *Journal of Religion* 40, no. 3 (July 1960): 220–22; and Beryl Satter, *Each Mind a Kingdom: American Women, Sexual Purity, and the New Thought Movement, 1875–1920* (Berkeley: University of California Press, 1999), 252. See also Donald Meyer, *The Positive Thinkers: Religion as Pop Psychology from Mary Baker Eddy to Oral Roberts* (New York: Pantheon, 1980), 252–64.

14. David Ray Griffin, ed., *The Reenchantment of Science: Postmodern Proposals* (Albany: SUNY Press, 1988), 13–14. There is a vast literature here. A good example of someone using quantum notions to argue for human and divine agency is John Polkinghorne, "The Nature of Physical Reality," *Zygon* 35, no. 4 (December 2000): 927–40. For an example of wide-ranging reflections on psychokinetic powers, see Rupert Sheldrake et al., *The Evolutionary Mind: Conversations on Science, Imagination, and Spirit* (Rhinebeck, NY: Monkfish Publishing, 2005), or Sheldrake's online location, www.sheldrake.org/homepage.html. For a partial summary of theological developments, see

Brooke, *Science and Religion,* 330–32. See also Albanese, *Republic of Mind and Spirit,* 507–10.

15. Shirley MacLaine, "The New Age and Rational Thought and a Rainbow of Expression," in *American Spiritualities: A Reader,* ed. Catherine Albanese (Bloomington: Indiana University Press, 2001), 482, 484; Deepak Chopra, *How to Know God: The Soul's Journey into the Mystery of Mysteries* (New York: Harmony Books, 2000), 9–12. For Chopra's advice on intentions and imaginative or devotional exercises, see 288–304. See also Hans A. Boer, "The Work of Andrew Weil and Deepak Chopra: Two Holistic Health/New Age Gurus: A Critique of the Holistic Health/New Age Movements," *Medical Anthropology Quarterly,* n. s., 17, no. 2 (June 2003): 233–50.

16. William Tiller, *Science and Human Transformation: Subtle Energies, Intentionality, and Consciousness* (Walnut Creek, CA: Pavior, 1997), ix, 60–92, 54.

17. This literature is vast. Some of it can be surveyed in recent psychology or psychology of religion textbooks, including, for example, Benjamin Beit-Hallahmi and Michael Argyle, *The Psychology of Religious Behaviour, Belief, and Experience* (London: Routledge, 1997). There is a host of other, more popular surveys. See also Harold G. Koenig and Malcolm McConnell, *The Healing Power of Faith: Science Explores Medicine's Last Great Frontier* (New York: Touchstone, 1999); Jeff Levin, *God, Faith, and Health: Exploring the Spirituality-Healing Connection* (New York: John Wiley and Sons, 2001); Harold Koenig and Harvey Cohen, *The Link between Religion and Health: Psychoneuroimmunology and the Faith Factor* (Oxford: Oxford University Press, 2002).

18. Chopra, *How to Know God,* 219–22, 195–96; Deepak Chopra, *Grow Younger, Live Longer: Ten Steps to Reduce Aging* (New York: Three Rivers Press, 2001), 102, 128; Chopra, *How to Know God,* 306; Gary E. Schwartz, William Simon, and Deepak Chopra, *The Afterlife Experiments: Breakthrough Scientific Experiments of Life after Death* (New York: Atria Books, 2003).

19. Benedict Carey, "A Neuroscientific Look at Speaking in Tongues," *New York Times,* November 7, 2006; Kelly Bulkeley, "Consciousness and Neurotheology," in *Science, Religion, and Society,* ed. Arri Eisen and Gary Laderman (Armonk, NY: M. E. Sharpe, 2007), 530–31. Christians are using psychology in ways too numerous to document fully here. Some working in the "positive psychology" movement argue that modern psychology reveals the benefits of Christian virtues; others, such as Justin Barrett, an experimental psychologist at Calvin College, and Frasier Watts, the Starbridge Lecturer in Theology and the Natural Sciences at Cambridge, are trying to correlate psychological perspectives and Christian doctrine. One best-selling author who has noticed the change in psychology from Freud's day to the twenty-first century is Patrick Glynn, who reads the psychological literature in the conventional religious way: as additional support that religiosity is natural and healthy. See Patrick Glynn, *God: The Evidence* (Rocklin, CA: Forum, 1999). I am indebted to Kelly Bulkeley for some of the information used in this paragraph.

# Index

abasement concept, 14, 17–18, 19, 25–26, 27
action: emotions converted into, 93–96; stimuli converted into, 82–83. *See also* athletics and exercise; neuromuscular system; reflex arcs (or actions)
Addams, Jane, 90
advertising, suggestion in, 165–66, 242–43n11
advice literature: on ameliorating spiritual and mental disorders, 190–91; on diverting woman's worry, 131; on effects of alcohol, 96–97; expansion of, 231n23; on nervous energies, 10, 75–101; optimism of, 207; on phrenology, 23, 220n35; on psychotherapy, 190; on sex and self-control, 100–102; on spiritual health and growth, 81–103, 105–8, 110–18, 120–29, 180–82; on the will and self-control, 123–29
affirmations: development of, 12; meditation of, 180–82; as physical forces, 183–85; recent reintroduction of, 206–7; thoughts as forces in, 192–93; as tool in controlling emotions, 190–91
African Americans, 148–49, 150, 175
agency: free will linked to, 107; James on, 60–61; quantum metaphors for, 207–8

agnosticism, 69
alcohol consumption: bad effects of, 96–99; loss of virility linked to, 99–100; nervous energies affected by, 90; use of will to avoid, 106
alienation, 14, 94, 133, 144–45
Alline, Henry, 14–15
*American Journal of Otology,* 52
*American Phrenological Journal,* 220n32
American Play Movement, 91
American Psychological Association, 201, 202–3
American Society for Psychical Research, 161
amusements and leisure: cautions about, 83–84, 93–96; debunking psychic phenomena as, 178, 179*fig,* 180; increasing religiousness via, 92–93; nervous energies stimulated in, 90. *See also* advice literature; play; rest and relaxation
*Andover Review,* 71, 93–94
Andover Seminary, 71, 80
animal magnetism concept, 76–77, 159
antinoise movement, 231n23
Arminian religions, 14–15, 218n19
Arnold, Matthew, 109
arts, cautions about, 93–95
asceticism, 79
associationism, 43

Richards, Graham, 166
Rieff, Philip, 5–6
Robertson, F. W., 108–9
Rogers, Carl, 206
Roosevelt, Theodore, 128, 129*fig.*
Rosen, George, 228–29n5
Ross, Dorothy, 238–39n2
Runnals, Bertram, 190

Sadler, William, 87, 88*fig.*, 184–85
Sage, Henry W., 40
salvation: body-spirit joined in, 117–18;
changing meanings of, 5; definition
of, 124; habits as key to, 125–26;
healing linked to, 187–90; physical
culture as distraction from, 118–19;
physical culture as means of, 114,
116; sinfulness and certainty in,
17–18; stages of, 163, 164*fig.*
Schelling, Friedrich Wilhelm Joseph
von, 159
Schleiermacher, Freidrich, 80
Schmidt, Leigh, 8–9, 243n16
school hygiene movement, 118
Schopenhauer, Arthur, 108–9, 124,
159
Schuller, Robert, 207
science: alienation experienced in,
144–45; believers unsettled by, 196;
conservation of energy law of, 62;
faith buttressed by, 3, 7; historiography on religion and, 2–7; new
physics in, 197–98, 207–9; nonmechanical concept of self tested in,
192; as pathological, 204; questions
about, 136; religious borrowings
from, 210–12; skepticism about certainties of, 60–61; spiritual forces
of nature proven by, 3–4; of suggestion, 182. *See also* experiments and
testing; scientific methodologies;
scientific psychologies
science and religion nexus: complexi-
ties of, 196–97; conflict narratives
on, 2–7; distinctions made in,
170–71, 243n17; subconscious as
mediating category in, 162–63.

*See also* psychologies; psychology
of religion; science
scientific methodologies: materialism
of, 68–69; mob-energy measures
in, 167–68, 168*fig.*; psychological
uses of, 135, 238–39n2; questionnaires and surveys as, 137–46,
150, 175–77. *See also* experiments
and testing
scientific psychologies: certainty
about, 31–32; discourses of, 11–12;
emergence of, 19–20; emotions
viewed in, 65–66; fragmentation
and diversification of, 12; Hall as
spokesperson for, 58–59; hopes for,
46–53; meanings of, 59–64; neural measurements in, 9–10; new
theologies juxtaposed to, 67–74;
as overcoming contradictions and
doubt, 24; possibilities in, 36–38,
39–40; spiritual innovators' uses of,
1–2, 6–7; Wundt as founder of, 42.
*See also* phrenology; physiological
psychologies; psychology of religion
Scopes trial, 99
Scott, Walter Dill, 165–66
*Scribner's* magazine, 64–65
Scudder, Vida, 93–94
secondary selves concept, 160. *See
also* unconscious, the
secularization, 5, 7, 214n6
self: alternatives to physiological
focus on, 6–7; building suggestibility in, 12; diagram of, 107;
gendered notions of, 129–33; habits as key ingredient in, 124–27;
inscrutable parts of, 75 (*see also*
nervous energies); as living,
active, purposive whole, 80–81;
model of spiritual development
of, 34, 35*fig.*, 36; new ways of
understanding, 13–14; phrenology as surfacing of, 21; reflex arc
as basic unit of, 42–43, 64–65,
82; scientific account of, 69; suggesting religious certainty to,
182–83; Tiller's recommendations